The Shape of Irish History

The
Shape of Irish History

A.T.Q. STEWART

THE
BLACKSTAFF
PRESS

BELFAST

First published in 2001 by
The Blackstaff Press Limited
Wildflower Way, Apollo Road
Belfast BT12 6TA, Northern Ireland

© A.T.Q. Stewart, 2001

A.T.Q. Stewart has asserted his right under the
Copyright, Designs and Patents Act 1988
to be identified as the author of this work.

Typeset by Techniset Typesetters, Newton-le-Willows, Merseyside

Printed in England by Biddles Limited

A CIP catalogue for this book is available from the British Library

ISBN 0-85640-691-0

www.blackstaffpress.com

To Anna

History would be an excellent thing
if only it were true.

LEO TOLSTOY

Contents

Preface

This book is not intended to be a concise history of Ireland, for many important aspects of Irish history are not discussed here. Nor is it only about Ireland. It is a personal inquiry into the shape of Irish history rather than its content, and, at a deeper level, into the nature of history itself, my own meditation on sundials. As such, it is part historical and part literary, a hybrid which may not recommend itself to orthodox historians. I began it with the intention of outlining what I took to be the dominant structures and patterns of Irish history; I wanted also to turn attention away from familiar topics and approaches, and on to the unlighted areas which were at least as formative, and in particular to the significance of prehistory, which academic apartheid now fences off from historians. This, in my opinion, distorts and restricts their very definition of history. As the book progressed, however, I found myself becoming more and more interested in the 'deeper silences' for their own sake.

Obviously the word 'history' has two meanings. It can mean either the past, or what historians write about it. They are not identical, but Irish people often act as if they were. And the reality of the past (even what little we know about it) is so intimidating that most historians steer clear of discussing it. This book deals with history in both senses, and here and there I have inserted a more conventional handrail for the reader made vertiginous by peering into 'the dark backward and abysm of Time'. I am fully aware that every syllable is open to contradiction by some historian with specialised knowledge of a particular period. But this is an exercise in painting with broad strokes, in the hope of illumining underlying patterns and shapes rather than surface detail. I shall, no doubt, be accused of wandering away from the herd, and even of renouncing the discipline in which I was trained. I can only reply that if I have articulated some of my reservations about modern historical study I shall, in Macaulay's words, 'cheerfully bear the reproach of having descended below the dignity of history'.

A work of synthesis like this must rest on the labours and conclusions of many scholars; only a small part of it is related to my own area of research. To attempt to acknowledge them all by name would be impossible, but I have tried to give in the references the sources of all quotations used in the text. I had the good fortune to be first the student, and later the colleague, of a very eminent Irish historian, the late Professor J.C. Beckett, and, though I suspect he would not have approved of everything in these pages, I owe a great deal to the inspiration of his teaching and the lucidity of his writing.

A more personal debt is owed to those who have given me so much help and encouragement during the writing of this book: to my publisher, Anne Tannahill, and her dedicated colleagues at The Blackstaff Press, in particular Wendy Dunbar and Patsy Horton; to my agent Frances Kelly; to Louis Lord, who read the first draft of the manuscript; to Gerry Healey who helped me to trace some elusive quotations, and to Finbarr O'Shea for his skilful editing.

A.T.Q. STEWART
BELFAST, MARCH 2001

The Walled Garden

The University is a Paradise, Rivers of Knowledge are there, Arts and Sciences flow from thence. Counsell Tables are *Horti conclusi* (as it is said in the Canticles), Gardens that are walled in, and they are *Fontes signati*, Wells that are sealed up . . .

JOHN DONNE[1]

The 10.14 from Clontarf

There is something wrong with the shape of Irish history. It is too short, too narrow, upside down, and it leans all over to one side. Sometimes it seems to be a circle, like the serpent in Celtic design which swallows its own tail; it is very difficult to see where the past ends and the present begins. For some people it is a burden, to be cast aside as soon as possible if the country is ever to prosper. For others it is a kind of Fermat's last theorem, a problem to which one day some clever person will find the answer.

For most Irish people, though, it is simply a family heirloom, a fine old painting in a gilt frame, which they would miss if it was no longer there. The varnish of time has darkened the scene, so that it is no longer easy to see exactly what is depicted. This hardly matters, because everybody knows that it shows a proud and independent nation emerging from captivity.

For some time now the experts have been concerned about the picture's cleaning and restoration. Much of the varnish has been carefully removed. Tiny particles of paint have been scraped off, and the layers subjected to microscopic analysis. Ultraviolet light has detected the over-painting and disposed of a few false signatures, while X-ray photographs have revealed interesting *pentimenti* – scenes and figures long ago painted out. As always, the experts are not in agreement. Many would like the painting restored to its pristine state. Others, finding the colours in the restored portions too harsh and bright, would prefer to leave it as it is. And now some of them have been gripped by a new fear – what if the whole picture should turn out to be a forgery? In one sense this is obviously true. History may be written by God, but historians have forged His signature.

Any schoolchild will tell you that the history of Ireland is not a picture but a railway line. We cannot quite see where the line begins but we know where it ends. Myles na gCopaleen,[2] in his relentless pursuit of the cliché, was wont to ask questions like 'In what are the round towers of Ireland shrouded?' and gleefully reply 'In the mists of antiquity'. It is in these vapours that we first dimly discern the outlines of the locomotive. The guard waves his green flag and it begins to trundle along the line, gathering speed as it passes through familiar stations – Clontarf, Limerick, College Green, New Ross, Union, Emancipation, Queenstown and Easter

Rising. The train is going somewhere, unlike its sister engine, stationary at the Boyne Water. The destination is often perceived as the Grand Central Thirty-Two County Republic. We know that most of us will get off before it gets there, but believe in the destination all the same, even unionists. This is what biblical scholars call eschatology, the doctrine of last or final things, such as death, judgement, heaven and hell. It is Christianity's legacy from Judaic religion, and it is hardly surprising to find it deeply ingrained in so Christian a country as Ireland. The history we learned at school was always linear, and sometimes there was even a scale, printed in bright colours to help us to remember where the Gaels ended and the Normans began.

Railway history has some obvious disadvantages. At night you can see nothing between the stations; most of the landscape is hidden. It is easy to assume that nothing dramatic or interesting happens between insurrec-tions, in those long, uneventful spells when Ireland appears to be quies-cent. Suppose we pull the communication cord and stop the train in open country, at a year chosen at random. The very first edition of the *Sunday Times* appeared on 20 October 1822, and contained reports from Ireland. This was not a year which figures prominently in textbooks of Irish history. We might assume that all was quiet on the western front. But was it? 'The state of this country was never more alarming than at present,' reported a Dublin correspondent. 'The spirit of disturbance has broken out in those very districts where so many victims were lately offered up to the vengeance of the laws. The worst apprehensions are entertained for the general peace of the ensuing winter; and it is thought there will be a greater demand than ever for special commissions and military executions.'

The editor, commenting on this report, does not neglect the customary rituals of breast-beating and guilt-ridden despair. 'Have not the privations and miseries, the penury and oppressions of the lesser island grown out of the political evils and cruel neglect of the greater? And what single prospect of amelioration presents itself to the most sanguine and self-flattering observer? What Englishman who does not prefer the suggest-ions of chimerical hope to the informing light of his understanding, can ever fancy that he sees the dawn of better days?'[3] (All this, it should be noted, twenty-three years before the catastrophe of the Great Irish Famine.) Nearly two centuries later, chimerical hope is still winning hands down over the light of understanding. In fact 1822 was a year of great scarcity and famine in Ireland, the harbinger of 1845.

The sense of some perfect and complete end to Irish history distorts everything that has gone before. A national will towards independence and unity is discerned in places where it did not exist, for example in the Confederation of Kilkenny of 1642, or in Swift's *Drapier's Letters*. Everything which seems to stand in the way of the train is viewed as a frustration, a deliberate and hostile attempt to prevent the Irish people from reaching their legitimate destination. Yet history itself knows nothing about railway lines. It gives no name to its final destination, nor does it travel in a straight line, or in any direction but its own, which is determined not by one will, or the will of a nation, but by the interaction of myriad events and causes.

At first sight there would appear to be a distinct shortage of level crossings on this railway line. Few influences from outside Ireland apart from the obvious and all-important one – domination by the sister island – are thought to cross the line or influence its direction. The whole of Irish history is imbued with a sense that Ireland is a holy and withdrawn place. Its well-known discontents bubble and simmer in a flask hermetically sealed from the rest of the world. Modern Ireland has clearly indicated that it likes well enough to cut a figure on the world stage, but always on its own terms. It is largely a one-way process, in which alien evils are kept at arm's length, mentally if not physically. Given the direction of Atlantic cultures in the twenty-first century, even the most determined of anti-nationalists may come in time to be grateful for this stubborn provincialism.

In reality, though, it is a kind of self-deception. Irish history has not been entirely a process of fermentation in a sealed flask. It is not true that all the ingredients of Irish history are home-grown, or that Ireland's troubles are in some way unique. Again and again – in 1641, in 1690, in 1798, in 1918 and in 1969 – outside influences can be seen operating massively on the course of events. This is one of the classic patterns of Irish history, manifest in the earliest days in migration and culture, and in later times in the rich interaction of ideas and influences.

There are certain dominant themes in Irish history that we may visualise as 'vertical'. They have grown up organically from earlier history, and are, or have long since become, peculiar to Ireland. At specific times Ireland is profoundly affected by powerful European or global influence which may be seen as 'horizontal'. At the point where these vertical and horizontal lines intersect a new and dramatic element is added to the island's history. The new product will be distinctively Irish, however, often modifying the outline and even the essential nature of the external influence, adapting it to specific Irish circumstances. At such times the vertical theme will appear to have taken on a new guise, while retaining its fundamental character. Republicanism is a very good example of this.

Thus we might think of resentment against English rule, or antagonism between Catholic and Protestant, as 'vertical' elements in Irish history, as demonstrable in the sixteenth century as in the twenty-first. Both of these vertical lines are crossed by the religious turmoil which engulfed Europe during the Thirty Years War (1618–48) to produce the Irish uprising of 1641 and the complicated alliance between Old English and Irish Catholic ruling families in the Confederation of Kilkenny. Again, the American and French revolutions crossing these lines at the end of the eighteenth century to produce the Volunteer and United Irish movements. Since that time the traditional hostility to England has worn a new face, one which might at the time have seemed alien and uncongenial. It has styled itself 'republican' in tribute to the two revolutions, one Protestant, the other anti-Catholic, in spite of the fact that the doctrines of republicanism were anathema to most contemporary Catholics. This was possible only because, for historical reasons which are no longer relevant, Catholics took over the empty shell of the republican movement in Ireland.

One can think of many other examples. The 1848 revolutions in Europe inspired the Young Ireland movement, and later the Fenian movement. The First World War ignited the Dublin Rising of 1916 and determined the character of the guerilla war of 1919–21. The civil rights movement in the United States provided the trigger for the crisis in Northern Ireland after 1969. The interaction of influences can be seen in the personalities of 1916. Patrick Pearse was steeped in the psychology of blood sacrifice which affected a whole generation of young men throughout Europe in 1914, a widespread belief that western civilisation had grown tired, effete and corrupt, and needed to be reinvigorated in the crucible of war, a feeling vividly expressed in the verse of the English poet Rupert Brooke. In Pearse's writings it took on the mystical force, not just of nationalism, but of religious symbolism as well. By contrast with so many of his fellow-countrymen, Pearse had no direct experience of war. He narrowed his mystical vision of blood sacrifice to the political needs of Ireland as he saw them. He was already the victim and martyr in another cause, the casualty in another war, before the bitter poems of Wilfred Owen and Siegfried Sassoon began to appear. If anyone could be said to have been subject to outside influences, and to have taken in consequence a wider view, it was Pearse's fellow revolutionary, James Connolly. Yet overnight Connolly's communism and dedication to the brotherhood of man was transformed into the most uncompromising kind of Irish nationalism, a denial, it might at first appear, of his cardinal beliefs. Their execution by the British united these two men of widely divergent outlook in the pantheon of Irish history, alongside St Oliver Plunkett and Theobald Wolfe Tone.

We must not forget that these vertical and horizontal lines, adopted to illustrate a pattern, are really not so much lines as huge intersecting, and interacting, webs of circumstance. The myriad influences at work on the inside collide with as many on the outside. Connolly was dead before the Bolshevik Revolution demonstrated how to make the conversion of communism to nationalism on the grand scale; for Russia communism became in the end merely an instrument of Soviet foreign policy. The lines give us only the framework on which we can see how these processes form. The significant point is that, to a remarkable degree, the ripples of global influence take on a very Irish colour when they reach Ireland. Always the vertical grain reasserts itself and the dominant direction is resumed.

Making a Statement

When, after years of studying Irish history, I first began to teach it, I saw it in a different light, and made three discoveries. The first was that, viewed as a whole, Irish history had its own very distinctive architecture, as instantly recognisable as the Taj Mahal or the Sacré Coeur. Moreover, the architecture was deeply incised with repeating patterns, such as invasions, insurrections, betrayals, secret societies, famines and funerals. Studying the structure can be, at different levels, both a help and a hindrance to the neophyte. To teach anything, you need first to understand it yourself, and if this necessarily involves the simplification of what is in truth complex, the compensation is that the student can get to grips with it at once and see it clearly. He can then move gradually to the complex as interest deepens. It is much more difficult the other way round.

But here the problem arises, for, as Flaubert observed, it is no small thing to be simple. The amateur in history may dine at an ample table, and choose according to appetite. The teacher, on the other hand, must select and present what he offers to his pupil, as a bird feeds her young. For most of us, this pabulum is the only food we shall ever know. We imbibe it early in life, and carry it with us as a fixed system of knowledge, like mathematics or chemistry. People often say 'I wish I had learned more Irish history' as if there was nothing they could now do about it. They even, on occasion, blame their schools, or the government, for keeping it from them for wicked political ends. There is not, in this age, much of the spirit which inspired weavers to learn Greek from a lexicon perched on the clattering loom.

The second discovery was that the architecture was far from complete. There were enormous empty spaces in it. Concentrating on the narrow demands of my own research, I had not particularly noticed them before. It was only gradually, as I went to look for information that was not available, that I became aware of them. Until then I had assumed, as most people do, that there was altogether too much Irish history in circulation, to the great detriment of the country and its inhabitants. This I found to be a myth, one perpetuated mostly by people who were not Irish. Even now the history of Ireland is a bit like the map of Australia, with a lot of names crammed into a small corner, and immense tracts of territory which are empty.

Subsequently I discovered that I was by no means the first historian to reach this conclusion. In an essay published in 1909, shortly after his death in an accident at Chamonix in eastern France, Caesar Litton Falkiner remarked on some of these empty spaces as they appeared in his time:

> If we analyse the Irish chronicle from the Revolution of 1688 to the present day, we shall find periods, sometimes covering a whole generation, which remain almost complete blanks upon the page of history. Thus in the nineteenth century there are the long silences which intervened between the Union and Catholic Emancipation, between the Repeal and Home Rule agitations. And in the eighteenth century, the pauses are still longer, and the silences yet deeper.[4]

Falkiner was of course talking only about political history, and in the ninety years since, most of those gaps in the nineteenth century have been filled. Whether they have for the eighteenth century is less certain. It must be said, too, that we now know a great deal more social and economic history, but the general application of Falkiner's observation remains valid. He deserves to be remembered as a pioneer in drawing attention to the 'black holes' in Irish history.

There also seems to be an engaging element of pure chance in the creation of some of the major works of Irish historiography. In March 1870 the Earl of Derby recorded in his diary that he had dinner with the historian J.A. Froude, and had remarked to him that the history of Ireland from the Battle of the Boyne to the Union was largely unwritten – at least there was 'nothing trustworthy' on the subject – and hinted that Froude might like to undertake it. 'He seemed to like the idea. His interest in Irish affairs is remarkable, and he has nothing else on hand.'[5] During the course of the next four years Froude published his three volumes on *The English in Ireland in the Eighteenth Century*. But it was a tendentious work, which goaded W.E.H. Lecky into writing his five-volume *History of Ireland in the Eighteenth Century*. The fact that four of Lecky's five volumes are devoted to the period after 1760 has given a permanent shape to our perception of Irish history in that period. This impressive work is still of immense use to historians because the footnotes contain so much transcription from records which perished in the destruction of the Four Courts during the Irish Civil War.

The third discovery was that Irish history was too important to be left to Irish historians, since they all seemed to agree more or less on its general outline and where it was heading. My first instinct had been, like that of most of my colleagues, to stand by to repel boarders – archaeologists, geographers, anthropologists, and social scientists of every description. This was born of our training, but I have come to believe that to unveil the past of Ireland the historian needs all the help he can get. Moreover the guerrilla war which has crippled the North of Ireland for the last thirty years has encouraged all the retrogressive tendencies in Irish historical writing, and even academic historians have been forced back into the mould of entrenched prejudice which a generation of young Irish historians had been confident of breaking in the 1940s.

In Ireland old attitudes can exist comfortably within the restraints of academic rigour. In any event, pressures of other kinds have meant that academic historical investigation is becoming more and more a police procedural, often with Inspector Plod in charge. One would like to think, however, that there is always room for the 'private eye' who will emulate the skills of Agatha Christie's hero, Hercule Poirot. He will regard no detail as insignificant, but he must also be able to see how the details add up to a pattern which may not have been previously noticed. He must be sceptical about the clues which everyone else finds lying around, and at the same time draw attention to the real clues which nobody thought were clues.

Captain Hastings, Watson to Poirot's Holmes, stands for the popular view of history. 'Ha!,' says Hastings, looking at the 1916 Easter Rising, 'This is the work of Sinn Féin.' 'On the contrary,' says Poirot, 'Sinn Féin is the work of 1916.' He knows that before 1914 Sinn Féin consisted of a small coterie of people around Arthur Griffith, who had the eccentric view that the Austro-Hungarian dual monarchy might work for England and Ireland as well, that is, that Ireland should be a monarchy not a republic. Hastings was misled because in 1916 British soldiers and the citizens of Dublin called every insurgent a Sinn Féiner. 'Or look here,' says Hastings, 'the formation of the Orange Society at Loughgall in 1795 fomented sectarian strife in County Armagh, and has done so ever since.' 'Not so,' replies Poirot, 'sectarian conflict between Protestant Peep O'Day Boys and Catholic Defenders had been going on in County Armagh since 1775 at least. So the Orange Order, whatever you might think of its opinions, is as much a consequence as a cause of these tensions. By the way, we may dismiss as nonsense the annual announcement by the media that Orangemen have been marching since 1690.' (There were, of course, many Orange and Williamite clubs throughout the eighteenth century, but the tradition of marching was born of the much more specific political circumstances of the 1790s in Ireland.)

The whole of Irish history is a challenge to Poirot in this way, not least the Case of the Missing Millennia, with which our investigations begin. Perhaps the investigator needs also something of the pertinacity of Inspector French, the irreverence of Inspector Dalziel, the thoughtfulness of Mr Campion, the patience of Miss Marple and the innocence of Father Brown. Confessing a taste for such escapist literature may invite criticism, but in it I have sometimes found, in whiling away the hours of a tedious journey, an insight denied to me in more serious works. With some audacity, therefore, I have made the odd allusion or quotation. I am more conscious of the daring of some of my speculations in areas which are not my own. An essay of this kind is a synthesis indebted to the labours of many scholars, and only a small part of it relates to my own research. I take some courage from these words of Fernand Braudel:

> The historian can really be on an equal footing only with the history of his own country; he understands almost instinctively its twists and turns, its complexities, its originalities, and its weaknesses.[6]

And I am still encouraged by Faulkiner's intuition that it is in the examination of hidden history that the origin of familiar events is most often revealed:

> The darker periods of history are not always the least attractive; the obscure is not necessarily the uninteresting. And the investigator is unfortunate, who delving in to the dead past, is not occasionally rewarded by the discovery of the secret springs of some long famous, but only half-understood event.[7]

A Letter of Instructions

The old-fashioned literary historians of the nineteenth century felt none of the restraints which press so heavily on academic historians today, and used their written evidence to discuss the human condition in the widest terms – explaining, moralising and preaching. Thus Carlyle, who is now often judged to be unreadable, but who once commanded a readership beyond anything a modern academic historian could dream of, was always ready to take the reader into his confidence, and share his opinions with him. Describing the death of Robespierre, he writes: 'He had on the sky-blue coat which he had got made for the Feast of the *Être-Suprême* – O Reader, can thy hard heart hold out against that?'[8] Dealing with the murder of Marat by Charlotte Corday, he notes in passing how Marat's brother had come from Neuchâtel to ask the National Convention if his deceased brother's musket might be given to him. 'For Marat too had a brother, and natural affections; and was wrapped once in swaddling-clothes; and slept safe in a cradle like the rest of us. Ye children of men – A sister of his, they say, lives still to this day in Paris.'[9] Academia has long since rejected Carlyle (as indeed it did in his own lifetime, when the University of St Andrews refused him a professorial chair, despite Goethe being one of his referees!), but it may have thrown the baby out with the bathwater, for Carlyle had imbibed a certain amount of German philosophy, and had an un-English fondness for speculating about what 'the past' really means.

In his darker moments Carlyle pictured the historian as a man with a storm-lantern stumbling over a vast rubbish tip and picking up here or there an object which caught his interest. He thought that a notice should be put up over every history library saying: 'Dry rubbish shot here'. At other times he envisaged the past more optimistically as a living forest:

> By its very nature it is a labyrinth and chaos, this that we call Human History; an *abatis* of trees and brushwood, a world-wide jungle at once growing and dying. Under the green foliage and blossoming fruit trees of Today, there lie, rotting slower or faster, the forests of all other Years and Days.[10]

In an early essay of 1833, however, he had found perhaps the most striking definition of all:

> History is the Letter of Instructions, which the old generations write and posthumously transmit to the new . . . it is the only *articulate* communication (when the inarticulate and mute, intelligible or not, lie around us and in us, so strangely through every fibre of our being, every step of our activity) which the Past can have with the Present, the Distant with what is Here.[11]

And a little further on he asks:

> Of the thing now gone silent named Past, which was once Present, and loud enough, how much do we know? Our 'Letter of Instructions' comes to us in the saddest state; falsified, blotted out, torn, lost, and but a shred of it in existence, this too so difficult to read and spell.[12]

It was to try to overcome the partial nature of history (partial in every sense) that the founders of the *Annales* school in France invented the concept of *histoire totale*. The historian must attempt the total picture. Fernand Braudel in particular tried to give his readers the sense of a past which reverberates 'so strangely through every fibre of our being, every step of our activity'. But *histoire totale* is self-evidently impossible, at best an ideal. The objection to it was succinctly stated by the anthropologist Claude Lévi-Strauss: 'Total history would cancel itself out.'[13]

The man who, more than any other, barred the layman from history was Carlyle's exact contemporary, the German professor Leopold von Ranke. Deeply shocked as a young man to find that Sir Walter Scott's *Quentin Durward* was not historically accurate, he devoted the rest of his life to establishing 'how it really was' (*wie es eigentlich gewesen*). By this he meant more than just accuracy. Ranke was by training a philologist, and he approached every historical document as a textual scholar. He taught that events in the past must be examined in the context of their own time, without the embellishment of later knowledge or understanding. For this reason the historian should confine himself to primary sources alone. All secondary work threatened the authenticity of the original, a rule which of course applied also to his own prolific output. In addition, the 'letter of instructions' had to be scientifically scrutinised for any sign of forgery, inconsistency, propaganda or bias. It was a counsel of perfection, but Ranke had many disciples, and his principles established history as a science, and gave it a respected place in university curricula.

Ranke's influence owed much to his longevity and phenomenal industry. He was Professor of History at Berlin from 1825 until 1871, and published more than sixty works, many of them multiple-volume histories, based on his own painstaking research in the archives of European chancelleries. At the age of eighty-two he began a 'History of the World', and managed to complete nine volumes by the time of his death eight years later. The Rankean legacy transformed the nature of historical study in Europe and America, fencing off academic work from all other forms of historical composition, which were relegated to amateurism, in the true sense of the word. Standards of accuracy and objectivity were set which improved the quality and usefulness of historical writing out of all recognition.

The drawbacks for historians have, however, also been considerable. Historical study in Ranke's day confined itself to certain select topics, chiefly politics and statecraft. A pecking order was established, with high politics at the top, and social and economic history and the history of ideas much lower on the scale. Military history has remained somewhere near the bottom, despite the obvious truth that all political history is underpinned by it. Even some of Ranke's own disciples exhibited unease at aspects of his teaching. Jacob Burckhardt declined an invitation to succeed him in the chair at Berlin because he felt that Ranke had drained all the poetry out of history, and Theodor Mommsen, the most rigorous of his pupils, preferred a wider cultural approach.

The greatest loss suffered by historians has been the defection of their popular audience. For the interested man in the street it is as if television had decided to abandon colour and go back to black and white. The history PhD industry annually turns out hundreds of monographs by young historians who, however diligent, give the impression that they have never read anything but other monographs. The treasures of experience in the other humanities are permanently locked away from them. Worse, they are no longer encouraged to think about the material they research; it is enough if they record it intelligently and draw the most obvious conclusions from it. The great bulk of historical writing is, in any case, now read only by specialists. To a large extent the historian whose research concerns, let us say, wool prices in fourteenth-century Tuscany will be read by a dozen other scholars who know what he is talking about. It is just too boring for the ordinary reader. One result of this is that when historians *do* make ground-breaking discoveries, these do not trickle down into school and college textbooks, not at least for a very long time. The papers of scientists may be just as unintelligible, but when someone finds a cure for a life-threatening disease you can be sure to hear about it in the media a week later.

Historical science now finds itself in a difficulty. It is too narrow, yet it attempts too much. It embraces the findings of all the intellectual disciplines of both science and the humanities. Its strength must always lie in selection and not in proof. Despite all claims to the contrary, the historian can never really be a scientist. He is like a man who dons a white coat and stethoscope and strides about the corridors of a hospital. Everyone assumes that he is a doctor, but he may be simply like Autolycus in *The Winter's Tale*, 'a snapper-up of unconsidered trifles'. The point is that he may adopt the methodology of the scientist, but his aims and conclusions are of a quite different kind. Even the simple word 'because' has not the same meaning for both. When you say that refrigeration preserves food because it inhibits the growth of bacteria, it is not at all the same kind of statement as saying that Hitler called off the invasion of Britain because Germany lost the air battles of September 1940. The first statement can be proved by repeated experiment; the second is essentially an opinion. 'What occurs in historical thinking,' wrote Sir Isaiah

Berlin, 'seems much more like the operation of common sense, where we weave together various prima facie logically independent concepts and general propositions, and bring them to bear on a given situation as best we can.'[14]

It is here that the historian's present difficulty resides. As with the medical imposter, general knowledge will carry him a certain distance, but he really needs the help of science. Paradoxically, owing to the spectacular advances in science and technology now occurring, historians are no longer the only, or the best, people to tell us the truth about the past.

The Night of Time

The night of time far surpasseth the day, and who knows when was the Equinox?

SIR THOMAS BROWNE[1]

The Case of the Missing Millennia

In 1642 Dr John Lightfoot, the Master of St Catharine's College, Cambridge, established by careful examination of the biblical evidence that the Creation had occurred on 23 October 4004 BC at nine o'clock in the morning. This opinion was repeated more memorably some years later by James Ussher, the Protestant Archbishop of Armagh.[2] Neither Lightfoot nor Ussher was a buffoon; they were scholars of international reputation, and they were meeting the most exacting demands of modern historical research, that is to say, they were using all the documentary evidence available to them *and no other kind of evidence*.

Scientists now assure us that, thanks to new and sophisticated methods of dating, they know that the Earth is 4,500,000,000 years old. For only a tiny fraction of this immense tract of time have there been humans on the planet, some 30,000 to 40,000 years. Even so, we know almost nothing about the earliest and longest period of human history. It began after the last Ice Age and ended with the Golden Age in Egypt of Pharaoh Amenhotpe III in 1360 BC. The first written records begin to appear about 3000 BC. The attempt is sometimes made to explain matters of this kind in terms that we can comprehend. Suppose that the scale involved is equal to a week of our time. Then mankind appears on the planet only a few seconds before midnight on the seventh day, and the birth of Christ occurs as the last chime of twelve dies away. It is little wonder that the human instinct is to reject knowledge of this kind altogether. The mind is not constructed for such a purpose. We are conditioned to measure time in a different way. The minutes passing as these words are written, the hurrying clouds which dapple the sunlight, these mark out the day. The days, weeks, months and years mark out our lives, and we measure time by the customary life-span. A century seems a very long time to us precisely because it is just beyond the normal. After that we think in terms of generations and genealogies. And then there is 'history', which we learned at school. No one can really imagine what a million years *means*.

The great attraction of the seventeenth-century computations was their precision. It allowed contemporaries to believe that if the Creation had not actually occurred in their lifetime, they could at least work their way back to it without too much mental distress. The precision has long gone, finally overthrown in the fierce controversies of the nineteenth century, but the cosy certainty lingers, consciously or unconsciously, and in un-expected places. Surprisingly, one of the places where it lingers is in the study of history. There is a reason for this. The essential framework of history was constructed long ago, and though the assumptions which underpinned it have perished, the framework can still be traced in many aspects of the subject because history cut itself off from archaeology and other disciplines with an interest in the past as such. The most sophisti-cated kind of historical writing today is no longer concerned with 'finding out about the past'; it devotes itself to solving problems which in essence are the same as problems encountered in any other intellectual pursuit. Historians ask one another 'Was there a general crisis in the seventeenth century?', 'Was Charles I the father of the modern welfare state?', 'Was the French Revolution a fall of snow on blossoming trees?'

Schoolchildren, who are not yet ready to debate these important questions, still learn from textbooks in which the framework is largely intact, and there are of course religious implications, not to say political ones, in departing from it. The textbook will devote perhaps three para-graphs on the first page to the whole of prehistory, twenty pages to the first millennium AD and most of the rest of the book to the history of the last two centuries. Where the history of Ireland is concerned, it may be thought there is some excuse for this. Ireland does not have much pre-history for the simple reason that it has not been inhabited for very long. The earliest traces of human habitation on the island are less than 10,000 years old. We really know only the history of the last two of these mil-lennia, and some of that is sketchy enough. Until recently four-fifths of our past was almost lost to us.

For at least two centuries, however, this lost past has aroused a lively antiquarian interest, and the ruins of these speculative theories still lie all around us. It is not too long since children were taught that the first inhabitants of Ireland were the Big Tomb Builders, those mysterious folk who littered the landscape with cromlechs and stone circles and then vanished again into infinity. They were thought to have come, in some way which was never exactly explained, from the Iberian peninsula. This was why we all had dark hair, flashing eyes and a mercurial tempera-ment. The fact that all they could do was pile large stones on top of one another proved that they were just about as primitive as it was possible to be. But then there was the puzzling question of how they managed to place these enormous capstones on top of the upright stones. What visions it conjured up of millions of slaves building huge earth mounds and rolling granite slabs on logs.

It never seemed to occur to our mentors that one reason the megalith builders left nothing else behind was that millennia of Irish wind and rain pretty well accounted for the disappearance of anything which was not stone. Older and wiser, we learned that the megaliths were constructed by Neolithic (New Stone Age) peoples who lived much later, and knew how to farm and weave and make pottery. They were far removed in civilisation from the earliest people. Now archaeologists are beginning to tell us that the Old Stone Age people were not primitive hunters after all; they too had mastered agriculture and a lot else besides – witness their astonishing cave art in other parts of Europe. Like Mark Twain's father, prehistoric man has learned an awful lot in the time it has taken us to grow up.

The rehabilitation of the caveman has proceeded with spectacular rapidity in the last few years, but, as so often happens, what the experts now know has not yet percolated down to the man in the street, who still cherishes the speculations of excited pioneers, the club-wielding caricature of comic cartoons. Yet the home life of the Flintstones may be closer to the truth than anyone realises. This can be illustrated by an example unconnected with Ireland – the Strange Case of Neanderthal Man. In 1856 in the Neander valley near Düsseldorf workmen building a railway line uncovered the remains of a skeleton. It appeared to be human, but the skull was abnormal in shape, and of remarkable size and thickness. It was long and wide, with a narrow and insignificant forehead, and large projecting ridges round the eye-sockets.

With that super confidence which brings joy into the lives of people deprived of a university education, a professor immediately pronounced the skeleton to be that of a creature who had lived before the Flood. One of his colleagues disagreed. On the contrary, he declared, it was the skeleton of a Cossack who had crawled into the cave to die when the Russian army crossed the Rhine in 1814. Artists soon began to produce their impressions of Neanderthal Man, and they have been drawing him ever since – a grotesque ape-like creature with a sloping forehead. When further skeletons of the same age were discovered in France, Marcellin Boule emphasised every feature he could find to distinguish these prehistoric skeletons from those of modern men, and in doing so produced the travesty with which we are familiar.

The original discovery had coincided with a critical moment in the history of science, just before Darwin published his book *On The Origin of Species*. In the great religious debate of the nineteenth century Neanderthal Man became the target of ridicule, and Neanderthal entered the language as a useful term of abuse for anybody with whose opinions you disagreed. Yet the whole thing is a myth, a premise resting on a misunderstanding. The fact is that every one of the abnormal features has been systematically disproved by unbiased observers in the course of the last sixty years. Neanderthal Man never existed; he was simply *a* man. Scientists examining a similar skeleton found at La Chapelle-aux-Saints in the Dordogne in 1957 concluded that if 'Neanderthal' Man could be reincarnated and placed in the New York subway – provided that he were bathed, shaved and dressed in modern clothes – he would attract no more attention than any of the other passengers.[3]

This is, to be sure, a somewhat ambiguous statement, but in the light of recent archaeological evidence, accumulating at an ever faster rate, we need to forget the drawings in our school textbooks and apply the New York subway test. The trouble is that it is so difficult to set aside the presuppositions which our education leads us to make about people in the past – not only in remote prehistory but in more recent centuries. One reason is that so many of our assumptions are still based on a mental framework of 'the progress of man', even though that theory of history has long since been disavowed. Instinctively we regard even a Swift or a Voltaire with sympathy because they were forced to live in an age more backward and benighted than our own. All the evidence suggests the contrary. One searches in vain in the eighteenth century for an Auschwitz or a Hiroshima.

If we are no wiser than they, are we not better informed? And, at least, we are cleaner and healthier. Well, perhaps, but progress is not on a broad front. If we measure it purely in terms of antibiotics and the dentist's chair, no one wants to travel back in time, and no doubt Swift would have enjoyed television and Voltaire had great fun with a personal computer, but neither they nor anyone alive today has out-written Shakespeare or out-painted Rembrandt. If we are to understand anything of the human mind we must approach the people of the past with humility rather than an overconfident superiority.

There is a difficulty here, and to help us with it we must turn to the anthropologist. In terms of technology mankind has advanced more in the last few years than in all of his previous history. Because for millennia prehistoric man did not advance beyond the use of implements of wood and stone, the assumption has been that, in comparison with us, he was of low intelligence. His brain was inferior to the modern brain. However, anthropologists tell a strange story. We are accustomed to take the same attitude to those 'primitive' peoples who occupy the planet with us in our own time. The naked forest dwellers of Papua New Guinea or the Amazon basin cannot be taught to use a computer, and even the simplest mechanical device is totally beyond their comprehension. On the other hand, Claude Lévi-Strauss tells us, they can without the slightest difficulty distinguish between more than 3,000 different species of forest plant, and describe the properties of each. No doubt they have many other skills of the same kind, including the ability to name hundreds of ancestors, and trace their history back to the Creation. There is strong evidence which would indicate that the capacity and functioning of the human brain are essentially the same throughout the species. Schoolmasters everywhere may shake their heads, but their experience is based on too narrow a range of examples!

Whatever the truth of this matter, it is undeniable that archaeologists are now beginning to find increasing evidence of the sophistication of our remote ancestors. The greatest obstacle to their investigations has always been the obliterating effect of time upon the evidence. And such evidence as survives has been extensively pillaged over the centuries. For anti-quaries every artifact found buried in the ground was treasure to be kept for gain or carted away to country houses and museums, where it generated wild speculations about past times. It was preserved, if at all, without order or system, or a reliable means of dating, its examination the pastime of the amateur and dilettante. It was not until the late nineteenth century that the meticulous labours of General A.H. Pitt-Rivers 'trans-formed excavation from a hobby into an arduous scientific pursuit'.[4] He insisted that the situation of every object found should be recorded, and made detailed plans, measurements, descriptions and drawings. These are the principles on which all archaeological investigation has since been conducted.

What we are faced with is a vast expanse of prehistory whose secrets are only now beginning to be revealed. Even the putative dating is almost beyond our comprehension. Archaeologists still work within the sections first labelled by the pioneers to indicate the typology of the artifacts discovered – Old Stone Age, Middle Stone Age, New Stone Age, and the eras of metalworking, Bronze, Gold and Iron Age – but these arbitrary labels are in many ways misleading. They cover millennia, and within them there are myriad problems of cultures and ethnicity with which archaeologists must wrestle. If history is measured in time, it is almost more convenient to measure archaeology in terms of the acceleration of scientific advance. Every day brings us closer to a definite answer to the question which the children ask of the fathers in the Book of Joshua: 'What mean these stones?'

Why Didn't They Ask Evans?

A t this point, if not long before, the reader is likely to say that this vast unrecorded human existence is all very well, but has it any relevance for the history of modern Ireland? More and more the progress of archaeology indicates that it has. Hardly a day passes without some new and startling revelation about the nature of prehistoric Ireland, but like so many other challenging pieces of information in that country, it receives little or muted publicity. It is not a matter for public discussion because it falls outside the framework of *perceived* Irish identity. It is not in any obvious way linked to religion, Gaelic culture, nationalism or partition. Therefore it does not command much attention, either in Ireland or abroad.

Archaeologists and historians may be divided by methodology, but the barriers are made higher by academic apartheid. Archaeologists used to complain that historians never listened to what they had discovered; now they don't even bother to tell them. A pioneer in breaking down the barriers was the late E. Estyn Evans, who was from 1945 to 1968 Professor of Geography in the Queen's University of Belfast. Evans, who had studied under the great historical geographer H.J. Fleure, had asked early in his career whether the purpose of history was to find out something about our past, or merely to argue about the finer points of politics in comparatively recent times. He suspected that the latter kind of history, in universities at least, commanded more prestige than the short and simple annals of the poor, though he lived to see that balance to some degree redressed. His early researches were therefore mildly, and always humorously, critical of academic historians, who, he felt, were too busy fighting off interlopers – geographers and such like – to see the obvious.

He came to believe that the Irishness of the Irish was a pre-Celtic heritage. This was a direct contradiction of popular belief, but, as he said himself, anyone who sets out to explode myths in Ireland must embark on 'an antagonizing reappraisal'. When he first came to Ireland from Wales and began recording rural folkways he was puzzled by the fact that almost nothing of this rich lore was reflected in the recorded history of Ireland, whether Irish or English. 'It was beneath the notice of the learned scribes, and the Irish laws ignored the common people.' Failing to find in such sources the evidence he sought, he began, in 1932, with a colleague, Dr Oliver Davies, to excavate prehistoric sites, starting with the megaliths, 'to see what evidence the spade could yield'.[5]

He could scarcely have imagined to what astonishing conclusions this archaeological research would lead him, and he was to devote a large part of his subsequent career to elucidating them in many books and articles, though even now they have not yet penetrated the general understanding of the subject. At the outset, he was warned off by the experts, who told him that everything that could be learned from the megaliths had already been discovered. He got no encouragement from his university, and later declared that he had faced 'open hostility from professors who regarded history and classical studies as the only ones fit for university teachers'. However, the excavations proved richly rewarding, and when, in 1937, he found a habitation site at Lyle's Hill near Belfast, the results exceeded his wildest hopes. Thirty years later he told an audience, with pardonable pride, 'You may not be moved by the discovery, on that hill top, of a hundred thousand Neolithic potsherds where almost none had been found in Ireland before, but this was the beginning of a series of discoveries which has excited archaeologists and made Lyle's Hill pottery one of the best known types of Neolithic ceramics in Western Europe.'[6]

Time and the labours of many other archaeologists have amply confirmed Evans's general conclusion, that the Irish Neolithic was a remarkably stable culture lasting some 2,000 years. 'The hundreds of megalithic sites which have been studied and classified tell us that a peasant culture deeply concerned with religious ideas, with votive offerings and magic ceremonies at wells, was already established in nearly every part of Ireland before 2000 BC.'

Even more important than the existence of a stable, unguessed-at Irish Neolithic culture lasting longer than the whole of perceived 'Irish history' was the ubiquitous evidence of continuity, a renewal of the old in contact with the new. Yet, as Evans complained, 'Gaelic scholars in general have shown little interest in these findings. Blinkered by their literary–historical training, they fail to see the significance of material culture and are critical of the work of the archaeologists.'[7] Nowhere was the continuity more visible than in agriculture. The most startling results of Evans's investigations were those relating to agricultural practice.

One example which can be cited is the Irish cultivation ridge. In areas where the soil is sticky and 'too tough for the plough' it is turned by the spade rather than the plough, to form broad ridges, generally called 'lazy-beds'. The spade ridge is still a favourite mode for the cultivation of garden and allotment crops. In the west of Ireland it was, into the twentieth century, a common method of growing field crops, especially potatoes, and even corn has been planted in this way. The spade ridges are not dug over – hence the name 'lazy-beds'. Instead, sods from the strips in between are inverted on to the beds, and further raised by shovelling soil on to them from the trenches. This method, so much easier than ploughing in difficult soils, is well adapted to the Irish climate and environment, and the narrow Irish spade is not primarily a digging tool but is designed to undercut the sod and invert it. Traces of old lazy-beds can be seen everywhere in Ireland. Older and fainter ones show up with a low sun or a light covering of snow.

Cultivation ridges of prehistoric antiquity have been discovered under several feet of blanket bog in County Mayo. Some of the most exciting work of this kind has been done by Seamus Caulfield, who at Bellderg Beg found unmistakeable traces of lazy-beds in fields enclosed by irregular stone walls, built long before the bog had begun to grow. Material found at the site confirmed a Neolithic date. Similar traces were found at Carrownalogh in County Sligo by Michael Herity, and since then further examples of pre-bog walls have been uncovered from Northern Ireland to County Kerry. It was seen, as Evans expressed it, 'that the narrow spade and the long-handled shovel, which have been the Irish navvy's passport overseas, have an ancestry of some forty centuries. Who can tell what profound consequences such aptitudes, an addition to hand implements and to small-scale units of social and economic life, have had on the nature of the Irish countryman and Irish society?'[8]

There are other, less tangible, ways in which one may sense the astonishing survival of very ancient cultures. Many Irish traditions and customs are so deeply rooted that sixteen centuries of disapproval by the Christian Church has not been able to eradicate them. Some of them have been adapted to Christian purposes. Others have been driven underground. Evans believed that the cult of holy wells, the worship of stones and the veneration of thorn trees were probably megalithic in origin. There are some 3,000 holy wells in Ireland, regularly visited at the (pagan) festival seasons, when devotees tie rags and strips of clothing to the tree which overhangs the well so that it may bear their ailments.

Significantly, a great many superstitions cling to the megalithic monuments themselves. The water which accumulates in the natural 'cupholes' or basins in the stones is considered to possess special virtues, such as the ability to cure warts. Offerings of pins and coins are often made in them. Some of the megalithic basins served as fonts in the early churches. More than once Evans was refused permission to inspect a site by a farmer fearful that such examination would bring bad luck. The megaliths were considered to be the haunts of fairies, which some authorities identify with ancestral spirits guarding the burial places. Others hold the theory that a belief in the fairies is the survival of some folk memory of an ancient people. The country people do not disturb trees on ancient burial sites, and will not even use the branches as fuel.

Curious beliefs still attach to prehistoric objects. Flint arrowheads are produced as evidence that cattle have been 'elf-shot' by the fairies, and polished stone axe-heads are supposed to have healing powers. When food is taken out of the house, some should always be left behind for the fairies lest the dreaded 'hungry grass' grow. An inordinate number of superstitions seem to attach to cattle, an indication of the importance of cattle-rearing and transhumance in early times. Such superstitions are held as tenaciously in Presbyterian County Antrim as in the Catholic south.

Of course these traditions and customs are not peculiar to Ireland. Many of the same ones are to be found in Scotland or Brittany, which may have shared a common prehistoric culture. But their survival seems particularly strong in Ireland, and has influenced the shape of Irish history. Behind the saints' days, and the Celtic festivals, lurk even older festivals associated with the four cardinal points in the year marking the change of the seasons. In Ireland great importance still clings to the first day of February, May, August and November. The festivals of February and November have been sanctified by the Church as St Brigit's Day and All Hallows. A swathe of timeless customs clings to each. On St Brigit's Eve children still pull rushes and take them home to make St Brigit's crosses. In the Glens of Antrim people make a small bed for the saint to come in and rest. In County Kerry the 'Biddy Boys' wear hats of straw on 1 February. The ceremonies of remembering the dead on All Souls' Day, 2 November, are preceded by the superstitions and rituals of Hallowe'en, which is particularly important as marking the death of the year, the time when the family unites after the bringing down of the cattle from the hill pastures. The other turning-point of the year is 1 May. In Ireland fires are lit on May Eve, the Beltane fires which may be connected to the ancient 'need-fires' found throughout Europe. With the beginning of August comes the Lammas festival, the beginning of the harvest, and for some reason associated with fairs. The significance of these confluences may sometimes be exaggerated, but they are not coincidence. They point at least to an ancient rhythm of life intimately connected to agriculture and the seasons, a pulse which modern industry and electric light have not entirely extinguished.

Evans soon came to be convinced of the existence of a long and very stable pre-Celtic culture in Ireland, and found ample confirmation in his study of Irish folkways for the revelations of archaeology. He knew that in expressing these conclusions he was throwing down a challenge to academic historians to reconsider their aproach to the subject. When they had become professional, he pointed out, 'they had only changed their methods and not their main interests'. Moreover, he felt that they had been 'preoccupied with the morbid phenomena of British rule in their country, "1169 and all that" done into academic prose', and he bluntly declared that he found this kind of history confusing and repellent.[9]

One might have expected Evans's work, increasingly confirmed by the discoveries of archaeology, to have influenced significantly the approach of historians and geographers, and transformed Irish thinking about proto-history, but this has not exactly happened. Though it won respect and academic honours, Irish scholars 'showed little inclination to move in the direction he suggested'. It may be that his conclusions went against the grain, for they did not appeal to the mind-set either of the independent state born in 1922 or of Northern Ireland where he lived and worked. Both populations were obsessed with their more recent history. Evans believed that the land made the people, but on all sides he found people trying to make the land.[10]

Scene of the Crime

'M ost Irish history,' declared Evans, 'has been written with little sense of geography.'[11] Modern history books do not mention geography, because Geography is four doors along the corridor or over in Block 10, and one would not dream of interfering in their strange preoccupations. Once again the Victorians allowed themselves a wider remit. Thus A.G. Richey began his *Short History of the Irish People* (a substantial book despite its title) in 1881 with this firm assertion:

> The progress and civilisation of a nation are mainly determined by its surrounding physical conditions: the situation of a country, the nature of its surface and coastline, its mineral and vegetable productions, the substances available for food, the proportion which the amount of food bears to the labour expended, and the peculiarities of the climate, affect the character of the inhabitants. It is therefore necessary to begin the history of the Irish people by a sketch of the physical geography and natural productions of Ireland.[12]

One could scarcely find a clearer expression of Evans's belief that land and people go together; the one cannot be understood without the other.

Nor, allowing for fashionable changes in measurement, could one improve on Richey's definition of Ireland's location:

> It is situated between the degrees of 51°26' and 55°20' north latitude and 5°20' and 10°26' west latitude, and bounded by the Atlantic on all sides except the east, where it is separated from Britain by the Irish Sea (138 miles wide), St George's Channel (47 miles at the narrowest) and the North Channel, where only thirteen miles separates Fair Head from the Mull of Kintyre. Its shape is rhomboid, the greater diagonal 302 miles and the less 210 miles. Its superficial area is 32,524 square miles.[13]

Unlike most islands Ireland is hollow in the middle and high round the edges. The central part consists of a shallow limestone basin, much of it covered by peatbog and barely above sea level. Its flatness is relieved by low hills and ridges (the moraines of glaciers) and a network of rivers and loughs. Round this central plain, except in part of the east, the land rises to mountains which form a coastal rim. The western coast is deeply indented, with long inlets where the sea has advanced through gaps in the mountains. We may dismiss, as putting too great a strain on the human mind, the speculations of some geologers that the island story began somewhere in the latitude of South Africa about 600 million years ago, and that Ireland moved steadily northward, crossing the equator 300 million years ago. It is enough to observe that the mountains of Ireland are constructed from some of the Earth's oldest materials. The geological structure represents the convergence of two great European mountain systems. The older axis of Scandinavia runs down through the north and west of the island to meet with a younger axis coming across through France and Spain. The crumpled and folded masses of Pre-Cambrian sedimentary rocks extend from the north of Antrim to Connemara. Ancient quartzites, mica-schists and marbles create the breathtakingly beautiful vistas of western Ireland. In the south are the parallel east–west foldings of Old Red Sandstone, called Armorican or Hercynian after Brittany and the Harz Mountains. Much later, igneous granite was forced up to form mountains in Galway, Mayo and Donegal, and the Mourne Mountains in the east. In Antrim young volcanic basalt poured out of the Earth's crust to cover and protect the underlying chalk, giving the north-east its distinctive black and white rocks. The central plain is a bed of Old Red Sandstone, thickly coated with limestone laid down over aeons by primeval marine life. Four great glaciations planed and eroded this geological complex, depositing moraines to form rich soil drifts, and the swarms of little egg-shaped hills which are called drumlins. These glaciations have given Ireland some of its most characteristic landscape features.

From the outset it seems to have been a very wet island. Water is everywhere. In addition to Ireland's long coastline, its inland loughs account for some 200,000 hectares of the entire area, and Lough Neagh in the north is the largest freshwater lake in the British Isles. Ptolemy's map, just about the first graphic definition of Ireland, indicates the chief rivers with some degree of accuracy. Over much of the island the water lies immediately below the soil level, seeping into the extensive peatbogs and mosses which cover a fifth of the total area.

All these reservoirs are continually fed by rain. It is Ireland's greatest secret, closely guarded by the tourist operators, but noted through the ages by every traveller and visitor. 'It generally rains four or five days in the week,' one eighteenth-century traveller noted, 'thus rainbows are seen almost daily.' A century earlier an anonymous French observer described it as 'seldom dry, but often running over, as if the Heavens were a wounded eye, perpetually weeping over it'. One consequence of this, as Edmund Campion noted in 1571, is that 'the inhabitants (especially new come) are subject to distillations, rheums and fluxes [colds and dysentery] for remedy whereof they use an ordinary drink of aqua vitae'. He thus neatly identified in one sentence the two most important liquid factors in Irish history.[14]

Humidity and wind are the chief features of Ireland's maritime climate. Unending depressions sweep in from the Atlantic on the prevailing south-west winds. The alternation of warm and cold fronts produces grey skies, with brief glorious intervals of sunshine and unforgiving rain, described by one French geographer as *quasi-horizontale*. The swiftly moving clouds precipitate most of their rain over the western mountains. The heaviest rainfall is in the west and south-west, and the driest areas are in the north and east. Passengers on aircraft flying in to Ireland are immediately struck by the intense green of the fields, the attribute which has given the island its national colour.

This is the climate of Ireland today, and we can reasonably assume its relative consistency in historic times, though there are some interesting variations which will be discussed elsewhere. But there was a much larger expanse of time when the climate was very different, and this is of considerable importance to archaeologists. The last great Ice Age was followed by a sub-Arctic climate, which gradually gave way to milder conditions. Flora and fauna entered Ireland even before the submersion of the land-bridge with Scotland. Ireland's first colonists were trees, the Arctic willow first, then birch, Scotch pine, hazel, elm, oak and elder.

The weather again deteriorated, becoming wet and stormy. The land sank, and coastal areas and inland hollows were inundated. This climate, from 5000 BC until 2500 BC, is called 'Atlantic'. A warm dry period followed, the 'sub-Boreal', which ended in the middle of the last millennium BC. Then the rainfall in the west, it has been deduced, was half or less of what it is now, and westerly winds were light. Once again, stormy weather returned, and Ireland became cooler and wetter than today. (It requires a suspension of disbelief to imagine this.) During this short 'sub-Atlantic' phase, from 600 BC until 100 BC, the peat was laid down, and the great forests were submerged in extensive peatbogs.

It is in fact because of bogland that all this is known. Peat has preserved the evidence as nothing else could, and it is valuable testimony for both climate and early human settlement. 'For the scientist', wrote Evans,

> the value of the peat-bogs lies in the fact that they preserve not only wood, twigs, and the seeds and fruits of plants but even the minute grains of pollen, so that as they accumulate they write their own record, a record which the pollen-analyst can read. Moreover the phases of vegetation and climate thus chronicled can be correlated with the story of Irishmen who, careless or forgetful, have left behind at different levels objects of stone, metal or wood, which the archaeologist can use as clues in his detective work. In this way a sequence of climate, vegetation and human industries has been worked out, and we now have an outline of the whole story from the time when the first layers of lake clay were laid down in the hollows of the surface while the ice still lingered in the mountain corries: they contain remains of arctic willow and the bones of the giant deer.[15]

Every one of these facts has influenced the course of Irish history – Ireland's insularity, its wide Atlantic shores, its separation from England and proximity to Scotland, its boggy terrain and inaccessible mountains, interspersed with fertile valleys which are ideal for cattle-rearing but not arable farming, its temperate climate and high rainfall. There is no such thing as an Irish race, as George Bernard Shaw observed, but there is an Irish climate.[16] It is what makes Irish people Irish. They are different from the people of Spain, who must shelter from the sun at noonday, and not quite like the people of Scotland, who have higher mountains and more snow in winter.

If the outlines of Irish history have been moulded by geography, it is true also that this history has a physical geography of its own, with mountains, plateaux, corries and ridges, plains, rivers and oxbow lakes. From these we can draw a contour map, and though the precise contours may be altered from time to time as the result of historical research, the map retains its distinctive shape. The names (or more often the numbers) of the highest peaks are known to us all – 1169, 1690, 1798, 1916, 1921. The plateaux of Anglo-Norman Ireland, the Old English, the Protestant Ascendancy and the Catholic nation stand out from the general background.

And there are valleys and featureless hollows which are only now receiving the attention they deserve. Through all flow the deep streams of Irish consciousness, past and present, bitter currents of strife and lawlessness, or simplicity and resignation. The landscape is touched with the beauty and grandeur which invest all divided nations.

Forensic

In the years immediately after the First World War archaeologists and historians were presented with an entirely new kind of evidence, the aerial photograph. A pioneer was the English archaeologist O.G.S. Crawford, a classical scholar who had turned to fieldwork. While serving with the Royal Flying Corps on the Western Front he came to realise the potential of aerial photography in archaeology. Later, as an archaeological officer for the Ordnance Survey, he did much to develop and popularise the science, and in 1927 he founded the journal *Antiquity*, which he edited until his death in 1957. Crawford's work was carried on by J.K.S. Saint Joseph, who served in the Royal Air Force Bomber Command in the Second World War and was eventually given a unique department of aerial photographic studies in Cambridge University, equipped with its own aircraft. His aerial survey of Ireland and its archaeological sites was, and continues to be, of the utmost value to the relevant disciplines.

Its usefulness is by no means confined to the archaeologists, for it has questioned some of the assumptions of historians about, for example, medieval fortifications. The truth was that the Earth's surface looked different from several thousand feet above it. In the words of the French aviator Antoine de Saint-Exupéry, 'For centuries the roads have been deceiving us.'[17] We naturally think of our history as it is revealed to us in our own patterns of settlement and habitation, at eye level. The aeroplane sees the earlier habitations that we cannot see. It restores to us the prehistoric ways and fortifications, the lost roads and trackways, the medieval villages wiped out by the Black Death, the most ancient patterns of cultivation. The growing crops, all unbeknown to us, betray the lines and ditches which lie under them, because 'interference with the ground for whatever purpose leaves its mark practically for ever'.[18] The long shadows cast by the sun in the morning and evening reveal most; the end of winter, the spring and early summer is the best time for aerial archaeology.

In 1949 an American chemist, Willard Libby, discovered a method of dating organic materials of great age. It was based on the fact that the radioactive isotope carbon-14, found in such material, decays at a known rate, halving every 5,370 years. This gave archaeologists for the first time a way of obtaining approximate dates for objects far back in prehistory. The declining radioactivity could be measured on a scale up to 50,000 years and beyond. Subsequently it was discovered that the assumption of a constant rate of decay was incorrect, and radiocarbon dates are now given on a calibrated scale with a *circa* prefix and several hundred or thousand years plus or minus.[19]

The uneven rate of radiocarbon decay was revealed by dendrochronology, the scientific study of the clearly defined rings found in the trunk and branches of a tree when it is felled. It proved that for some reason organic material was more exposed to carbon-14 before 1000 BC than after. The beauty of tree-ring dating is its simplicity and accuracy. Every summer a tree acquires a new outer sheath as it is permeated by nutrients and moisture rising from its roots. Each time this happens, a new ring is formed; a tree is therefore its own calendar, and must always tell the truth about its age. Moreover, since the rings are thin in dry years and thick in moist ones, the tree rings also tell the expert a great deal about variations in climate and weather through the centuries, information which is beginning to reveal some startling gaps in our historical knowledge.

The principle is simple, but the analysis of thousands of timber samples from many parts of the world demands scientific work of great skill and complexity, and now owes much to the use of computers. The pioneering research of Michael Baillie and his team at the Queen's University of Belfast has enabled a database to be created from trees in many parts of the world, against which a sample from any source can be compared and accurately dated. This accuracy is of incalculable value to both archaeologists and historians. Baillie has constructed a tree-ring chronology for the Irish oak as far back as 5289 BC.[20] This means that any piece of oak, whether it is found under a prehistoric habitation site or in a Tudor manor house, can be related to a certain summer long ago, and we can say something about the weather that summer. This is truly an example of a breakthrough in our investigation of the past.

The latest weapon to be added to the detective armoury is DNA 'fingerprinting'. Nothing to do with fingerprints, this is a convenient shorthand for the discovery of the genetic code, which is an even more effective way of identifying individual human beings (and all other animals and plants) by the pattern of their genes. No two examples are identical, but DNA fingerprinting allows comparison of homogeneous groups in different regions and at different times. This has revolutionised the gathering of forensic evidence in police work; it is now revolutionising archaeology. Already it has produced some startling results. The first genetic map to be prepared for the whole of the British Isles has shown that there is no significant genetic variation. We all share a common gene pool, which is many thousands of years old. The Institute of Molecular Science at Oxford profiled 6,000 people and compared their blood samples with DNA extracted from the remains of Stone Age people. There was a 99 per cent correlation. This suggests that the original gene pool has hardly been disturbed by the waves of invading Celts, Gaels, Romans, Vikings and Normans.

These findings have predictably not been well received by enthusiasts for national and regional identity. A member of Plaid Cymru insisted that 'the Welsh are distinct in *every* way', while the Anglo-Saxon Society declared that genetic mapping 'demeaned and insulted' traditional views about Britain. 'This casts us all back into the Stone Age. I am not sure that I want to go there.'[21] The genetic map has not been warmly welcomed by the Scots and the Irish either.

All such techniques have been rapidly advanced by the widespread use of computers in the sciences. We are only at the beginning of a very exciting process, and in the twenty-first century the revelations of scientific archaeology may change the face of history.

Footprints

N o trace of human habitation in Ireland before the ninth millennium
BC has yet been found, though archaeologists still hope that the
advance of science will eventually reveal signs of Palaeolithic (Old Stone
Age) settlement. Ireland was in fact one of the last places in western
Europe to be inhabited. The earliest people in Ireland appear to have been
fishers and hunters who lived by the water's edge and used the resources
of the woods, rivers and lakes to survive. They have left faint traces of
their existence in worked flints and bones, often found on the sea or lake
shore. Although this inevitably suggests a very primitive form of life and
a simple technology, archaeologists are impressed by the fine craftsman-
ship involved in producing these blades and arrowheads. Attempts to
date early human artifacts were beset with false trails and disappoint-
ments in the twentieth century but are now more successful. The earliest
radiocarbon date of *c.* 7490 BC was established by Swedish archaeologists
at Woodpark, County Sligo.[22]

The picture became clearer in 1973 when an astonishing discovery was
made at Mount Sandal near Coleraine in County Londonderry. A very
early human settlement was found and excavated over the next four years
by Peter Woodman. He established radiocarbon dates from 7010 BC to
6490 BC. More interestingly, in occupation levels spanning 500 years he
uncovered ('contrary to all expectations') the remains of roughly round
houses about six metres in diameter, which not only are the oldest
Mesolithic (Middle Stone Age) houses to be discovered in Ireland, but also
predate any so far found in Britain.[23] The phrase 'contrary to all expectations' rings through the story of the progress of human knowledge.
It was 'contrary to all expectations' that the Earth was found to be re-
volving round the sun, and not the other way round, and that a mould
growing in one of Dr Alexander Fleming's dishes was found to be capable
of destroying bacteria. When in 1989 the spacecraft Voyager 2 got close
enough to the planet Neptune to take detailed pictures of the surface, they
were 'contrary to all expectations'.

The existence of houses at Mount Sandal was determined from round
stains left in the ground, caused by the decay of the timbers they had once
held. These holes were not vertical, but angled inward, showing how the
houses had been constructed from saplings, converged in a domed roof,

like the igloo of cartoonists' imagination. Inside the houses were hearths, 1 metre wide and 30 centimetres deep. The narrow-bladed flints (microliths) and the small bones of birds and fish found on the site suggest that the occupants spent most of their time fishing and hunting game. There were other surprises, including the presence of a number of stone axes. It had hitherto been assumed that these had not been introduced into Ireland until the coming of the first Neolithic (New Stone Age) agriculturalists several millennia later, so it would not be surprising if even earlier Mesolithic settlements lie waiting to be uncovered.

No skeletons of these Mesolithic people have yet been found, but undoubtedly they formed the original genetic stock of 'the Irish people', to which all subsequent stocks were added. There is a gap in our knowledge at the end of the early Mesolithic, coinciding with a change in the technique by which flints were shaped. A sharp line used to be drawn between the early Mesolithic hunters and the Neolithic people who had learned how to farm, and who were assumed to be invaders from mainland Europe. Academics are good at drawing sharp lines, but now the whole theory is crumbling. Archaeologists are coming to think that the late phases of Mesolithic culture overlap with the earliest traces of agricultural activity. While it is probable that the so-called Neolithic Revolution does coincide with invasions and an influx of new people into Ireland, there is no *compelling* reason to assume that the original inhabitants were exterminated. It is far more likely that they were assimilated into the new stock over a very long time, and gradually adopted their more settled lifestyle.

The Neolithic agriculturalists were the builders of the megaliths, the great stone monuments which are their lasting memorial. There are more than 1,200 of them in Ireland, and they pose the most perplexing questions of all about Irish prehistory. The huge Neolithic passage tombs of the Boyne valley were too impressive to be ignored by later peoples, and this fact must constantly be borne in mind when their contents are examined. At Newgrange, material from secondary settlements built round the monument has given radiocarbon dates of 2100 BC to 1925 BC, the beginning of the Bronze Age, but the most intriguing discoveries there have been of numerous Roman coins and gold jewelry of the early Christian centuries. It has been suggested that these are the votive offerings of many generations of pilgrims to the site. It is all too easy to see how the first antiquarians to explore these monuments were misled, and in their turn misled their successors. Only now can scientific methods of dating sort out the confusion. These edifices were in active use, for whatever purpose, for at least three millennia, which is a very long time. We know, for instance, that in the ninth century AD Knowth was the seat of the northern kings of Brega, the area which corresponds to County Meath.

The proto-scientific investigation of Ireland's past begins only in the last year of the seventeenth century, when the Welsh antiquary Edward Lhuyd made his first visit to Ireland. Lhuyd, who was Keeper of Antiquities at the Ashmolean Museum in Oxford, wrote the first detailed and scholarly account of the great megalithic tombs at Newgrange, which had been opened by accident in the same year. Lhuyd's interest in Irish antiquities, however, was subordinate to another enthusiasm. He was one of a group of Welsh scholars who, at the very end of the seventeenth century, put the history of Wales on an entirely new footing by showing that Welsh was the language of the Ancient Britons, and a sister language of Irish, Scots Gaelic, Cornish and Breton. All these in turn descended from the language of the Celts. Lhuyd was a careful scholar, but like many of his contemporaries, he was anxious to establish a living continuity with the classical world, especially for the 'Celtic' peoples. His contemporary Henry Rowlands believed that the megalithic stone circles found all over Wales were Druid temples, and the cromlechs sacrificial altars.

In Ireland, as in Wales, this antiquarian revival of the eighteenth century was closely bound up with the Druids and the Celts. The influence of these misdirections not only lasted to the second revival of interest in the Celts in the nineteenth century but has grown in strength ever since, so that even hard-headed business people talk unselfconsciously about 'the Celtic fringe', 'the Celtic tiger' and so on, and separatist groups in Brittany, Scotland, Wales and Cornwall proclaim their solidarity with the Irish struggle against the Saxon. Yet the astonishing fact is that no one in Ireland claimed to be a Celt before 1700.[24] Even today, relatively few of the Irish megaliths have been excavated, and it is by no means established that they were 'tombs' at all. During the last thirty years, however, enough has come to light to bring about a complete reassessment of traditional views. The more one reads the reports of fieldwork on the Neolithic period, the more convinced one becomes that this research is still only in its infancy.

There are four major types of megalithic structure – court cairns, portal tombs or chambers, passage tombs and wedge tombs. Most of them have been disturbed, even in prehistoric days, and this always has to be kept in mind when their possible function is considered. There is, for example, nothing to stop people from placing bones in 'tombs' which are already thousands of years old. It has been suggested that the court cairns may not be burial places but temples, where the ritual involved would have taken place in the forecourt, some magical or religious activity at which we can only guess. Each might have served as a focal centre for a scattered population, as the parish church does for the rural population of the Irish countryside today. 'The court cairns give the impression,' writes Peter Harbison, 'of being the product of an egalitarian society, broken down into groupings of perhaps no more than 50–100 people, who were using the cairns to establish ancestral rights over the minimum amount of land they needed to survive.'[25] The implications of this kind of research are far-reaching. A hazy outline of society begins to appear, something which economic historians could get their teeth into by comparing these patterns with more familiar ones in later times.

We no longer need to imagine an invasion of megalith builders from sunny Spain in order to explain so many court cairns. We generally underestimate the immense lapse of time over which assimilation takes place. After all, we do not need to draw the conclusion from the prevalence of electric light-bulbs or Japanese television sets that Ireland was once successively invaded by Americans and Japanese. Ten thousand years from now it may be difficult to measure the time gap between the arrival in Ireland of these two products. The idea of an 'economic invasion' is perfectly feasible in prehistory, and the court cairns can be explained as the adaptation of a ubiquitous European idea by an otherwise indigenous population.

The Passage Tombs

It is when one turns to consider the huge passage tombs that speculation gives way to awe. They have been described as the first great achievement of monumental architecture in Europe, and in the Boyne valley Ireland has some of the finest of them. The builders seem to have arranged them within hilltop cemeteries. The outstanding cemetery is located about 12 miles upstream of the mouth of the River Boyne. The tombs there are remarkable for their size and the evidence of the engineering skill that went into their construction. They indicate great sophistication of burial ritual, and some are most elaborately carved with complex and mysterious iconography of abstract symbols.

The now thoroughly excavated tumuli in the Boyne valley raise enormous but fascinating questions. Are these tombs huge monuments to the dead, or are they temples of an esoteric cult? The motive for their construction must have been as compelling as that for building the pyramids. As Liam de Paor writes, this implies complexity in social organisation.

> There must have been experts of various kinds – priests, engineers, gaugers, carvers. There must have been . . . an organisation of society more open and complex than that of extended families communally farming. And, about the passage-type megalithic tombs in particular, there are features which, oddly, suggest an almost urban background, the formal monumentality, the grouping of the tombs, the specialisation implied and the underlying questions about food supply and the direction of labour.[26]

The three famous mounds which make up the cluster in the Boyne valley are Newgrange, Dowth and Knowth. The large mound at Knowth has produced 'a number of astounding surprises' during the course of excavations since 1962. It was found to contain not one but two passage tombs, built back to back at about the same time, one pointing east, the other west. It has been suggested that they have a deliberate equinoctial orientation (sunrise on 20/21 March and 22/23 September) associating them with sowing and harvest. A remarkable macehead of flint was found in one of the recesses of the eastern chamber. It seems clearly to be carved in the shape of a human face, with the mouth as a hole for the wooden handle. The same chamber yielded another astonishing find, an elaborately decorated stone basin. And it must always be remembered that these sites were thoroughly pillaged by Vikings in search of treasure, which, for all we know, they found.

The eastern tomb at Knowth is the longest passage tomb in the whole of Atlantic Europe. Its roof is corbelled, that is, constructed from large flat stones placed one on top of another in ever-decreasing circles until the gap can be closed with a single stone. There are a considerable number of decorated incised stones over the whole site. One, placed at the entrance to the western tomb, has a series of boxed triangles, with a vertical line in the centre; another, on the southern side, has what looks like the radiating lines of a sundial.

Dowth is a less interesting mound. It was systematically excavated in the nineteenth century, and yielded few finds of interest, mostly of a later date than the tomb. Archaeologists now wonder if Dowth might, like Knowth, have a second chamber, but Michael J. O'Kelly looked for it from 1962 until 1975 without finding it. The dryness of the Dowth chamber is testimony to the engineering skill of its builders, and still excites the admiration of modern engineers.

The third of the three great passage tombs is Newgrange, situated on a hill overlooking the River Boyne. Early Irish mythology identifies it as the burial place of the kings of Tara, and also as the home of the Tuatha Dé Danann, a race of supernatural beings devoted to the goddess Danu. They had gone underground, where they continued to perform feats beyond the powers of mortals, an echo perhaps of some episode of conquest or resistance. The mound was opened in 1699 in an attempt to quarry stone for road building, and it was this event which first roused the interest of Edward Lhuyd.

Newgrange's most remarkable feature, one which has made it known to archaeologists throughout the world, is the deliberate orientation of the central line of the passage. At sunrise on the winter solstice every year, a pencil-thin ray of sunlight lights up the whole passage for exactly seventeen minutes. Since the passage slopes gently upward, the sunlight entering by the doorway shines only about half-way along it. There is, however, a small opening above the doorway which allows the sun's rays to enter horizontally and penetrate the whole passage to the very centre of the chamber.[27]

We have come a long way from the historian's dismissive nod to the Big Tomb Builders, all the way to a richly complex and apparently quite advanced early Irish society. Here theories evolved from modern ethnographic parallels may help solve some of the riddles of the megalithic peoples. Prehistory was shaped from the paucity of the evidence, and this predicated our mental attitude to it. With the help of scientific investigation we are beginning to learn that we are not dealing with simple primitive societies at all. It is as if, finding a single mouldering timber from the deck of an Armada galleon, we concluded that in the sixteenth century men sailed the seas on planks.

The Palimpsest

From the fifth millennium BC until the fifth century AD Ireland is a palimpsest on which not one, but many, civilisations write their story. Even the terms we use for them are now outworn. The Beaker folk, whoever they were, take their name from the highly distinctive pottery which spread across the British Isles from the Low Countries after 2000 BC. It was called 'Beaker' pottery because early antiquaries assumed that it was used for quaffing alcoholic beverages. The rise of new metalworking cultures introduced new technologies. Outside Austria, only a handful of prehistoric copper mines have ever been identified, and some of these are on the slopes of Mount Gabriel, near Schull in County Cork, twenty-five mineshafts in all. Examination of some of these in the 1960s and 1970s threw light on the mining methods. Adits were apparently dug into the hillside. Then charcoal fires were lighted as far as the supply of oxygen would permit, and when the walls were sufficiently heated, water was thrown on them, which would shatter them so that the copper ore could be detached by the use of crude stone mauls. The debris in the adit shafts yielded charcoal and mauls fashioned from pebbles, some with grooves for rope handles. The charcoal gave a radiocarbon date of c. 1500 BC. The radiocarbon dating is vital because there were still mining operations in Cork and Kerry during the last two centuries. In 1793–4 copper mines were opened at Ross Island near Killarney by Rudolf Erich Raspe, who is better known as the translator into English of *Baron Münchhausen's Narrative of his Marvellous Travels and Campaigns in Russia.*[28]

Copper ushered in a new era after the Stone Age. There is evidence that it was plentiful in Ireland. Early Bronze Age objects there consist largely of heavy axes, which are not found in anything like the same profusion in England, Scotland or Wales. Metalwork is for the archaeologist the sole link between the Early Bronze Age and the Late Bronze Age, which is calculated to begin about 1000 BC. 'From the technological developments and advancements in bronze and gold working,' writes Harbison, 'we try in vain to fill out the political and social history in the 600 years from, say, 1400 to 800 BC.'[29] It can be assumed that only the tiniest fraction of the objects produced at this time in copper, bronze and gold have yet been discovered, certainly less than 1 per cent. Many will almost certainly have been exported, but who knows how many still lie hidden under the peat of Ireland?

The richness, variety and sophistication of this prehistoric metalwork, which flourished for a span of centuries, are a challenge to the achievement of later ages. The awe inspired by Ireland's 'Golden Age' is indeed one of the factors which has, in the popular mind, thrown the earlier ages into darkness. Irish civilisation begins with the glory of its golden ornaments. A single example may illustrate what is involved. A gold hoard found at Gorteenreagh, County Clare, in 1854 included two small ornaments called 'lock-rings' (though their precise use is unknown). The lock-ring is made from two cones joined at their base, with a central tube and a break or slit at the side of the cones, suggesting that it might be used to hold in place a lock of hair. The outside of these gold cones is decorated with minute concentric lines almost too fine for any but the youngest eyes to see. It was at first assumed that these lines were incised, but when the lock-rings were examined under a microscope, it was discovered that the lines were in fact made up of minute wires only 0.33 millimetres in width. This is the kind of prehistoric achievement which must transform all our attitudes to the past. It is a feat which jewellers today say they would find difficult to perform, even with the most powerful lenses and the most modern tools.[30]

Increasingly archaeologists are uncovering evidence of the most startling nature which indicates a link between remote periods and later, recorded, Irish history. Among the curiosities found by archaeologists are the traditional cooking places called, in Irish, *fulachta fiadh*, horseshoe-shaped mounds usually found beside streams. Two excavated by Michael J. O'Kelly of University College Cork were dated to the second millennium BC. They were used in this way. A trough was filled with water, and a fire was lighted close by to heat stones, which were then thrown into the water; when it reached boiling point joints of meat could be cooked. O'Kelly found that he could bring the water to the boil in thirty to thirty-five minutes. This method of cooking is described in detail by Geoffrey Keating in his *History of Ireland* in the seventeenth century.[31]

Recently archaeologists have made the astonishing discovery of a stretch of wooden road under the blanket bog at Corlea, County Longford. No one knows where it was intended to lead, or why it was suddenly abandoned. The peatbog has preserved it intact for over twenty centuries, but once it is uncovered the timbers must be rushed to a conservation laboratory if they are not to perish. It consists of shaped and adzed planks like railway sleepers laid on top of parallel lines of trimmed birch logs which support it. It is sophisticated road building in difficult wet terrain. The planks are morticed and secured in place with oak pegs cut for the purpose. When the first timbers were sent to Belfast, Michael Baillie was able to date them at 148 BC. What form of transport used such a trackway? Fragments of what might be a cart were also found nearby. How many skilled people were needed for this work, and where did they live – not, one presumes, in the bogland itself, where there would be no resources for normal existence? How were the timbers transported to the site? Other, less impressive, examples of wooden trackways, called toghers (from *tóchar* in Irish), have been discovered from time to time. This one was discovered only through the operations of the Irish Turf Board (Bord na Móna).[32] Perhaps there is a whole network of prehistoric roads waiting to be discovered. In any event, the date of the Corlea timbers brings us at last to those enigmatic people, the Celts.

The Vanishing Celts

Round about 600 BC the Greeks began to notice the presence in Europe of a strange new people they called *Keltoi*. They had come from the East, and in a series of waves they spread throughout most of Europe, eventually reaching central Italy, south-western Spain, France and the British Isles. They were noticed even more forcibly in 387 BC when they sacked Rome and left it in flames. Rome survived by buying them off, and began its rise to military power, always aware that one day it would have to conquer the Celts in the field. To the Greeks and the Romans these people were barbarians, not because they were uncouth, but because they were alien, and a threat to established civilisation. Three hundred years later Julius Caesar would lead his legions into battle with them in France and Britain, and refer to them as *Galli* or Gauls. From the account in his *Gallic War* we know a good deal about them. They were fierce warriors, organised in local tribes, and they had a developed culture in which religion played a dominant role, with many holy places, and priests (the

Druids) who exercised great power over the people. They liked song and dance and legends of fighting prowess.

It is generally believed that these people occupied and colonised both Britain and Ireland, and that, at some stage, those in Britain invaded France again and established the colony which gave Brittany its name. Apart from the references in classical Latin and Greek, however, we know practically nothing of the history of the Celts, for they left no records of their own. The chief evidence for their unmistakeable presence is provided by the traces of their culture. Their arrival in Europe coincides with a period of rapid social and, above all, technical change which we call the Iron Age. The distinctive metalworking culture of the Celts is found everywhere in Europe, and it is very rich in Ireland.

In the form most familiar to us, this is usually called the La Tène culture, after an archaeological site in Switzerland where a hoard of 2,000 artifacts was found on the shore of Lake Neuchâtel in 1846. The La Tène culture, with its characteristic frond-like patterns and designs, is the one we recognise most readily as Irish. By now we are in an era of very elaborate Celtic design and decoration, found on a wide variety of objects from carved stones to swords and scabbards. This splendid flowering of Celtic art has been adopted somewhat arbitrarily as the basis for Irish culture. We are so accustomed to it that when we see it we think of it as essentially Irish, yet this conclusion would have astonished our ancestors. While it is also found in France and England, we do not think of it as characteristic of either of those countries.

There are other signs of Celtic influence in Ireland. It is from about the seventh century BC that we get the great circular enclosures that are believed to be the sites of royal courts. Although the Celts left no historical records as such, there exist still the collections of ancient tales in Irish. They have come down to us in the form of twelfth-century 'recensions', texts edited and retold by monks who were also steeped in the Scriptures, Latin and Greek authors, and the writings of the Fathers of the Church. Under this learning and sophistication are preserved ancient tales of gods and heroes, kings and queens and warriors, which come down, undoubtedly by long oral tradition, from the Celts themselves. For a long time archaeologists have been trying to match these tales with the testimony of the spade.

The most important of the royal sites is Navan Fort near Armagh in Northern Ireland. Archaeologists identify it with Emhain Macha, the royal seat of the Ulaid, whose most famous king was Conchobar mac Nessa. His chief warrior Cú Chulainn is the hero of the series of early Irish tales which make up the Ulster Cycle. The best known of them, *Táin Bó Cuailnge* ('The Cattle Raid of Cooley'), tells how Cú Chulainn helped his king to repulse invaders from the south, the men of Connaught, led by Queen Medb. Another of these sites is Dún Ailinne in County Kildare. Both sites show evidence that they were built on earlier Neolithic settlements.

The whole question of the Celtic presence in Ireland, and indeed in both islands, has become a source of controversy among archaeologists. It has always been assumed that the 'Atlantic Celts' were invaders who became an élite warrior caste, conquering and eliminating the original Neolithic inhabitants along with their language and culture. The problem is that the archaeologists can find no trace at all of an invasion at any point during the Iron Age. What does this mean? As an explanation for cultural change, 'invasions' are no longer in fashion, and the experts have turned more and more to the theory of 'cumulative Celticity', first put forward by archaeologist Christopher Hawkes.[33] Could it be that the Neolithic population absorbed Celtic culture and learned to speak a Celtic language without there being a sudden influx of foreigners?

The language itself has always presented problems. The tongue spoken by the Celts belonged to the Indo-European family, as did Greek and Latin. We cannot believe that earlier people spoke *no* language, but it has completely vanished, except for a single example, the unique language of the Basques in the Pyrenees. The ancient Celtic language has been reconstructed and is called Proto-Celtic. It is in two forms, Q-Celtic and P-Celtic. P-Celtic is so called because it has changed the original Indo-European sound /kw/ into 'p', as it occurs in Welsh. Where the Atlantic Celts are concerned, Q-Celtic is believed to be the earlier influence, and is called Goidelic or Gaelic. This is the one from which Irish and Scots Gaelic descend; P-Celtic, or Brythonic (British) Celtic, is the form associated with Wales, Cornwall and Brittany. According to linguistics experts Q-Celtic came into Ireland in the fourth century BC.[34]

There are other problems. The artifacts of the La Tène culture are found mostly in the northern half of Ireland; in Munster and south Leinster there is no trace of it, yet the whole of Ireland had an Iron Age culture of some sort. None of this has deterred people from the elementary mistake of confusing 'race' with language, yet, as E. Estyn Evans wrote, 'not only politicians and journalists but historians, linguists and perhaps geo-graphers too have been known to refer to the Irish as a Celtic race because they once spoke Gaelic'.[35] The question then remains: did the Celts con-quer Ireland, or did Ireland conquer the Celts? Only since the eighteenth century has Gaelic civilisation been seen as the *fons et origo* of the Irish nation, but today the assumption is all but universal. As J.R.R. Tolkien wrote, Celtic is a magic bag 'into which anything may be put, and out of which almost anything may come'.[36]

The debate among scholars on this question is lively and ongoing, and can be tracked through the pages of the journal *Antiquity*. It is not free of contemporary political influences, not all of them Irish. Beliefs about identity, origins and history are passionately held, and historians and archaeologists, used to quiet libraries and museums, have found them-selves accused of 'ethnic cleansing' and even 'genocide', an example of how history is often viewed through the distorting lens of today's preoccupations.[37]

The Great Roman Mystery

At the very threshold of Ireland's recorded history we are faced with a mystery. Why did the Romans not come? It is a fact of major importance. Ireland has no straight Roman roads, or Roman villas, or mosaics, or the rectangular *castra*, the bases of the Roman legions. Yet Britain was part of the Roman Empire, not for a few years or decades, but for four centuries, a stretch of time equal to that from the reign of Elizabeth I until today. How is it possible to believe that for all that time Rome ignored an island only thirteen miles away at the narrowest crossing? Consider for a moment all that has occurred in Anglo-Irish relations since Tudor times – how much settlement and colonisation, how many military expeditions and encounters. On the face of it, it does seem very odd. Experts in Roman history are less impressed, and tend to point out that our surprise is based partly on a misunderstanding of what the expansion of Roman influence implied. We ought not to think of subalterns with legionary shoulder-flashes anxiously scanning the waters of the Irish Sea. What is wrong with honest trade? But partly, too, they are weary of turning the evidence over and over and not finding out the answer. The subject is talked out.

Among other things it means a tantalising gap in written records. Yet there are frequent references to Britain, and sometimes to Ireland, in Roman literature. With the poets, including Vergil and Horace, a mention of Britain was almost *de rigueur*. The problem is that these allusions are literary devices rather than statements of historical fact,[38] indicating the extent of Roman majesty and influence, rather like the Victorian hymn-writer's

> From Greenland's icy mountains
> To India's coral strand

Specific detail is harder to come by. Julius Caesar in the first century BC accurately located and identified Ireland (Hibernia) and the Isle of Man (Mona), but after that Ireland almost disappears from the Roman record.[39]

There is only one moment in all that time when the mists part. In AD 97 Tacitus was writing the biography of his father-in-law, Gnaeus Julius Agricola, who had been the military governor of Britain between AD 78 and 84. He records that in the fifth year of Agricola's campaigning the whole side of Britain which faced Ireland was lined with his troops preparing to invade the island, and it is clear from his account that they already knew a great deal about it.

> Ireland is small in extent as compared with Britain, but larger than the islands of the Mediterranean. In soil, in climate and in the character and civilisation of its inhabitants, it is much like Britain. Its approaches and harbours are tolerably well known from merchants who trade there. Agricola has given a welcome to an Irish prince, who had been driven from home by a rebellion; nominally a friend, he might have been used as a pawn in the game. I have often heard Agricola say that Ireland could be held by a single legion and a few auxiliaries, and that the conquest would also pay from the point of view of Britain, if Roman arms were in evidence on every side and liberty vanished off the map.[40]

The opinion is often expressed that here Agricola claimed his place as the first in a long line of military optimists where Ireland was concerned. In the event he was never called upon to police the Shankill and Falls, or station his ballistae at Drumcree. The invasion of Ireland was called off, apparently at the highest level by the Emperor Vespasian in Rome. Instead, Agricola turned eastward up into the Highlands of Scotland, where he eventually defeated the Calidonii at the Battle of Mons Graupius. Until fairly recently the account of Tacitus was the only evidence of Roman activity in Galloway and Ayr, but in 1949 aerial photography yielded startling evidence to confirm the invasion plan. Fortlets could be discerned at several locations, including Gatehouse of Fleet, and a Roman road was traced heading for the coast and disappearing under the streets of Irvine.[41]

The Irish coast is clearly visible from this part of south-west Scotland, and on a day threatening rain one can see houses on the other side. 'This explains,' writes I.A. Richmond, 'why Agricola should have considered, with such vivid longing, the conquest of Ireland, and, conversely, why an Irish chieftain should have pinned his hopes on Roman backing.' For a brief period in his career Richmond had been a lecturer at the Queen's University in Belfast, and he adds that 'only those who have viewed the opposite coasts from either Larne or Portpatrick can realize how imminent the threat of conquest, or how bright the opportunity must have seemed'.[42]

Ireland was destined to escape invasion until the days of the Vikings and the Normans. As time went by it was the Irish who invaded Roman Britain, as the story of St Patrick shows. The Picts, who were so troublesome to the Romans in Scotland, made allies of the Irish. The Romans called these raiders Scotti (confusingly enough), and it was thus the Irish who gave Scotland its name. They came, it would appear, from a tribe in north-west Ireland who were to become the scourge of the coast of Britain from the Solway Firth to the Bristol Channel. At first their raids were spasmodic but developed in strength until they were led, not merely by tribal chieftains, but by High Kings of Ireland.

In AD 395 Niall of the Nine Hostages sacked Chester and Caerleon in a raid of unprecedented fury. In general the Irish made no permanent settlements, but they caused an enormous amount of devastation, burning and looting Romano-British villas as far south as the Severn estuary. The British monk Gildas describes 'the groans of the Britons', a series of desperate appeals for help.[43] It may have been in answer to these that the Roman general Flavius Stilicho (himself by blood a Vandal) came to Britain in AD 399 with reinforcements. He tried to create a local defence system that would be strong enough to lift the burden from the imperial shoulders, and after a time his troops were withdrawn. In AD 405 the British won a battle against the Irish in which Niall was killed. It was during these dark years that the Roman poet Claudian imagines Britannia crying 'I was perishing at the hands of neighbouring peoples! For the Scots brought the whole of Ireland against me, and the sea foamed under hostile oars.'[44]

For a brief period in Anglo-Irish affairs the boot was on the other foot, and received opinion is that Ireland escaped both the blessings and the burdens of the *pax Romana*. But there is in fact no necessity to believe this. The quantity of Roman material found in Ireland is greater and more varied than one might at first imagine. Interest in it was kindled in the middle of the nineteenth century when the antiquary Henry Clibborn recorded in his scrapbook (now in the Royal Irish Academy) some objects which a Mr Perry had found at Stonyford in County Kilkenny, namely a beautiful plain light green glass urn with human bones in it, a glass lachrymatory very rudely made, and a bronze mirror, silvered or tinned on the convex side.[45]

Archaeologists now believe this to be a first- or second-century Roman burial, probably of a woman, perhaps the wife of a Roman merchant. The site may be significant as being within easy reach of Waterford harbour. The possibility that there may have been a trading station here, and at other locations along the east coast, is strong. In the early 1800s a number of skeletons in long stone cists, with coins of the reigns of Trajan (AD 98–117) and Hadrian (AD 117–38), were found at Bray Head, County Wicklow. A similar set of inhumations was found at Beraghstown, County Meath. The people in these graves were incomers, provincial Romans from elsewhere, or perhaps even Irish auxiliaries who had returned after years in Roman military service. A large amount of Roman material has been unearthed at Newgrange, but does not indicate any form of settlement or occupation. All the evidence indicates that the site became 'a magnet for travellers from the Roman provincial world' and that the coins and objects found there are in the nature of votive offerings.[46] Nearby, on the hill of Tara, the Roman presence is felt even more strongly. Fragments of pottery from Gaul, Roman glass beads, a part of a brooch, a pair of bronze dividers, two iron padlocks, a lead seal and miscellaneous objects of iron and bronze have been uncovered. Barry Raftery thinks they might be the possessions of Roman provincial settlers.

Although a wide range of Roman material has been found in Ireland, this does not mean that all of it, or indeed that more than a fraction of it, has been there since Roman times. Archaeologists have learned to be very cautious, and only the most careful analysis enables them to isolate the authentic from the spurious. If you find an interesting Roman figurine buried in the garden of an old house in Dublin, you will be well advised to check that the dwelling was not once the home of an antiquary, or any kind of enthusiast for Ireland's past. Of the very large number of Roman coins found in Ireland, by far the largest proportion were brought home from the Middle East or elsewhere by Irish soldiers in the British army.

The material judged to be genuine, however, includes some very interesting items, such as silver ingots with official Roman stamps, a silver plate depicting horsemen with spears, either in battle or hunting, iron padlocks, a large key and a rectangular slate tablet with an inscription 'For the son of Marcus Tutianus an eye salve misy for his old scars'.[47] (Misy was a kind of yellow eye ointment.) Does it suggest an occulist practising in County Tipperary, or an army doctor at a military base? Analysis of the material yields some interesting results. It falls into two distinct categories according to date, a first/second-century group and a fourth/fifth-century group, with hardly anything in between. Roman finds are concentrated in the area around Dublin and the northern coasts of Antrim and Donegal, with another line of discoveries extending westward from Kilkenny. The coastal areas might indicate the activity of traders; the inland discoveries are more intriguing, though it has been suggested that they might well be the loot of Irish raids on Roman Britain.

Enough confirmed evidence remains to pose interesting questions about the nature of Roman influence on Ireland during this long period. The Roman ignoring of the island preserved its 'Celticity' right down to the Middle Ages, no small factor in the shaping of Irish history. Ireland may never have been officially part of the Empire, but were there Roman travellers, tourists, and pilgrims, as well as sailors and traders, whose presence may be taken as certain? Great excitement was generated in the late 1990s with the reported finding of a Roman military camp near Dublin, but it was dismissed at once by the archaeological experts. The hope of discovering some such evidence will always remain. 'We have taken our arms beyond the shores of Ireland,' wrote Juvenal in the second century AD, 'and the recently conquered Orkneys, and Britain of the short nights.'[48]

In one sense Ireland was, in the end, conquered. The tree rings indicate that something very strange happened in or about AD 540 which caused a darkness over all the land. Sources as diverse as Gildas, Zachariah of Mitylene, Procopius and the Chinese chroniclers record mists and ever-lasting gloom, unprecedented cold, and flashing lights in the sky. At first the dendrochronologists thought that these phenomena might be explained by massive volcanic eruptions, but recently Michael Baillie has suggested that they coincided with the close approach of a comet and a shower of meteors, falling perhaps in the Irish Sea.[49] One thing they undoubtedly coincided with was the first terrible visitation of bubonic plague, usually called 'the Yellow Plague', or 'Justinian's Plague'. It reached Ireland in AD 544.

This marks the beginning of that ill-lighted stretch of European experience which historians have called the Dark Ages. It may literally have been dark. But the last breath of Roman influence in the West carried with it the spark of Christianity, and the fire took hold. Where Ireland was concerned, it created the distinctive Celtic Church, a beacon of light which was to send its beams throughout Europe, despatching Celtic monks not only to Iona and western Britain, but to Luxeuil in the Vosges, to Bobbio in Italy and to St Gall high up in the Swiss Alps. St Columbanus and his disciples founded over a hundred monasteries on the Continent, Helen Waddell reckoned, 'some of them the greatest strongholds of learning in the Middle Ages'.[50] The Irish were to keep alive the flame of Latin literature and Roman civilisation in the dark years.

The Monk's Tale

The first framework of Irish history was the creation of Celtic scribes and churchmen, and we have not yet abandoned it. The whole culture of modern Ireland since independence draws its strength from a Gaelic past revived in the late eighteenth century, and to a large extent reinvented in the nineteenth. That in itself is an accident of history, the chance convergence of a second Gaelic revival with a particular set of circumstances in Anglo-Irish politics. The political activists of the period deliberately sought an Irish culture in the past which would have no taint of Saxon England about it, though on the same amount of evidence both countries might have claimed a Celtic past. Moreover, as a deeply religious people, the Irish did not want to hear of a too-distantly pre-Christian heritage. It was more comfortable to go back no farther than the Celts, those warlike but cultivated and artistic people who inspired Ireland's first literature, and who linked the Irish ethnically to other 'oppressed' and anti-English people on the English periphery – the Scots, Welsh, Bretons, Manx and Cornish.

It is not that Irish scholars, with some notable exceptions,[51] reject the whole of prehistory; on the contrary they write about it with increasing attention. But the accumulated weight of Ireland's literary history is difficult to shake off, and its psychological influence remains, even when it is replaced by a more extended perspective. When Columbus set out to reach India by an alternative route, he stumbled upon a whole new continent in the west, but he still called it the Indies, and its indigenous inhabitants are referred to as Indians to this day, a usage likely to survive 'political correctness'.

Besides, the problem is far from being a simple one. All students of early history (the period when written evidence as distinct from other kinds of evidence really begins) have to come to terms with the fact that the motivation of the earlier chroniclers was very different from that of the historian of today. To begin with, their cosmography was essentially that of Dr Lightfoot and Archbishop Ussher, and central to it was the need to prove continuity from the Creation to the moment of writing. They constructed it from such materials of record, myth and memory as were available to them, and it had to meet certain specific criteria. It had to have a chronology which was remote enough to be a wonder to men, but not so remote that the tribe collectively could not remember it. In a word they needed a history which would place their own community in the order of things.

The scribe was a monk, and his primary task, so obvious and universal that it was instinctive rather than deliberate, was to reinforce the Christian cosmography at every point, uphold the social order, praise the pious ruler and condemn the wicked, say what needed to be said about strangers, aggressors and invaders, and outline the suffering of God's people at their hands. Often he wrote to flatter a patron or advance his cause, to justify a claim or establish a genealogy. His methodology was almost the opposite of that employed by a modern historian. He moulded and distorted his evidence to suit his purpose rather than letting it dictate to him. Occasionally he loaded his narrative with as much partisan malice as the ink would bear. Credulous as well as selective, he recorded the birth of a two-headed calf alongside a raid by the Norsemen.

The *evidence* used by the monks is a different matter. In the nature of things they had to use the materials which lay to hand, and this meant a mixture of detail from many sources, some ancient, others recent or hearsay. The pre-Christian sources were thin but tantalising, and somewhere in the mishmash of credulous record are the echoes of real events, the shadows of real people. The difficulty is that scholars have had frustratingly little success in correlating the events narrated in the literary sources to the findings of the archaeologists.

At the stage where the annals could no longer be taken to be a reliable historical record (which is quite a late stage) early Irish history fell into the hands of the philologists. It is easy to see why. The earliest chronicles were in Irish, and no one was better placed to interpret them. Few, if any, historians were then competent to follow the linguists into the labyrinthine recesses of their specialism. To a large degree the determination of certain questions came to depend on the nuance of language.

There was a further advantage. With the coming of independence, and even more after its achievement, the study of the ancient language, and all aspects of Gaelic culture, ceased to appear to the general public to be an abstruse and academic branch of knowledge and became the badge of patriotism. Gradually the whole of Irish life took on a golden tinge, the inherited nobility of a distant Gaelic past. The specialists themselves did not at first always see it in quite this light. Scorning any weak-kneed view that scholarship, like virtue, was its own reward, they complained that theirs was the least acknowledged and rewarded of all academic endeavours, far behind those of the historians in glamour and public acclaim.

While the contribution of the philologists has been considerable, their approach and working methods have been different from those of either the historians or the archaeologists. Like the former, but to an even greater degree, they are restricted in their investigation of a remote past by the essentially literary nature of their evidence. However, Celtic scholars and historians worked for a long time in isolation from each other, and when their efforts were compared it was found that they had been travelling on roads which did not converge.

As late as 1968, reporting on the state of historical research for pre-Norman Ireland, the distinguished historian F.J. Byrne could still write:

> It is a sad admission that the historical work of the last thirty years on the first seven centuries of Irish history can be very rapidly surveyed. Eoin MacNeill, who first laid the foundations for the serious study of early Irish history ... expanded his scholarship in many learned articles and brilliant essays. The task of weaving a consecutive narrative was left to the over-enthusiastic hands of Mrs Alice Stopford Green, since whose time no one has ventured to write a full-scale history of the period before the Norman invasion.[52]

This revelation is fairly eyebrow-raising for a modern academic historian, but it is not as bad as it sounds, quite apart from the fact that a good deal of research has been undertaken since 1968 and recorded in articles and contributions to co-operative surveys. The simple truth is that today no historian *dares* to write a full-scale history of pre-Norman Ireland, because since 1939 they have all been trained in a discipline which insists that the entire infrastructure of documentary research must be in place before the task of synthesis can be undertaken. On that principle none of the great interpretive works of the nineteenth century would have seen the light of day. 'It may well have been felt,' Byrne continued, 'that the time was not ripe for such an ambitious attempt: much research had yet to be done, many monographs written, and nearly all the basic texts published before the historian could undertake his proper task of narrative, analysis and interpretation.'[53]

Byrne then turned to the language problem, the chief reason why Celtic scholars and historians have worked in isolation from each other. 'Since the historians are not bold enough to challenge the pretensions of the philologists, early Irish history was relegated to the realm of philology', and given 'the curious forms of academic apartheid', the paths of the investigators were bound to diverge further.[54] From all this Byrne concluded that in 'the difficult terrain of Irish proto-history, the linguist, the archaeologist and the historian must advance cautiously, and as a team, to work out possible or plausible correlations of significant phenomena'. This is easier said than done, however, since no one can hope to master all the disciplines involved, 'all of which are growing in complexity and specialisation, and each of which has attracted a circle of satellite auxiliary sciences'.[55] Moreover, the individualistic temperament of Irish scholars does not help. Teamwork is even less congenial to them than to academics generally.

Nowhere are the problems of early Irish history more clearly illustrated than in the quest for the historical St Patrick. Evidence for the events of Patrick's life are so hazy that he has been given two distinct lifetimes in the fifth century. We know that he was born in Britain at Bannavem Taberniae, a place never satisfactorily identified, though claims have been entered for Kilpatrick near Dumbarton and even for Boulogne-sur-mer. Thereafter his biography consists of phrases like 'it is thought' and 'probably'. Legend tells that as a boy of sixteen he was carried off into captivity by Irish raiders and sold into slavery in County Antrim. After six years he escaped, went to France and became a monk, first at Tours and then at Lérins. He was consecrated as a bishop and returned to Ireland, where he converted his old master Michu and other chieftains to Christianity. He eventually fixed his see at Armagh, where, probably, he is buried.

The traditional account puts his return to Ireland at AD 432 and his death at 465, and within that time he is supposed to have traversed the whole country in his missionary endeavours. The Christianisation of Ireland was accomplished peacefully, with no recorded martyrs. More recent scholarship has placed his birth at 423 and his abduction at 434. It is thought that he returned to Ireland as a bishop in 456 and died in 493 and that the area of his missionary endeavours was more restricted than tradition would have it.

The only authentic literary sources for Patrick's life are his own spiritual autobiography, the 'Confessio', and his 'Letter to Coroticus'. Both are in rudimentary Latin. The letter is a sharp rebuke to the British chief who had carried some of Patrick's converts into slavery. Coroticus has been identified as Cenedig Wledig, a ruler of Strathclyde, and the saint tells him that it is outrageous that he should have joined with the heathen Scots and apostate Picts to make a raid on Patrick's baptised converts, not only because he was himself a Christian, but also because he was a fellow Roman citizen. This is an observation of great significance. One of the few things we know about Patrick's background is that his father, Calpurnus, had the titles of a Roman magistrate.

Hibernia Antiqua

Old Mortality, the ruins of forgotten times.

SIR THOMAS BROWNE[1]

The Book of Invasions

'I am a genuine typical Irishman,' George Bernard Shaw once declared, 'of the Danish, Norman, Cromwellian, and (of course) Scottish invasions.'[2] The oldest pattern in Irish history is created by the continual arrival of newcomers through 'invasions'. The early migration of peoples across Europe seems to be inexorably westward, and sooner or later they must come to Ireland, which until the discovery of America was the western edge of the world. Once there, they had to stop, and help form the reservoir of population into which the next westward-moving wave would inevitably spill. The original Irish gene pool was created by the first Mesolithic and neolithic dwellers, but the subsequent process is one of continuous mixing. The Irish must be among the most heterogeneous of peoples, yet they behave politically and culturally as if the precise opposite were true.

This ceaseless mixing of the population makes nonsense of all the familiar assumptions of 'Gaelic origins' or 'the Irish race'. The distinctive nature of Irishness arises specifically from the interaction of newcomers with natives (the perennial cliché of Irish historical writing). Strictly speaking, there are no natives; or, to put it the other way round, *all* the Irish are natives. 'Irish', if it means anything, simply means being born in Ireland, even if, like Swift or the Duke of Wellington, you did not want to be. Many of the characteristics which are regarded as 'typically Irish', for instance, are demonstrably the legacy of the Old English, or the Anglo-Irish or the Lowland Scots just as much as they are of the Celts, whom we now call the Gaels. Interest in the Gaels, in their language which Irish people still spoke, in their literature and culture generally, revived in the eighteenth century. More specifically, both Protestants and Catholics, though divided from each other politically by the penal laws and structures based on them, tried to establish a connection with the Gaelic Irish culture, which was still extraordinarily healthy. By the middle of the nineteenth century it was in decline, and speaking Irish was regarded as a mark of social inferiority, something associated only with backward rural communities. Then, by the end of the century, a revival was under way, and Gaelic culture was being presented to the Irish population as the indigenous culture.

Relatively speaking, the Gaels are quite late 'invaders', not the first but merely the first of the most recent series – Gaels, Vikings, Normans, Old English, Welsh and Scots, and modern Scots. They are the first of which we have *written evidence*, and this of course gives them a high value in the eyes of historians. And the Irish language is the key element in the survival of their traditions. We simply do not know what language was spoken by their precursors, but it is no longer possible to believe that they spoke no language at all. As we have seen, some archaeologists now think the invasion was that of a culture and not a people, for they can find no trace of invasion in the military sense.

Because they were 'consumed by a curiosity to find out what happened in their country before the dawn of history',[3] early Irish Christians made considerable efforts to establish the succession of peoples who had come to Ireland at various times, and in the eleventh and twelfth centuries these were drawn together in the so-called *Book of Invasions*. It was largely from this source that the Irish derived the idea of Ireland's history as a series of hostile incursions, starting with the followers of Mil or Milesius from Spain, who was to retain a powerful hold on the Irish imagination. In the nineteenth century Daniel O'Connell was to be presented with a specially designed Milesian hat, which appears in cartoons of him.

The Gaels were the first example of a people who were assumed to come as fierce warriors and establish themselves as a dominant caste, imposing their customs, laws and, in the long run, their language upon a pre-existing population. Even if this were true, it was a long process, stretching over many centuries, and complete perhaps, in the last respect, only after considerable interbreeding. But 'invasion' has a wider meaning for archaeologists than for medieval monks or military men; and at least some of the uncertainty hangs over later invasions also.

There can be no doubt about the initial hostility of the Vikings, and Ireland was not their only prey. At the end of the eighth century, obeying one of those outward urges which from time to time manifest themselves in populations, and which some experts associate in this instance with climatic changes in Scandinavia, Norse raiders began to attack the coastal areas of Europe to the south of them. During the next two centuries they settled and became a significant, though largely overlooked, element of the population in many of the Atlantic countries and even in Russia. Their long, shallow-draught and highly manoeuvrable warships gave them command of the seas and enabled them to extend their influence from Constantinople in the east to North America in the west, where evidence of their settlement is only now coming to be accepted. They conquered England in 1013, giving English history King Canute (Knut) with his obsession about waves. In Ireland the longships first sailed up the Bann to Lough Neagh, and the Shannon to the very centre of the country. Their earliest forays were for gold and land, and the Irish Christian monasteries were an easy target. In consequence the monks gave them a bad press, which has persisted ever since.

There was, however, more to the Norsemen than savage warfare. They had a sophisticated literary heritage and system of government with an assembly (from which English derives the useful word 'thing', its Scandinavian name). Their later settlements gave Ireland its first towns, at Dublin, Waterford, Cork and Limerick, and established a trading economy for the island. The existence of these Norse settlements was a complicating factor in the ceaseless internecine wars of the Irish Gaelic chieftains. The Vikings (or Ostmen as they called themselves) of the enclaves intervened in these wars, taking sides and making treaties, until they were finally defeated at the Battle of Clontarf in 1014 by Brian Boru, who was killed in the battle. His success in establishing supremacy over all the warring factions to make himself High King of Ireland, establishing Armagh as the primatial see and giving a semblance of unity to the whole country, has invested him with a special significance in Irish history, but that cohesion would not be recovered for a long time to come.

The Norsemen were to have a second chance when they re-entered Irish history in their later, and much better publicised, guise as the Normans who conquered England in 1066. Another century would elapse before they would take a serious interest in Ireland, but their first landing there is for nationalists the beginning of 'the eight centuries of English oppression'. The erroneous assumptions to which the use of the word 'English' in this heart-warming cry gives rise are legion. Quite apart from the fact that the speaker will in all probability have an English name, and Anglo-Norman blood coursing in his veins, it takes for granted that, when we are talking about the twelfth century, 'Ireland' and 'England' mean what they mean today, distinct countries with distinct histories (even if this is a hazy concept where England is concerned). It soon becomes clear that the point at issue is the much more recent occupation and domination by the English since Tudor times, and that for the last three centuries the Normans have been dragged in to give the argument historical ballast. Eighteenth-century patriots, who were in the main Anglo-Irish

Protestants, complained about the Norman 'invasion' at considerable length, though they rather gave themselves away by beginning the history of the Irish nation in the twelfth century, at least until the end of the eighteenth century when they began to take an interest in the Celts. This is not, of course, an unfamiliar story in other countries, and there is a parallel in many ways with Wales, where the conquerors also begin to adopt the indigenous culture.

That the coming of the Normans should be associated in the popular mind with the beginning of Anglo-Irish difficulties is perhaps understandable. It is more worrying that academic historians often accept it too. One historian has recently complained that even in academic conferences, traditional assumptions underlie the whole topic. He is led to conclude that the academic view seems to concur with the popular one, and that therefore 'it behoves historians to examine from time to time the largely unquestioned assumptions upon which their scholarly edifices are built'. One of these assumptions is that the coming of the Normans marked a turning-point in Irish history.

Traditionally the Irish question is held to have begun on a day in May 1169, when three shiploads of knights in chain-mail landed at Baginbun Bay, near Bannow on the coast of Wexford. These chain-mail men laid the foundations of English power in Ireland, and they appear in Irish history as the first English invaders. 'At the creek of Baginbun,' runs the old Irish rhyme, 'Ireland was lost and won.' Yet they were neither English nor invaders. Their leaders, Maurice Prendergast, Henry de Montmorency and Robert Fitzstephen, were Norman lords from the Welsh marches. They and their followers were a mixture of Anglo-Normans, Welsh and Flemings. It is doubtful whether any of them could speak English, the language of the Saxon. What they had in common was that they were all subjects of Henry II of Anjou, who ruled over an empire stretching from Scotland to the Pyrenees. It was not a state ruled by a centralised English government, but a random collection of fiefs, owing greater or less allegiance to a feudal king, along with some more loosely attached dependent territories. One of these peripheral territories consisted of the Welsh marches, the adopted home of these restless and land-hungry frontiersmen. They came to Ireland, not as invaders or as conquerors, but merely as mercenaries hired by Dermot MacMurrough, the King of Leinster.[4]

Ireland was not then, nor would it be for centuries to come, a united country. Dermot was but one king among five. His position as ruler of

Leinster became precarious when his rival, Rory O'Connor of Connaught, was chosen as High King of Ireland in 1166. In desperation he obtained Henry II's permission to enlist allies among the marcher lords of south Wales, and with their assistance he regained his territory, but lost the good opinion of his compatriots for all time. Even the Anglo-Irish of the eighteenth century heaped obloquy on him as the quisling who let the English in.

The most important of his allies was Richard de Clare, Earl of Pembroke, whom history remembers as 'Strongbow'. MacMurrough sealed his compact with him by giving him his daughter Eva (Aoife) in marriage, and when Dermot died in 1171, Strongbow seized and held the Kingdom of Leinster, including the Norsemen's town of Dublin. It was this action which alerted Henry II and forced him to intervene.

Beyond the Pale

The tragedy of Ireland, it has often been pointed out, is not that the English conquered it but that they failed to conquer it, a failure which would in time create the 'Irish question'. From the twelfth century onward the inhabitants of the larger island have desired both to rule Ireland and to leave it alone, and often they have succeeded in doing both at the same time. Already by Tudor times English statesmen were using the same expressions of weary despair we are familiar with in later days. The government of Ireland was a 'Hydra's task';[5] as soon as one head of rebellion was cut off, two more shot up in its place. They wished that the whole island could be submerged in the Atlantic.

The ambivalence was present from the beginning. When Henry II landed with a large army in 1171, his intention was not to conquer Ireland but to bring some of his most powerful barons back under control. He asserted his authority over all the lands they had occupied, and made it clear in confirming the grants to Strongbow and others that they held these lands as tenants and not as independent warlords. The Norse towns were retained under royal control, a sign of their economic and strategic importance. At the same time most of the Irish chieftains willingly accepted Henry as overlord. In all this Henry had prudently secured the full backing of the Church. His intervention in Ireland was prospectively legitimised by the bull *Laudabiliter* of Pope Adrian IV, the only Englishman ever to accede to the papacy. It called upon Henry to reform the deplorable condition of religion in Ireland. To this end Henry summoned a synod of all the Irish clergy at Cashel, where many reforms were promulgated, the main result of which was to bring the Irish Church more into line with the English.[6]

Thus was established the 'Lordship of Ireland', which would last for four centuries until Ireland became a kingdom in the reign of Henry VIII. These events have been given enormous significance in the canonical writings of Irish nationalism, and are seen in a misleading modern context. The Lordship fell far short of the whole island, and had continually to be patched and repaired with new treaties and compromises. It was a practical arrangement of a kind that was made by medieval rulers everywhere when they were powerful enough to make them, and it was not viewed at all in terms of nation states. That concept so colours all our thinking about such matters that modern historians, even when they are well aware of the problem, find it difficult to think themselves into a time when there was no barrier to migration except physical geography.

The intervention in Ireland was therefore 'English' only in a geographical sense. For the Angevin dynasty, as their name implied, home was in geographical France not England. Henry's soldiers were a mixture of Normans, Norman Welsh and Flemings. The Irish did homage to Henry as King, not to an abstraction thought of as the English Crown, and Ireland, or part of it, became another ingredient in the patchwork quilt which was the Angevin empire. A few years later Henry gave the Lordship of Ireland to his son John, who was not heir to the throne. (John did, however, by the accident of history eventually become king.)

Moreover, by no means all the rulers of Irish lands were included in the Lordship. Rory O'Connor, who declared himself to be High King of Ireland, did not formally submit to Henry, though he made a treaty with him in 1175, with the blessing of the Church. The attempt at dual government which formed the basis of the agreement did not work, for O'Connor had more enemies than the King, and had no successor as High King. The situation of the Norman colony was, and remained, ill-defined. Even within the Lordship there were large areas ruled by Irish potentates, and in the course of the next century or so very complicated political and military structures evolved, with cross-cultural manifestations which have come in time to be regarded as peculiarly Irish. Some of the Anglo-Norman barons bold enough to carve out kingdoms of their own in remoter areas adopted Irish customs and Hibernicised names. They were the first element in the population to be described as 'more Irish than the Irish themselves'.

One might assume that the arrival of the Normans in Ireland marked the start of an inexorable process which made the whole island an Anglo-Norman colony. The reality was different. It is true that for the first two centuries after 1169 Norman power expanded until it covered almost two-thirds of Ireland. By the fifteenth century, however, the Lordship was no longer expanding and had begun to shrink. The Gaelic lords had re-covered a large part of the lands which the Normans had seized, and English influence was increasingly restricted to the Pale and some of the seaport towns. The Pale took its name from the ditch which originally surrounded it, and it came to mean the area in which only English law prevailed, that is, in which the King's writ ran. By the middle of the fourteenth century it consisted of Dublin, Louth, Meath, Kilkenny and Kildare, but by 1500 it had shrunk to an area extending roughly 50 miles north and 30 miles inland from Dublin.

Beyond the Pale lay a congeries of native Irish fiefdoms which existed alongside it in a state of frequently disturbed equilibrium. From time to time the Irish descended from their mountains to attack the Pale and exact heavy tribute as the price of peace. The Gaelicisation of the tributary Norman lords was a continuing process. Nevertheless the Lordship in-troduced to Ireland elements of English law and administration which proved to be secure and firmly rooted. One of these was the institution of parliament, which was to play a central role in Irish history until 1800. Its introduction to Ireland happened at a stage when it was still the King's council and was beginning to evolve as part of the English governmental system, with the result that in Ireland it followed a curious parallel history with its English counterpart, acquiring all its privileges and powers without being allowed to use them to the full. These powers were ac-quired, but not, so to speak, earned, by a struggle with the Crown. From an early stage the freedom of the Irish parliament was impeded by special checks, most notably Poynings' Law (called after Sir Edward Poynings, sent over as Lord Deputy in 1494). The intention of this measure was to prevent the Irish parliament being used against the King's interest – this was at the time of the Yorkist plots against the Tudors – but it came to be the most notorious shackle on the liberty of the Irish parliament until its repeal in 1782.

One reason for the erosion of royal authority in Ireland during the fourteenth and fifteenth centuries was the continual drain of resources in the series of wars between the English and the French, which has come to be known as the Hundred Years War. 'There was,' writes Robin Frame, 'an inverse relation between activity on the continent and the troops, money and commanders who could be spared for Ireland.'[7] A familiar pattern was developing, too, for military expeditions in Ireland. When campaigns *were* organised they tended all too often to collapse 'because the weather was so wet and windy, and on account of the great difficulty of the mountains, bogs and woods'.[8] The years 1315–17 were ones of terrible famine, and it was at this precise moment that Edward Bruce, brother of the victor of Bannockburn, landed in County Antrim with 6,000 Scottish soldiers. In 1316 he was crowned 'King of Ireland' at Dundalk, but Bruce mustered little support from the Irish, and in 1318, excommunicated by the Pope, he was defeated and killed at the Battle of Faughart. The Irish remembered him only as 'the destroyer of all Ireland ... both foreigner and Gael'.[9]

But there was another reason for the decline in English authority, which the history books mention only in passing. The worst of Ireland's invasions was silent and invisible, and today we call it the Black Death, though it was not called that at the time. It came ashore in the summer of 1348 in ships from Bristol and Chester. In Bristol 'almost the whole strength of the town had perished, as it were surprised by sudden death, for few kept their beds more than two or three days, or even half a day. Then this cruel death spread on all sides, following the course of the sun.'[10] It had come to south-west England from France, where it was part of the European pandemic, and soon it was raging in Wales and Scotland. The plague appeared in Dublin and Drogheda by August, and continued until 1351, though with diminished strength. The mortality rate in the coastal areas was high. A friar, one John Clyn, who died in 1349, probably a victim of the plague himself, recorded that 'in scarcely any house did only one die but all together, man and wife with children and household, travelled the same road, the road of death'. By the end of 1348 the Great Plague of Ireland had reached its height. 'It is Christmas night,' begins the prayer of an educated young Irishman, 'and I place myself under the protection of the King of Heaven and earth, beseeching that he will bring me and my friends safe through this plague.'[11]

The deadly bacillus was spread by the bite of fleas living on the black rat. Within two to eight days of the flea-bite the victim developed a high fever and the characteristic buboes, which gave bubonic plague its name, swellings of the lymphatic glands in the armpits and groin. Purple patches under the skin led to bacterial infection of the nervous system, delirium and wild frenzy (the 'dance of death'), and finally death itself. The bubonic plague was worst in warm spring and summer weather; its even more deadly variant, pneumonic plague, was active in cold and damp weather. One of the persistent myths of history teaching is that nobody washed in the Middle Ages, except the King, and then only on the three great festivals of the Church year. In fact frequent washing was one of the many attempted remedies, all of them ineffectual because the means of transmission was not suspected. As late as the nineteenth century diseases were thought to be spread by miasmas in the atmosphere.

When these pandemics wane they do not die out entirely but leave 'reservoirs' of infection which can last for centuries. The plague of 1348 stemmed initially from a reservoir in Central Asia, and the reservoirs exist there and in parts of Siberia, Mongolia and China to this day. The mortality rate among those infected is still the same as in the fourteenth century (50 to 80 per cent) unless treated with antibiotics within twenty-four hours. The persistence of these reservoirs meant that the plague returned at intervals during the later Middle Ages and into the seventeenth century. Epidemiologists tell us that one visitation of plague does not usually cause a continuing demographic decline, but repeated outbreaks do, and this is what happened everywhere in Europe during the late medieval period. High mortality rates were followed by low birth rates. 'For whatever reason', writes one historian, 'there was some kind of fertility crisis in late medieval England', and he suggests that probably it was the result of later marriage, 'as women found a sudden and temporarily liberating change in their economic status'; the discussion among experts is complex, but 'plague remains at the centre of the debate about changes in late medieval society'.[12] As Johan Huizinga observed in *The Waning of the Middle Ages*, 'An everlasting call of memento mori sounds through life.'[13]

The effect of plague was compounded by a deterioration in climate beginning about 1300 and lasting until the first decades of the nineteenth century. Meteorologists have called it the Little Ice Age, and we are only just emerging from it. The Annals of Connaught for the first half of the fourteenth century record a litany of disaster:

1317   Great famine throughout this year in Ireland ...
1318   Snow the like of which had not been seen for many a long year ...
1322   Great cattle-plague throughout Ireland the like of which had never been known before ...
1324   The same cattle-plague was in all Ireland this year ...
1325   The cattle-plague throughout Ireland still ...
1328   Much thunder and lightning this year, whereby much of fruit and produce of all Ireland was ruined, and the corn grew up white and blind ... A great and intolerable wind this summer with scarcity of food and clothing ...
1335   Heavy snow in the spring, which killed most of the small birds of all Ireland ...
1338   Nearly all the sheep in Ireland died this year ...[14]

Such were the conditions of life in Ireland between the Bruce invasion of 1315–17 and the arrival of the Black Death in 1348, and they are confirmed by Michael Baillie's oak-tree-ring evidence. Now they were about to get much worse. It was observed at the time that the English of the Pale suffered more from the onset of the plague than the native Irish. The English towns and seaports were hotbeds of infection, while in the mountains and open country the risk of contact with the lethal germ was less, or at least delayed. According to Geoffrey Le Baker it laid low the English, but did not reach the 'pure Irish' in the mountains until 1357.[15] The plague returned six times before the end of the century, and it has been estimated that it reduced the population of the colony by almost half.

Bubonic plague was to visit Ireland again in the late sixteenth century. It broke out in Dublin in the summer of 1574, and spread over eastern and southern Ireland during the next two years. The summer was unusually hot and dry, optimum conditions for the spread of the disease, and its virulence continued into the autumn, when it was checked by the cooler weather. In the spring of 1575 it reappeared. By now there is evidence of a more co-ordinated medical and administrative response, at least in Dublin and the major towns. Ordinances were passed threatening penalties for concealing plague victims, because it was felt that their isolation was the key to controlling the outbreak. To some degree it was, but again the lack of knowledge of the true cause rendered it ineffectual. The victims were housed in temporary buildings, and a physician was appointed to look after the mayor and citizens, the first public health appointment of this kind in Ireland.

The plague then vanished as mysteriously as it had come, and the last quarter of the century was free of it. In the year following the death of Elizabeth I, an epidemic affected the whole of the British Isles, lasting for most of the decade. It reached Dublin in the summer of 1604, and once again, as had happened in 1574, there was a mass exodus of the wealthier citizens. The sick were isolated in a special pest-house outside the city boundary, and guardians were employed to supervise the inmates and bury the dead. All travellers arriving in Dublin were required to produce proof that they had come from plague-free areas. The infected were re-strained from 'running abroade' through the streets of the city, and all citizens were ordered to light fires before their doors, 'for better purging of the aire'.[16] The last visitation of bubonic plague in Ireland took place in 1650–1, possibly introduced by a Spanish ship sailing in to Galway. From there it spread eastward across the country to Dublin. This time the sick were cared for at the city's expense. A surgeon was appointed by the town assembly (his own family died of the plague). As soon as the pestilence subsided it was followed by a most severe famine which caused a high mortality among Ireland's poor, starvation being followed by diseases other than bubonic plague, chiefly dysentery and typhus. In the future these two would create their own havoc.

The Long Divorce

In retrospect we can easily see that events in Ireland in the sixteenth century had much to do with a wider process, the emergence in Europe of the modern nation state. The accession of Henry Tudor to the English throne after the Battle of Bosworth in 1485 seemed at the time just one more twist in the everyday life of medieval magnates, specifically a change of fortune in the Wars of the Roses, but to us the transition from medieval to modern is sharply marked by the accession of his son, Henry

VIII. Henry VII had paved the way by dealing successfully with his 'overmighty subjects', rivals who might be tempted to do as he had done and wade through slaughter to a throne. But in one part of his dominions the 'overmighty subject' survived and flourished. Ireland was still ruled to all intents and purposes by the Yorkist Lord Deputy, the Great Earl of Kildare, and it was from the base of Ireland that Perkin Warbeck launched his three invasions of England, claiming falsely to be the son of Edward IV, and the younger of 'the princes in the tower' who disappeared in 1483.

Forced to concentrate his energies on England, Henry left Kildare alone, and later came to an agreement with him to continue as Lord Deputy so long as he remained loyal to the House of Tudor. Kildare kept his vow because the title of Lord Deputy was very important to him. Without it he could have caused the English Crown an immense amount of grief; with it he was omnipotent in Ireland. Garret More, as he was known to the Irish, was the head of the most powerful of the Anglo-Norman families of the Pale, the Fitzgeralds. His lands in the Pale were extensive, but they stretched far beyond it, and his influence rested also on a network of treaties and marriage alliances with the Gaelic lords. With the seal of the deputyship giving him control of the King's council in Dublin, he was unassailable, and no one could be better placed to rule Ireland in the King's name.

This system, which had many advantages, was continued at first by Henry VIII, and when Garret More died (in a skirmish with one of his rivals) his son Garret Oge succeeded to the deputyship as if it were hereditary. It was clear, however, that this method of governing Ireland could not be allowed to continue indefinitely. Cardinal Wolsey is given the credit of drawing Ireland to Henry's attention, and of beginning to collect information about the situation with a new thoroughness, but it was his successor Thomas Cromwell who drew up the plans for dealing with it in ways we would recognise as modern. He was, above all else, one of the first of the high-level civil servants. The most malign stroke of British history was that Henry's experiments in Ireland would become entangled forever with his matrimonial difficulties. Not the least of the consequences of this was that Ireland became a pawn on a Europe-wide chessboard.

The opportunity to reform Ireland came in 1534 when Garret Oge was summoned to London, leaving his son Thomas, Lord Offaly, to rule in his place as Lord Justice. Less patient than his father and grandfather, and swayed by false rumours of his father's execution, 'Silken Thomas' flung down the sword of office and rebelled against the Crown. His rebellion, so prominent in the history books, had little chance of ultimate success. It was in a sense a pre-emptive move, for the fall of the House of Kildare was inevitable. In a little over a year the war was over. Garret Oge died in prison. Silken Thomas was captured and executed with five of his uncles at Tyburn. The Leinster Geraldines were all but wiped out.

The rebellion dictated a new policy in Ireland, even if Henry had not already resolved on one. The second Tudor monarch is remembered today as a caricature, a fat evil man with six wives, two of whom he beheaded. No one remembers the slender Renaissance prince who was hailed on his accession as the most accomplished in Christendom, a scholar who could debate with the learned theologians in Latin, and compose an air like 'Greensleeves'. In the same way his Irish policy has been entered in the register of history as yet another grievous wrong inflicted on Ireland, yet it was in many ways conciliatory and far-sighted, and bears favourable comparison with those of his successors.

With the Geraldine power broken, there was by 1540 no obstacle to the complete reconquest of the island. But Henry's quarrel with the Pope had exposed him to so many dangers abroad that, for the moment, he hesitated to become embroiled in an expensive campaign in Ireland. Instead Sir Anthony St Leger was sent over to negotiate a series of agreements with the Irish chiefs by which they would surrender their lands to the King and receive them back to be held by knight-service. The principle was not new, but this time the policy was crowned with success, and by 1541 every Irish chief had been brought into a formal relationship with the Crown. The more important were given English titles. In the same year parliament conferred on Henry the title of 'King of Ireland'.[17] The Bill was read to the assembly in the Irish language, and the chiefs gave it their 'liberal consents'. The new title was proclaimed after solemn Mass in St Patrick's Cathedral, celebrated by the Archbishop of Dublin. Thus did Henry shake off the tradition that he was ruler of Ireland by virtue of the papal bull *Laudabiliter*. Ireland was given a new green flag and the harp as its national symbol. 'In this policy,' wrote one historian,

> Henry showed a more enlightened statesmanship than many of the Englishmen who have had to govern Ireland. His main objects were conciliation and fusion; the conciliation of the great by confirming them in their

lands, granting them new titles and sharing with them the spoil of the religious houses; the fusion of the colonial and native populations by a complete abandonment of the policy of segregation and by the extension of English law to the whole country.[18]

The trouble was that in the long run it did not work. The principle of 'surrender and regrant' ran counter to the Gaelic laws of land-holding. The English system of primogeniture conflicted with the Irish custom of gavelkind, whereby the land was communally owned by the tribe and the chieftainship was to some degree a conferred honour. The chiefs who were ambitious exploited the law of primogeniture, and this was a source of friction with their kin and their rivals. In general the Gaelic system was attuned to war rather than peace, and gradually it became obvious that Henry's blueprint would work only if it were preceded by reconquest. For the rest of the century the Crown was to be preoccupied with that goal, but it was not achieved until the very end of Elizabeth's reign, when the last and most formidable rebellion, that of Hugh O'Neill, was crushed. It proved to be an enormously expensive undertaking, but one which became ever more imperative as time went on. Armies fell sick in the damp, unfamiliar climate or were ambushed in the bogs and mountains. Food and military supplies regularly ran short, and Irish allies could not be depended on. In more fertile and defensible areas plantations were begun with high hopes that were rarely fulfilled. Above all, the process was complicated by the Reformation.

Henry VIII died a Catholic, but the Reformation parliament of the 1530s, which he had used to break England away from Rome, had put in place all the legislation to allow the spread of Reformed doctrine, and in the brief reign of Edward VI the country became Protestant. His sister Mary Tudor tried to bring it back into the bosom of the Catholic Church, and married Philip II of Spain, but even she dared not take back the monastic lands from England's rising gentry class, now overwhelmingly Protestant. When Elizabeth came to the throne she faced many enemies abroad, the most formidable of whom was Philip II, but England was still dangerously divided in religion (about a quarter of the population was still Catholic), and the compromise which expediency then dictated is still fairly visible in the Church of England.

In Ireland these vertiginous changes did not have the same consequences. There the Reformation did not take, because the Protestant clergy were able to introduce the religious changes only in areas where English secular authority ran. In this respect Ireland was like a child's colouring book: once painted in, it showed up, more than anything else had ever done, just how limited the power of the Crown was. The vast majority of the population were unaffected by the doctrinal revolution, and remained in the old faith, as they have done to this day. Moreover, Ireland became a fertile field for the evangelising agents of the Counter-Reformation, in particular the orders of preaching friars, and strong links were forged with the Catholic countries of Europe who were now England's enemies.

Flavit Deus et Dissipati Sunt ('God blew and they were scattered') – so runs the Latin motto on the Dutch medal struck to commemorate the defeat of the Spanish Armada in 1588. This, our schoolbooks told us, marked the climax of Elizabeth's war with Spain, the moment when Spanish sea-power was broken, as the galleons were driven from the Channel to perish one by one on the desolate western coasts of Ireland. They did not tell us about the Spanish armadas of 1596 and 1597. On 13 October 1596 a fleet of ninety-eight ships and 16,000 men (only a little smaller than that of 1588) sailed from Lisbon under the command of Don Martin de Padilla. Unknown to Elizabeth its destination was Ireland, and its purpose to bring aid to all those who had sworn 'to pursue that all-out war, wholeheartedly against all the enemies of the Catholic Church, especially the English Protestants'.[19] Once again God seemed to be on the English side. The armada was scattered by a ferocious storm off Cape Finisterre, but this time two-thirds of the galleons struggled home safely to Spain. They formed the core of the armada of 1597, larger than that of 1588, but with a more limited aim. 'Moved by the universal outcry of the oppressed Catholics of these nations', Philip ordered it to invade Cornwall and take Plymouth, a first step towards a general rising and the reuniting of the two crowns.[20] Once more Philip insisted that it sailed in the autumn, too late in the year. It was only 30 miles off the Lizard on 12 October when a violent gale blew up and, after battling with it for three days, the armada turned for home. Eleven days later the alarm was sounded in an England that was totally unprepared, its fleet away in the Azores, no land defence in place, and no Drake playing bowls on Plymouth Hoe. Truly, as Sir William Monson wrote, 'the Spaniards never had so dangerous an enterprise on us'.[21]

The dominant topic of Anglo-Irish relations, which has so distorted

Irish historical study, derives first from geography. Ireland is an island hidden from Europe behind a larger one (*L'île derrière l'île*, as the French have called it), and with the emergence of the modern nation state, and still later, the rise of Great Britain to the rank of world power, a pattern developed in Irish history which continues down to the present. The accident of history which determined that most of Ireland should remain in one faith, while most of England and Scotland chose another, sealed the difference between the islands, but its roots go back farther, perhaps to the pre-Celticity of the Iron Age, bypassing Rome and Saxon England. It is already manifest in the missionary expeditions of the so-called Dark Ages and in the Irish medieval clerk's desire to 'walk the white roads of France' for the love of learning.

From the sixteenth century onward the 'otherness' of Ireland was to England's enemies not just an opportunity but a constant temptation. The Spanish were the first to exploit it, in their expeditions to aid Hugh O'Neill, and the pretext of religious solidarity made it the most dangerous challenge to English authority in Tudor times. Fortunately for England, the Spanish landed at the wrong end of Ireland, received little support from the local population and were closely besieged by the English army. Not only were they of little use to O'Neill, but he had to move his army right across the island from north to south to establish contact with them, and was heavily defeated as a consequence. The Spanish surrendered on terms, and were allowed to return home.

In the seventeenth and eighteenth centuries the challenge was taken up by the French. Louis XIV's regiments intervened substantially in James II's war against William of Orange, and, a hundred years later, the eagerly awaited arrival of French troops was the chief factor in the United Irish plans for an uprising. Historians who have worked in the military and naval archives of France aver that in almost every year of the eighteenth century the French had an invasion plan for Ireland. In 1760, though to a large degree by chance, François Thurot invaded County Antrim with some of the cream of the French army, seized and held Carrickfergus and threatened Belfast, before departing, only to be intercepted by the British navy. At Christmas 1796 a large French military and naval expedition to aid the United Irishmen reached Bantry Bay, with Wolfe Tone on board. They were driven off by atrocious weather, high winds and heavy snow, which inflicted more damage on the fleet than any military reaction. On this occasion the French repeated the Spanish mistake of landing on the wrong side of Ireland, as they were to do again in August 1798, in County Mayo. At that time the heart of the United Irish conspiracy was to be found in the Presbyterian north around Belfast.

The pattern of foreign intervention concealed ambivalences. The Spanish episode had the backing of the papacy, the intervention of Louis XIV on behalf of James did not; and whereas the French support for Irish rebellion in the 1790s came essentially from the French Revolution, all the earlier French attempts were associated with the *ancien régime*, and were motivated by Catholic solidarity and enmity to England more than by the novel idea of the brotherhood of man. In other words, the pattern transcends the changing ideologies, and becomes a shaping element in Irish history. The intervention of foreign powers, for their own political ends, becomes the hope and expectation of dissident Irish nationalists.

In the early twentieth century France was succeeded by Germany. The European ambitions of Kaiser Wilhelm II, and his hostility towards the land of which his grandmother was Queen, stimulated an interest in Ireland's troubles. In 1913 he questioned Sir Edward Carson closely about the situation in Ulster.[22] The guns which were landed to arm the Ulster Volunteer Force were German, though no evidence has ever been produced to reveal an official hand in what seems to have been a commercial transaction. German support for, and assistance to, the 1916 Rising is a matter of record and now part of Irish history. The Kaiser does not seem to have contemplated an invasion of Ireland. A very different situation prevailed during the Second World War when the independent part of Ireland remained neutral. Already, before the war, there was in place a network of Nazi spies on the island. One of them was the distinguished scholar Dr Adolf Mahr, the Director of the National Museum in Dublin who left Ireland in August 1939 and worked for German intelligence in Berlin. During his time in Ireland he became friendly with E. Estyn Evans, and they co-operated on many aspects of Irish prehistory and archaeology. Long afterwards Evans remembered that Mahr had shown a special interest in coastal sites of the Lecale area of County Down.[23] In 1940, when Hitler was seriously contemplating the invasion of the British Isles, General K. Student, the Commander-in-Chief of the German Airborne Forces, drew up elaborate plans for the rapid occupation of Belfast, after the dropping of thousands of parachute troops on the surrounding hills.[24]

Holy Disorders

Men have lost their reason in nothing as much as in their
religion, wherein stones and clouts make martyrs.

SIR THOMAS BROWN[1]

Confederates

The seventeenth century is very popular with journalists, politicians and clerics who, despite all evidence to the contrary, think we are still living in it. Thirty years ago it was the consensus that we should be taken out of it and 'dragged screaming and kicking into the twentieth century'. A scream might seem appropriate for anyone brought into the century of Auschwitz and Hiroshima, and Edvard Munch's famous image its very logo, but as the century ended, Kosovo succeeded Rwanda, and plague succeeded famine, the phrase began to sound hollow and dropped out of fashion. Like 'mindless violence' or 'Freedom!', it is a thing people say when they cannot bear the pain of a nanosecond's thought.

The bad news is that we *are* living in the present and all the things that are happening in Ireland are happening now. In some respects they may remind us of the darker episodes of the seventeenth century and its wars of religion, but there is a barrier between us and the people who lived then, a glass wall through which we can see but may never travel. Once again a familiar figure wanders unbidden into the debate. Carlyle puts his finger exactly on the difficulty.

Sifting through the voluminous background material in order to edit the correspondence of Oliver Cromwell, he despairs of the task of scaling the 'paper mountains' of political and religious pamphlets – thirty to fifty thousand of them in the British Museum alone.

> There, all vanquished, overwhelmed under such waste lumber mountains, the wreck and dead ashes of some six unbelieving generations, does the Age of Cromwell and his Puritans lie hidden from us. . . . our spiritual notions, if any notion of ours may still be called spiritual, are fatal to a right understanding of the seventeenth century. The Christian Doctrines which then dwelt alive in every heart, have now in a manner died out in all hearts . . . Nay, worse still, the Cant of them does not dwell alive with us, little doubting that it is Cant . . . Thus the old names suggest new things to us – not august and divine, but hypocritical, pitiable, detestable.

In other words we cannot any longer even distinguish sincerity from hypocrisy in what people said then: 'all Puritanism is grown inarticulate . . . The fashion of this world passeth away.'[2]

The seventeenth century was an age of religious wars, treachery and barbarity, very complicated and bad for almost everybody. Ireland shared these horrors to the full; other people's troubles were indeed the cause of most of the confusion in Ireland, and make it one of the most challenging periods of Irish history to study. In Ireland it was an era of turmoil and upheaval, and for half of it the country was ravaged by war. Historians tend to measure centuries less by the exact calendar dates than by the congruity of trends within them, and the significance of events on either side of their portals. Thus, according to taste (or prejudice), one may speak of the period between the Flight of the Earls in 1607 and the Battle of the Boyne in 1690, or choose instead the 'long century' from the death of Elizabeth I in 1603 to that of Anne in 1714. Either way it was a complex and confusing period for Ireland, and for Anglo-Irish relations.

The century began with an extensive, and ultimately successful, plantation in the north of the country, which changed its essential character in some ways but not in others. This episode, along with the civil wars in the middle and at the end of the century, brought about large transfers of Irish land from Catholic to Protestant ownership. By 1700 only a fraction of the land was still held by Catholic landlords. Land on this wet and boggy island was from the earliest times of vital importance, and, from this point on, it became the dominant issue, mixed as it now was with religion.

At the same time, political and administrative power in Ireland, under conflicting kinds of English suzerainty, passed from the hands of the Old English (descendants of the medieval settlers) into those of the New English (the incomers associated with the newer plantations and military campaigns). It did not happen all at once, and the forum in which the shifts took place was the Irish parliament, but it was a major cause of tension in the period. The chief attempts to reverse the process, during the Confederate and Jacobite wars, brought defeat and ruin on those elements of Irish society which (paradoxically) supported the English monarchy against the English parliament in both cases.

For twenty years between 1640 and 1660 there was a complete breakdown in the normal structures of government and allegiance, a period of confusion and demoralisation, in which, at one time or another, every recognisable interest could be found fighting on the side one would least expect, and individual commanders changed partners as in an elaborate dance. Since things could hardly have got worse, the Restoration of Charles II in 1660 marked the beginning of a spell of marked improvement for Ireland, both politically and economically, marred only by the execution on trumped-up charges of the Catholic Archbishop Oliver Plunkett at the height of the religious fury known as 'the Popish Plot'. The century ended with a Catholic king, deposed from his English throne, but reigning legitimately in Ireland, at cross-purposes with his Irish subjects, while his Protestant subjects flocked to the banner of a foreign monarch, who happened to be his son-in-law and also his nephew.

Are there clues to guide us through this maze? Land, loyalty and religion will take us part of the way. At the beginning of the century Ireland became for the first time an administrative unit totally under the control of the new Stuart monarchy. The county divisions were determined, as we know them today, and the King's writ ran in all of them. It is easy to forget, when we try to survey the whole period from 1171 until 1603, that at no point in this stretch of time was Ireland entirely or effectively subject to a centralised English government. James VI and I was the first British monarch who could say not only that he was King of Ireland but that there was a Kingdom of Ireland which he might rule.

Of course we must remember that this was true of James's rule in Scotland also. It was only during his reign that the monarchy deliberately and successfully extended its authority into the Gaelic western isles. This was not without significance for Ireland. For centuries the MacDonalds, as Lords of the Isles, had ruled over a thalassocracy which embraced both sides of the North Channel, only thirteen miles across at its narrowest point. When they came under pressure from the kings of Scotland, the chieftains could rally, or take refuge among, their own clansmen in Ulster. James was determined to close this bolt-hole, and replace it with an anvil, on which the MacDonalds of the Isles and the MacDonnells of Antrim might be fashioned into good subjects.

The centralisation of government was not, however, his primary objective. After the surrender of O'Neill, he showed that he was more interested in the security of Ireland than in total victory over the Gaelic system, which he understood better than most Englishmen. Not only were O'Neill and Hugh O'Donnell pardoned and confirmed in the possession of their lands, and given English titles as Earl of Tyrone and Earl of Tyrconnell respectively, but an Act of Oblivion was passed to remove any fear of the prosecution of former rebels. That policy was destroyed by the abrupt and unforeseen action of O'Neill and O'Donnell in taking flight abroad in 1607, an episode which was by no means as simple and irreversible as legend has made it appear. The precise motivation of the earls remains obscure. It now seems unlikely that they were animated solely by a sentimental patriotism or religious fervour. Driven by bad weather to take refuge in Normandy, they made their way to the Spanish Netherlands and then circuitously to Rome, but neither the Pope nor the King of Spain felt disposed to support their claims to restoration. Historical research has suggested that the younger man, O'Donnell, was the instigator, and that the flight was against O'Neill's better judgement. Whatever its causes it came in time to be seen as a national tragedy, the end of the Gaelic system in Ireland, and it opened the way for an extensive plantation in the north of Ireland.[3]

The Plantation of Ulster is the subject of great misunderstanding in Irish history. To paraphrase a similar verdict by Alfred Cobban on the French Revolution, most people know only three things about it, and not one of them is true. The native Irish were not completely driven off the land, the Plantation did not coincide with the six counties which constitute Northern Ireland today, and it was not the cause of the 'Ulster problem'. Nationalist rhetoric always depicts it as a rape or violation of Gaelic Ireland by planting colonies of English and Scottish strangers on confiscated Irish land, and unionist rhetoric often accepts the same interpretation, though with satisfaction. The historical facts are rather more complex and indeterminate. In practice the Irish often remained as tenants; and the Scots expanded on to the portions reserved for English settlers but not taken up by them. Thus was created the extraordinary mosaic of population which underlies modern Ulster, and which is so little understood outside Northern Ireland itself.

The difficulties and conflicts which make this mosaic a 'problem' today arose from later history when religion was fatally intertwined with land and national allegiance. The territory of the present Republic of Ireland has a patchwork of earlier English plantations which now present no political problem. Their Protestant populations remained minorities, but this was not so in the north. In the late eighteenth century the Presbyterian Scots became the chief object of concern to the British government, and many of them combined with Catholics in opposition to, and finally in revolt against, British rule in Ireland, but they were never regarded by Catholics as other than an alien population, and this has stoked the intensity of sectarian hatred ever since. Nevertheless, if the influx of Scottish population is held to be the origin of the Ulster problem, then the blame cannot be laid solely at the door of James I, or of any British government, for that influx had been under way for centuries before, and continued for a century after, the Plantation. Moreover, the counties of Antrim and Down were not included in James's plans, deliberately so, since they were already densely settled.

Against all this it might be argued that the plantation which began in 1609 was the most thorough and well-planned of all the schemes of plantation in Ireland. Had it been possible to implement as it was mapped out on paper, it might indeed have entirely replaced the native Irish population in six (though not Northern Ireland's six) counties with Scottish and English planters. But, like most Irish enterprises, it was only half accomplished. The interplay of changing circumstance and private interest, greed and opportunism, and the perennial lack of finance altered it into something else, and left the ruins for future generations to attack or cling to. Only the vigorous private enterprise of the London companies seemed for a while to justify the effort.

The chief contemporary consequence of the Plantation was to strengthen what came to be known as the New English interest in Ireland, the post-Reformation planters of the late sixteenth and early seventeenth centuries. Their acquisitiveness, along with their unequivocal loyalty to the English Crown, was in time to create a heartbreaking dilemma for the Old English, the descendants of all the strains of medieval settlers who collectively formed the garrison through which England had attempted to govern the island from the days of the Lordship. They were not of course all English in the narrow sense, but Normans, Welsh and Scots too. At the core of this population there was now a native Anglo-Irish aristocracy, but allied with an extensive and prosperous Catholic merchant class. The Old English were strongest in the Pale, which had been the cradle of their caste, but they also exercised considerable influence in the seaports like Cork, Waterford and Galway.[4] These two factors made their influence paramount in the Irish parliament when the century began.

They now became locked in a power struggle with the New English. The vital difference, and the one which was to prove decisive, was that the Old English had not changed their religion at the time of the Reformation. Already by the end of Elizabeth's reign they were under pressure because of their religion, and in retrospect we can now see how they gradually defined themselves as a group as the seventeenth century progressed. To begin with, it was somewhat amorphous, and, at its periphery, not sharply distinguished from other elements in the population. There was a nucleus of families with a proud tradition, including the Palesmen, but also embracing families with great estates beyond the Pale. Around them, we have a series of concentric circles, the outermost circle being the most difficult to define. By the end of the century, however, the stand which the Old English had been forced to take on a whole series of issues defined them sharply, and qualified them as a doomed ascendancy.

The Old English thus became that favourite object of Irish sympathy, 'the dying breed'. This was to be the classic paradigm of Irish history. In their fall they prefigured the fate of the Protestant Ascendancy which largely replaced them, as a consequence of the century's religious wars, and re-enacted the fate of the Gaels and Normans who preceded them. James I called a parliament in Ireland in 1613, and in order to increase the power of the New English he created a large number of new boroughs by royal charter (including incidentally Belfast). The Old English vainly petitioned the King to suspend the new charters, and made a determined effort in parliament to halt the erosion of their privileges. It was the beginning of a process which was eventually to equate loyalist with Protestant, and force the Old English to cross the fatal line which divided the planters from 'the King's Irish enemies'.

The process was further advanced during the deputyship of Thomas Wentworth, Earl of Strafford (1633–40). Wentworth was an able and conscientious royal servant who endeavoured to make Ireland peaceful and efficient, and, even more ambitiously, to make it pay. A strong man, if somewhat lacking in diplomacy, he had been plucked from the English parliamentary opposition to Charles I to become a pillar of the monarchy. He was nevertheless the very prototype of the insensitive proconsul in Ireland, grappling with problems and a people he did not in the least begin to understand, though he thought he did. He succeeded in some of his short-term objectives by the ruthless application of the policy of 'Thorough', but at the cost of alienating every element of Irish society, from the Old English to the Scots Presbyterians of Ulster. Like countless other viceroys he imagined that the right course in Ireland was not to show sympathy to any particular group. As a result he appeared cold and alien to them all, and earned their intense hatred. There was a significant Irish element in the hostile agitation which enabled the Long Parliament at last to pull him down. Charles I sacrificed him in a vain attempt to save his tottering throne, and he went to his execution with the bitter words 'Put not thy trust in princes.'

The sudden rebellion of the Irish chieftains in 1641 followed closely on Wentworth's removal. The date fixed for the uprising was 23 October 1641, and the plan was to seize Dublin Castle, the headquarters of English authority in Ireland. The plan was betrayed and the Castle saved – a blueprint for all future rebellions – but in the north the native Irish rose and seized most of the towns, then turning to massacre thousands of the colonists spread thinly over the Plantation. At first only the English were attacked and the Scots left alone, but gradually the killing took on the familiar trappings of a holy war. Londonderry became a place of refuge for the planters, while Enniskillen, Carrickfergus and Belfast also remained in Protestant hands.

Nevertheless the Plantation had been all but overwhelmed. The drums and bonfires which warned the Protestants to rally to their own defence have, so to speak, entered the bloodstream of Irish Protestantism. The atrocities committed by the Irish were luridly detailed in depositions taken by parliamentary commissioners some years later under the Commonwealth. The memory of these events, and the savage retaliatory massacres they provoked, have increased sectarian tension ever since, though many people would earnestly deny this. The authenticity of the depositions, which are preserved in large folios in the library of Trinity College, Dublin, was the subject of heated controversy in the last quarter of the nineteenth century, and is still challenged. There is naturally great sensitivity about allegations of genocide in Ireland, though no fair-minded historian would ever attribute a monopoly of slaughter to any religious sect.

The nineteenth-century debate, however, tended to follow the line of sectarian division, and it was hardly a coincidence that it should coincide with the furious public debate over Home Rule for Ireland. This is a very obvious illustration of the way in which historians are influenced by the issues of their own time, but there are many more subtle and less ostentatious ways in which this influence operates. Since the revolution which took place in Irish historical studies in the mid-twentieth century the subject has not attracted the attention of many historians, and has, until recently, been studiously avoided. That the documents themselves are genuine can no longer be seriously doubted; their actual content, and their use as parliamentary propaganda, are another matter. The consensus of opinion among historians is that the figures for the massacre are greatly exaggerated.

The 1641 insurrection in Ireland was strongly influenced by the course of events in Great Britain, in particular the revolt in Scotland against Charles I's religious policy, and the frustrations built up during the period known as 'the eleven years tyranny', when the King tried the experiment of ruling without parliament. The fall of Wentworth indicated a further weakening of royal authority in Ireland, but the rising must also be viewed against the background of a more general crisis, the religious wars in Europe. No account coming out of Ireland exceeds the horrors inflicted on the German peasantry as narrated in the pages of Grimmelshausen's *Simplicissimus*. Irishmen in exile returned to play a significant role in the rising, and Cardinal Richelieu sent aid to the insurgents.

If these were the powerful 'horizontal' influences on 1641, the 'vertical' roots went back to the conquest and confiscations of Elizabeth I's reign. The cause was not so much that all the Gaelic Irish had lost their lands as that those who *were* dispossessed adopted a pattern of life which inevitably led to a *revanche* mentality. The petty chieftains, obeying perhaps ancestral instincts and patterns of behaviour connected with the ancient pulse of transhumance, took to the mountains and woods, accompanied by their dependants and followers, forming an irregular army that would in time become the 'secret army' of Ireland. This tradition of secret military societies, from the tories and rapparees, through the agrarian secret societies right down to the Irish Republican Army (IRA), is of immense significance in the working out of Irish history.

Sustaining themselves on song and legend, Gaelic poetry, and the memory of ancient wrongs and more recent dispossession and exile, the native Irish longed for the day when they could take back their own. Above all, the unifying effect of the old religion, that fatal fusing of all the elements in the population who were placed, or placed themselves, outside the law, in a common outlook and purpose, would ultimately replace the law. It could at least be represented as a defence of Catholicism and the Gaelic heritage. They established a pattern, a way of looking at things, which still powerfully influences the people of Ireland, and shapes their politics. And yet the Gaelic heritage was only one kind of Irish heritage.

The rebellion of 1641 can be seen on two levels of significance. First it may be considered as the consequence of plantation, the inevitable result of half-hearted attempts at subjugation, conversion and colonisation. It may also be seen as the proximate cause of the English Civil War. The failure of the monarchy to deal with the Irish situation was the last straw on the camel's back, the ultimate financial burden which put Charles I at the mercy of parliament and changed the British constitution. In its origins 1641 was the work of a handful of discontented gentlemen and soldiers, but at a later stage a popular element entered into it, as was the case again, to a far greater extent, in 1798.

One aspect of 1641 which has received very little attention from historians was the fear which it gave rise to among the population in the western parts of Britain. In some areas it amounted to wholesale panic at the prospect of imminent invasion by hordes of murderous Irish. Sir Phelim O'Neill, who led the rebellion in its initial stage, had falsely claimed to be acting on the King's authority, and nothing did more damage to Charles's cause during the first civil war than Ireland. 'To the day of his death,' wrote J.C. Beckett, 'Charles was never able to shake off completely the imputation of complicity in the rising.'[5] This raw nerve would be touched again at the end of the century, and would lose James II his throne. It is a good example of the way in which Irish history continually interacts with English history. It is a fact of geography.

The 'Irish' significance of 1641 is that it was a critical moment for Protestant consciousness, the coming of 'a tempest long foretold'. It was St Bartholomew's Night, the Domesday situation. Fires are lit, church bells toll, drums beat, men rush to arms, women and children are led to shelter. A pattern of behaviour is established for the future, to be reactivated again and again – in 1689, in 1798, in 1912 and 1920, and after 1969. But in Northern Ireland the course of history has altered the pattern so that each religion fears the other.

In 1641 the Pale was thrown into confusion. Sir John Borlase and Sir William Parsons, the Lords Justices (acting officers of state), appointed the Earl of Ormond to command the royalist forces. Ormond was a Butler, a member of one of the most ancient of the Old English families, but he had been brought up as a Protestant on the orders of James I. The guiding principle of his life was loyalty to the doomed House of Stuart. At first Ormond was obliged to remain on the defensive. Dublin had to be made secure. Later he wished to take the field against the rebels, but the Lords Justices would not allow him to do so. They had a reasonable concern about the attitude of the Old English of the Pale. The Old English had proclaimed their loyalty to the King, but in the circumstances Borlase and Parsons hesitated to arm Catholic recusants. In the end the lords of the Pale settled the matter in an extraordinary way – they joined the rebels.

Their hope was to be able to control the Irish, and then bring the whole military coalition over to the King's side, thus removing the danger to him by strengthening his hand against parliament, while regaining their old influence, so eroded in the previous reign.

The turmoil in Ireland was immensely complicated by the outbreak of civil war in England a year later. 'The War of the Three Kingdoms' which occupied the next seven years upset all the constant equations in Irish history. Interests and parties, and even individuals, were obliged by abnormal circumstances to take the side opposite to that on which one might expect to find them. It may be useful, therefore, to identify at least the main interests involved. They were: (1) the Old Irish, most of whom were in rebellion, but against the Plantation interest rather than against Charles I; (2) the Old English, strongly represented in the Pale, in some towns and seaports, and a few areas elsewhere, who had thrown in their lot with the Irish, but who protested their loyalty to the King; (3) the New English, Protestant settlers in towns and ports and on the Ulster Plantation, who were divided in loyalty between King and parliament; (4) the New Scots, densely settled in eastern Ulster and spread more thinly over the Plantation; one might have expected them to take the Puritan side on idealogical grounds, and initially they did, but the twists and turns of the King's negotiations with Scotland led many of them to support his cause, and they protested at his execution in 1649.

Meanwhile in 1642 the rebels, under the guidance of the Catholic bishops, set up a central government of Ireland at Kilkenny and called a 'general assembly', a parliament in which both Irish and Old English interests would be represented. They also appointed a supreme council to carry on the war, and to make arrangements for justice and administration. As regards long-term objectives, the Irish wanted the policy of plantation to be reversed, but they also demanded the recognition of the Roman Catholic religion. In effect they wanted the re-establishment of the Catholic Church as the Church of the Kingdom. The Old English were uneasy at being technically in rebellion, and they sought to return to allegiance without exacting religious concessions from the King. They understood his difficulties, though they did not waive their demands for more sympathetic treatment. Despite a difference in emphasis, both groups protested loyalty to Charles I, fearing that their lot would be a good deal worse if parliament should win the war. The two interests were fused by the Catholic religion but by little else, and sooner or later a divergence of views was inevitable.

This coalition of Irish and Old English is generally known as the Confederation of Kilkenny, but, as Beckett pointed out, this is a historian's term, of modern origin. When the word was used in the seventeenth century it did not have the meaning of an alliance of parties or communities. The 'Confederate Catholics of Ireland', as they described themselves, were individuals who had sworn a binding oath of association 'to carry on the war for our faith, our king and our country'.[6] This serves to remind us that friction, distrust and feelings of racial and social distinction were built into the assembly and supreme council. These bodies were at best instruments of expediency, and in the end they gave way under the strain.

In Ulster the rebels were commanded by Owen Roe O'Neill, nephew of the Great Earl of Tyrone. In Leinster the forces of the Old English were commanded by Sir Thomas Preston. The Pale was held for the King by Ormond, while Lord Inchiquin led the Protestants of Munster. The King wanted to make a treaty with the rebels, and Ormond worked hard to bring it about, concluding a cessation of arms in 1643. But Charles could not grant the Confederates' full demands, and in the north the Scots, as usual, looked after themselves. After the first shock of the 1641 massacres refugees had arrived in the west of Scotland, arousing anger and sympathy there. The parliament of Scotland promised to send troops if the English would pay for them, but it was not until 1642 that 2,500 Scottish soldiers landed at Carrickfergus, under the command of General Robert Munro, a seasoned veteran of the Thirty Years War. (This event also brought about the consolidation of Presbyterianism in the area into a distinct Church when the Scottish army chaplains established the first congregations along the Sixmilewater.)

The arrival of the Scots restored the morale of the settlers, and created an uneasy peace, but they ignored the cessation of arms and subscribed to the Solemn League and Covenant. Ormond could negotiate only for the forces directly under his command, and to make matters worse, the Munster Protestants now deserted him and went over to the side of the English parliament. Ormond was betrayed also by the duplicity of the King. Charles I opened his own secret negotiations with the rebels, through his emissary, the Earl of Glamorgan, an English Catholic. However, the terms of the agreement became public, and Charles was forced to repudiate it. Then in March 1646 the Old English, who dominated the supreme council, made a new treaty with Ormond, without telling their Irish allies or their powerful advisor, the Papal Nuncio, Giovanni Battista Rinuccini, the Bishop of Fermo. Pope Innocent x had sent an envoy to the Confederates in 1643 (Pietro Scarampi), but the money and supplies he brought with him were of little use, so when Rinuccini landed at Kenmare in October 1645 the Confederates were overjoyed to receive a fully accredited nuncio as an earnest of the Pope's active support. Rinuccini was a formidable ally, a brave and determined man driven by zeal, but rash and impulsive, with little skill at conciliation, and he played a large part in bringing about the downfall of the Confederacy.

Rinuccini was suspicious of Ormond from the outset, and in August 1646 he condemned the treaty in a synod at Waterford, threatening all who had signed it with excommunication. The supreme council and the aristocracy were willing to defy him, but he had the support of the ordinary Catholic people who made up the rank and file of the Confederate army, and who were provoked into riots against the agreement in Limerick. Rinuccini had arrived with a large supply of money and arms, which he used to support the campaigns of Owen Roe O'Neill, whose prestige was now at its height. In the summer of 1646 Munro and the Scots advanced towards Armagh, eager to engage O'Neill's army, and were lured into an ambush in unfavourable terrain near Benburb in County Tyrone. Here on 5 June O'Neill inflicted a crushing defeat on the Scots army. They left their standards and most of their artillery on the battlefield, and Munro's wig was found hanging on a bush. 'For aught I can understand,' Munro later wrote, 'the Lord of Hosts had a controversy with us.'[7]

At Rome the victory was celebrated with a *Te Deum* in S Maria Maggiore attended by the Pope. Benburb altered the balance of power in the supreme council, putting Rinuccini in control, and though O'Neill failed to follow up his advantage, his supporters were able to repudiate the Ormond peace. Thus by 1647 Ormond's position had become impossible. No further help was to be had from Charles, who by then had lost the first civil war in the field. On 19 June Ormond surrendered Dublin to parliament, and six weeks later sailed for England.

The royal cause was not yet entirely lost in Ireland. In a second astounding switch of loyalty Inchiquin and the Scots declared for the King in early 1648. Ormond hastened back to Ireland in late September and reopened negotiations with the Confederates. At first O'Neill ignored these overtures and toyed with the idea of supporting parliament, but then threw in his lot with Ormond. It was too late. In August 1649 Oliver Cromwell landed in Ireland with 12,000 battle-hardened troops and parliament's commission to act as Lord Lieutenant of Ireland.

Ironsides

The conduct of the war now changed. Parliament was ready to put an end to the confusion in Ireland, and Cromwell was the chosen instrument. Whatever else may be said about him, we now know that he was a military genius. Beside him Ormond and Inchiquin appear almost as amateurs. In the short term his two Irish military campaigns were successful, ending anarchy and giving Ireland a stability which lasted until 1689. Unable to raise an army against him in the field, Ormond secured some of the strongholds and put the rest of his army into Drogheda.

Cromwell stormed Drogheda on 11 September 1649 and Wexford on 11 October, sending a detachment to relieve Londonderry, which was then enduring a siege by the Presbyterians (the opposite of the situation in the more famous siege half a century later). At Drogheda, after his first attack had been repulsed, he gave the order to spare none of the garrison. By the rules of war at the time he was justified in refusing quarter to a town taken by storm after it had rejected a call to surrender, but this was a rule sparingly invoked. The garrison and such recusant clergy as could be found were slaughtered, a savage act of war without doubt, but 'there seems to be no foundation for later stories of an indiscriminate slaughter of the whole civilian population'.[8] This is an area in which it is very difficult to arrive at the truth. Another massacre accompanied the taking of Wexford, but here Cromwell was not directly responsible.

Whatever the facts, the sack of Drogheda has earned Cromwell the undying hatred of the Irish people ever since. Even scholarly Irish historians express views of him which place him in the same category as Hitler or Pol Pot, though one can never escape the suspicion that his religion compounds his lack of compassion.

In one way this is quite unhistorical, to select one episode from a war and a century which overbrims with sacked towns and massacres; the Thirty Years War which had ravaged Europe had just come to an end. But all Irish historical memory is like this, and indeed derives its special vitality from the ability to select without balance. Drogheda is lamented and 1641 played down. Drogheda might just have slipped into the semi-oblivion which engulfs most sieges had it not been for Cromwell's ostentatious lack of pity, and his justification of his actions as divine retribution on the Irish people. 'I am persuaded,' he told parliament, 'that this is a righteous judgement of God upon those barbarous wretches who have imbrued their hands in so much innocent blood, and that it will tend to prevent the effusion of blood for the future; which are satisfactory grounds of such actions, which otherwise cannot but work remorse and regret.'[9]

In the long run his harshness was a political blunder. Drogheda established yet another pattern in Irish history, setting a deadly historical trap for the British soldier in Ireland. Wherever he goes in that country, Cromwell walks by his side. Cromwell's second campaign in 1650 extended parliament's authority inland. Kilkenny surrendered in March, and Clonmel was taken in May. Then Cromwell was recalled by parliament to prepare for imminent war with the Scots. The campaign was carried on by his son-in-law Henry Ireton, and by other Cromwellian officers when Ireton succumbed to the plague in 1651. Galway, the last stronghold to resist, fell in April 1652.

Conquest was followed by confiscation. In 1652 the English parliament passed 'an Act for the settlement of Ireland'. Every proprietor who could not prove 'constant good affection to the interests of the Commonwealth of England' was to forfeit a proportion of his estate. This proscription included almost everybody who was either loyalist or rebel, and the Old English were finally classified with the enemies of the English state. To clear the way for a new plantation, all the forfeiting landlords were required to remove themselves west of the River Shannon, where they would be granted an equivalent portion of land. Cromwell did not, of course, say 'To Hell or Connaught', nor did anyone else at the time. That was the rallying cry of Protestant extremists in County Armagh at the end of the eighteenth century, in the effort to drive Catholics out of the county; but the whole of Irish history is an all-purpose arsenal of abuse.

This harsh measure was largely dictated by financial expediency. It seemed to be the only way of meeting the debt to the Adventurers, the merchants and financiers who had advanced money for the conduct of the war in 1642, and it was a convenient way of settling the arrears of pay to the soldiers, a constant source of complaint, and the well-spring of much of the revolutionary agitation in the parliamentary army. Many of the new landlords were its officers, and in time would be the progenitors of many of the Ascendancy families of the eighteenth and nineteenth centuries. There was also a political motive, however, for this was an effective way of making Ireland safe for the Commonwealth, of solving the 'Irish question'. If fully implemented, it would mean removing all potential rebels into Connaught. Then the soldiers would be settled among the rest of the Irish population as a permanent English garrison. Henceforward 'Protestant' would mean 'loyal', and Catholics (even planters and Old English) would automatically be categorised as 'disloyal'.

The Cromwellian settlement (as it is somewhat misleadingly called, for it was parliament's settlement) radically altered the balance of power in Ireland. Before 1641 the majority of landlords had been Catholic; after 1652 the majority were Protestant. Once established, this plantation was not disturbed. As with the Plantation of Ulster in the north, it did not, contrary to popular belief, bring about a large-scale transfer of the non-landowning bulk of the population. Not that the Commonwealth government baulked at the prospect; a displacement of population, every bit as thorough as those carried out by Stalin or Hitler in the twentieth century, seems to have been the intention, and at one stage it was proposed to move the entire Presbyterian population of Antrim and Down to Tipperary, but the logistics of these plans defeated the parliamentary commissioners. The military landlords were new, but in many instances the old tenants remained undisturbed.

The sack of Drogheda and the land confiscations have combined to give Cromwell his unenviable place in Irish history, though these are scarcely comparable episodes, and Cromwell was not personally responsible for the confiscations. There is much more to be said, however, about Ireland in the Cromwellian period. For a brief spell, the only time before the Act of Union, Ireland and Britain were united in one state. The Commonwealth attempted a vastly ambitious programme of reform and modernisation which would have completed the task begun by Henry VIII, that of pulling Ireland out of the Middle Ages. But the desire to make a *tabula rasa* and start from fundamentals is the chimera of the truly radical mind in all ages, and the process is coincidentally so closely entwined with religion in Ireland that it is scarcely possible to argue such a proposition rationally. The period after 1653, when Cromwell became Lord Protector, is in many ways as close as one can get to one of the blank pages of Irish history, a subject which has attracted few Irish historians. There is only one recent book, the scholarly study of administration by the English historian Toby Barnard, and in his preface he relates how his colleagues greeted his decision to write it 'with incredulity if not derision'.[10]

Oliver Cromwell died on the afternoon of 3 September 1658, murmuring passages of Scripture. His son Richard was proclaimed Lord Protector in Dublin on 10 October, four days after his other son Henry had been appointed Lord Lieutenant of Ireland. Henry Cromwell was an honourable and amiable man, and Ireland was to owe him a considerable debt (whether acknowledged or not), but he was not politically ambitious. His chief wish was to retire and live quietly in the country.

Of the four provinces of Ireland, only Leinster strongly supported the Commonwealth. In Ulster the army, and therefore the province, was under the control of Sir Charles Coote, who was prepared to obey, but without enthusiasm. In Munster the Cromwellian soldiery were commanded by Roger Boyle, Lord Broghill, the son of the great Earl of Cork who had fallen foul of Strafford. He was, like his father, notoriously an opportunist. Connaught, filled with refugees from Cromwell's vengeance, was completely royalist, and waiting on events. It was a major threat to the government.

In Ireland as in England people were tired of the Puritan regime, of the army controlling politics, and above all of the endless wrangling between the army and parliament. Cromwell had given Ireland efficient government, and had cleared up the confusions of the Civil War. The irony was that his Irish dispositions had put in power men who now wanted to see the monarchy brought back. Once Cromwell's strong hand was removed, the keys to the situation were held by the army commanders, Coote and Broghill. Thus it came about that, contrary to all expectations, Ireland took the initiative in the restoration of Charles II. Coote and Broghill, who were jealous and mistrustful of each other, had separately made secret contacts with Charles in Brussels. The last complicated rounds of the long boxing match between the army and the Rump Parliament brought both men to power after their appointment as two of the three parliamentary commissioners for Ireland.

A convention was called in Dublin in February 1660, consisting of representatives of the constituencies as they had stood in Strafford's time. It was dominated by army officers and Cromwellian planters who by this stage were interested only in preserving their landed interests in the impending constitutional change. The royalists, led by Coote and Broghill, persuaded them that this could best be achieved by restoring the King. In March the Rump dissolved itself and a convention was summoned at Westminster on the Irish model. General George Monck, who commanded the army in Scotland, then with the support of the Irish army officers, invited Charles to return to England as King. These officers thus played a key role in the whole affair, and considered that they had a special claim on the monarchy. For the rest of the century the dominant issue would be the possession of land.

The character of any land settlement would be determined by the Dublin convention, where, as mentioned, the Cromwellians were in the majority. In England the restoration of confiscated lands to the royalists who had served Charles I was a relatively straightforward matter. This was not so in Ireland, where the shifts in power since 1641 had been so complicated. Not all those who had lost their land could claim to have lost it in the King's service, and it was by no means clear that all who had been loyal could be reinstated in their own property. Already Charles II had issued many letters to claimants who had been with him in exile, but it was obvious that a comprehensive land settlement was needed. The scheme was set out in a royal Declaration of 30 November 1660. A commission was appointed to deal with all claims, but it had no statutory power and achieved little. Reluctantly Charles had to submit the whole land question to a parliament now called in Dublin, and the settlement passed decisively out of his hands.

In the summer of 1662 the Irish parliament passed the Act of Settlement, which gave statutory force to the Declaration, and set up a Court of Claims to implement its provisions. By this Act all land confiscated since 23 October 1641 (the date of the outbreak of the Irish rebellion) was vested in the Crown as trustee for the various interests. The enormous and complex task of deciding thousands of claims, from the 'innocents', who were given top priority, to the various degrees of soldiers – ''49 men', 'ensign men', 'letterees' (who had the King's letter) and 'nominees' – totally overwhelmed the court. When it ended its hearings in August 1663, some 800 cases had been heard and 700 decrees of innocency had been issued, but this represented only a fraction of the cases outstanding.

Meanwhile the Cromwellian proprietors were becoming very alarmed. Many decrees of innocency were being granted on false evidence, and they feared that if this continued, the whole Protestant plantation would go. The Duke of Ormond, who was now Lord Lieutenant for the second time, summed up the impossible situation. 'There must be new discoveries made of a new Ireland, for the old will not serve to satisfy these engagements.'[11] He himself favoured a policy of compromise, and indeed it soon became clear to everyone involved that compromise was inevitable.

It was eventually embodied in the Act of Explanation in 1665. By that Act all decrees of innocency so far issued were confirmed, but no more were to be granted. Instead certain persons named in the Act were to be given full or partial restoration of their estates. To provide the land needed for this the Cromwellian Adventurers and Soldiers were to give up one-third of what they had received by the Act of Settlement. This was a tremendous blow to the Protestant interest, and the Bill was passed in the teeth of bitter opposition in the Irish House of Commons. Even after the Act of Explanation there was not enough land for those named in it.

Such was the Restoration land settlement, later to be described as 'a tragedy in three Acts'. It was an exercise in expediency, not justice, but what else could have been done, given that the King had been restored to his throne by the Cromwellians? The settlement is one of the unlighted areas of Ireland's history. Since its essence is legalistic, and the details rebarbative, it tends to occupy little space in elementary textbooks. It was to cause much trouble in future, providing the dynamic for the war in the next reign, and making its presence felt subterraneously throughout the nineteenth century and beyond. The fact that Charles II was restored to the thrones of Britain and Ireland (they were separate) largely by the actions of Cromwellian planters, and that therefore the Cromwellian confiscations were not substantially reversed, was a factor of the utmost importance in the shaping of subsequent Irish history.

Buried Treasure

O ne day in 1655 Samuel O'Neale began to set down a careful and detailed description of the townland of Kells in County Meath.

> Here is also a large church, but ruinous; one end is covered, wherein the horse quarter that are in garrison there. The said church hath also a fair square steeple which stands about 2 perch from it. About 20 perches from the said church on the north-west side thereof stands a little house about 30 foot high, 25 foot long and 18 foot broad, built of great stone without any timber about it. It had therefore no light, only a little hole at the top looking in to the east. The house, they say, was the cell of Columbkill, one of the chief patrons of Ireland. From this house to the church is a passage, so that from the cell to the church, to his devotion and back again, was all his recreation. The inhabitants of this town have for many hundred years past had the keeping of a large parchment manuscript in Irish, written as they say by Columbkill's own hand, but of such a character that none of this age can read it.

To this description O'Neale added an aside. 'The said writing was about a year and a half ago sent to the late commissioners of the Commonwealth by the governor of Kells.'[12]

The information was collected for the rather misleadingly named 'Down Survey' prepared for the Commonwealth government by the statistician Sir William Petty, its name apparently deriving merely from the fact that it was 'set down'. Its purpose was to facilitate the re-apportioning of estates to Cromwellian settlers, and it is of great useful-ness to historians because of its topographical detail. The Protestant church of St Columba has replaced the ruins where the Cromwellian cavalry were quartered in 1655, but the ancient burying ground still has its round tower and Celtic crosses, and visitors come to see the small 'House of Colmcille'. The parchment which the Cromwellian officer re-moved and sent to the commissioners in Dublin was not in Irish but in Latin (which O'Neale admitted he could not read), and it was not in Colmcille's hand. Today it is called the Book of Kells, a national icon and one of Europe's greatest artistic treasures. Reverently preserved in the library of Trinity College, it is studied by scholars from all over the world, and is cautiously on display to the wondering gaze of visitors, the pages being regularly turned.

It seems clear that the magnificently illustrated copy of the four Gospels was brought to Kells to protect it from marauding Norsemen, but scholars do not really know exactly when it was made, or where, at Iona, or in Ireland or somewhere else. It lay for a very long time on the altar of the church at Kells, before being sent to Cromwell's commissioners, which might reasonably have been expected to have been the end of its history. Were these not the men who tore down religious statues and smashed the stained-glass windows of the churches in their own land? Yet the manuscript survived.

What happened to it after 1653 is obscure. For a long time it was believed that it had somehow been acquired by Archbishop Ussher, with whose library it was eventually catalogued in Trinity. He was certainly well aware of its existence in 1621 when he was just about to become Bishop of Meath, for he wrote this graffitto in his own hand on Folio 334v of the manuscript: 'August 24, 1621. I reckoned the leaves of this book and found them to number 344.'[13] Ussher went to England for a short visit in 1640, but the sudden outbreak of the Irish rebellion, closely followed by the war between Charles I and parliament, prevented his return to Ireland, and he remained in England until his death in 1656. He managed to rescue his library, which he had shipped from Drogheda, and subsequently bequeathed to Trinity College. Scholars have convincingly shown that the Book of Kells was not part of it, and indeed Ussher himself explicitly states in 1639 that the men of Meath still held the book in veneration in Kells. From internal evidence in O'Neale's account it is clear that the transfer to the commissioners took place in 1653. Ussher's library arrived at Trinity in 1661, after the Restoration. Whether the Book of Kells was then part of it or not, it came to the university through the efforts of Cromwell's son Henry, who was chosen Chancellor of the university in 1653, and became Lord Deputy of Ireland in 1657. He was a generous benefactor to Trinity, and it was he who secured Ussher's bequest. It seems more than likely (though it cannot be proved absolutely) that he oversaw the transfer of the Book of Kells to the library of Trinity in 1653.[14] The name of Oliver Cromwell is execrated in Ireland, to such an extent that a proper historical evaluation of the period is hardly possible, yet in all probability his son, by the authority of the Commonwealth, saved for posterity one of Ireland's greatest treasures.

There was an earlier, and more comprehensive, survey, undertaken 'for the better discovery of the interests of the Commonwealth into lands held by English and Protestants'. The Civil Survey was, as J.G. Simms wrote, 'the essential preliminary to the Cromwellian confiscation, and like the Domesday Book was a stocktaking made by the conquerors with the help of the conquered'.[15] Considered as a document, it was less fortunate than the Book of Kells. Since it no longer exists, historians are forced to rely on copies of copies of part of it. It is like looking at the image of something in a mirror with the aid of an even smaller mirror. The original Civil Survey for twenty-seven counties of Ireland disappeared in the fire which burned down the Surveyor-General's office in 1711. For the next hundred years it was believed that no fragment of the Civil Survey had survived.

Then, in 1817, the Irish Record Commissioners discovered, in Lord Headfort's library at Kells, a set of Civil Survey barony record books covering the greater part of ten counties. Lord Headfort's ancestor Thomas Taylor had three copies made for his own use when he was a sub-commissioner in the Restoration Court of Claims in 1666. The Headfort books were bought in 1837 by the Commissioners of Woods and Forests and subsequently kept in the Quit Rent office in Dublin.

From there they were transferred to the Public Record Office of Ireland, on condition that copies should be made for the Quit Rent. The transfer was made in 1910. In the days before photocopiers and computers the making of those copies was a slow and laborious business, but, as it turned out, these precautions were well worth while. The Headfort books, along with most of the medieval records of Ireland, were destroyed in 1922 when the Four Courts in Dublin were blown up by the IRA. There could be no greater irony: the Book of Kells saved by a son of Cromwell, and Ireland's medieval heritage wiped out by patriots. This is truly Carlyle's Letter of Instructions, which comes down to us 'blotted out, torn, lost, and but a shred of it in existence'.

A Tragedy in Three Acts

Catholic hopes of a more tolerant religious policy after the Restoration were soon dashed. An attempt was now made by some of the Old English to win the government's confidence by collecting signatures for a

statement of loyalty to the Crown, a legal formulary of Irish Remonstrance, which would, it was hoped, allay the old Protestant fears of
Catholic disloyalty.[16] Many prominent laymen, and some of the clergy,
signed the Remonstrance, but it ignited controversy among Catholics. In
the end most of the clergy rejected it, and its fate was sealed by the
opposition of the Vatican.

Ormond was removed from office in 1669, at the time of the Earl of
Clarendon's fall from the King's favour in England, to make way, it was
suspected, for a new royal policy. Charles now surrounded himself with
the new ministers of the so-called Cabal – Clifford, Arlington, Bucking-
ham, Ashley and Lauderdale. One result was a perceptible change in
attitude towards Catholics in Ireland. The Vatican made new ecclesiastical
appointments, taking note of the King's wishes. Peter Talbot, a member of
one of the illustrious Old English families, became Archbishop of Dublin.
His soldier brother Richard was in the forefront of the campaign to win
back the royalists' lands. Another man of Old English stock, Oliver
Plunkett, became Archbishop of Armagh, not a popular choice as it
happened, since he had made an enemy of the Franciscans and alienated
some of his own clergy.

By 1677 Ormond was back in favour, enjoying the unique distinction of
becoming Lord Lieutenant for the third time. His immediate predecessor,
Sir Arthur Capel, Earl of Essex, an ex-Cromwellian, had proved a steady
and sensible governor. Much of his vice-royalty had been taken up with
countering the financial and political intrigues of corrupt courtiers. He
also had to deal with the special problem of the Presbyterians of Antrim
and Down, who had close links with their brethren in south-west Scotland. When Lauderdale began the persecution of the Covenanters in
Scotland, and they rose in rebellion, the government kept an anxious
watch on the Ulster Presbyterians, and a frigate was sent to patrol the
North Channel, rather like the frigate which patrolled these waters in the
1970s to prevent guns being run in to the Protestant paramilitaries.[17]
While one or two Covenanters briefly sought refuge in the Antrim up-
lands (the famous 'Prophet' Peden hid on a farm near Glenwherry), the
Dissenters in general made no move to assist the Scottish insurgents in
more active ways.

On the whole the early Restoration years were a period of increasing
stability and prosperity, though the tensions created by the land question
always lay just under the surface. Disaster fell suddenly on the Catholic

Church in 1678, when the 'revelations' of Titus Oates, a perverted and mendacious scoundrel, were used by Ashley (now elevated as Earl of Shaftesbury) and the Whig party to bring pressure on the King and his brother, James, the Duke of York, who had converted to Catholicism. It was alleged that a whole series of plots to assassinate Charles and put James on the throne had come to light. A wave of anti-Catholic hysteria swept over England. James was forced into temporary exile, and Charles, terrified at the prospect of 'going on his travels again', submitted to the most extreme demands of parliament, where the Whigs were in full cry.

Ireland was inevitably involved in any 'popish' scare. Peter Talbot, accused of a plot to assassinate Ormond, was arrested and imprisoned in Dublin Castle, where he died. Ormond, who did not believe in any of the plots, tried to hold firm in the storm, to Shaftesbury's exasperation. The most notable Irish victim of the 'Popish Plot' was Archbishop Oliver Plunkett, and even the authority of the Lord Lieutenant could not protect him. Plunkett was accused, on absurdly fabricated evidence, of plotting a landing of the French in Carlingford Lough. To save him Ormond allowed the trial to be held at Dundalk, but orders came that he was to be sent to London to stand trial there. At the second attempt he was found guilty of treason and executed. The Church beatified, and more recently canonised, the innocent archbishop, but long before that he had taken his place in the pantheon of Irish martyrs.

With his execution the Popish Plot reached its climax, and the storm blew itself out. For the rest of his reign Charles was able to be his own master. Ormond's prestige grew steadily, and in 1680 it was at its height. Two years later the King received him in London with every mark of favour and advanced him to a dukedom in the English peerage. Then, following his return to Dublin, he suddenly received a letter from Charles telling him that he was to be replaced. Puzzled and put out of countenance, Ormond obeyed, as always, without murmur, but the public, and particularly the Protestant public, interpreted his dismissal as a sign that a new Catholic policy had been adopted, one dictated by the King's brother, James.

Charles II died on 6 February 1685, apologising politely for the unconscionable time he was taking over it. He had allowed Ormond to stay in office until the spring, but within days of his accession James ordered him to hand over the government of Ireland to Lords Justices, specially appointed deputies. The move further alarmed Protestants and elated

Catholics, especially when it was learned that Richard Talbot had been given command of Ormond's regiment of horse. This was followed by the rapid appointment of Catholic officers throughout the Irish army, an indication of the use which James might ultimately make of it. Now it was the turn of English Protestants to become alarmed.

The fatal destiny of the House of Stuart was nearing its fulfilment. Every step which James II now took prepared the way for his overthrow, but for the present purposes we need only consider the implications for Ireland. James had appointed Henry Hyde, now second Earl of Clarendon, as Lord Lieutenant. It was a calming move; his sister Anne had been James's first wife, and the Hydes were staunchly Church of England. In fact, however, the government of Ireland was sliding into the hands of Talbot, and in 1687 he succeeded Clarendon at the head of the administration. 'Fighting Dick Talbot' was a brave but impulsive man, and he made no secret of his chief political aim. ('By God, my lord,' he told Clarendon, 'these Acts of Settlement and this new interest are damned things.'[18]) Ennobled as Earl of Tyrconnell, and already in command of the army, he set about regaining the Catholic lands and restoring the primacy of his Church. But these aims were not quite the same as those of his sovereign.

This was to be amply demonstrated after William of Orange landed at Torbay in November 1688 and James fled his British throne. Ireland was held secure for James by Tyrconnell. It was in constitutional law a separate kingdom, so that, even after his formal deposition in Britain, James was able to rule there, call parliament, raise taxes and organise armed forces to win back the throne he had lost. And it was this which obliged William, with some reluctance, to lead an army into Ireland to defeat him. For William it became a minor theatre of his European war against Louis XIV. That conflict might seem at first sight to be a very unequal contest, but William III had powerful allies, and one of them was, rather surprisingly, the papacy, which was then at odds with the French King.

Even before James arrived in Ireland, Tyrconnell had taken the first steps to try to make the north secure, but the result was to frighten the Protestants, who were wrestling with the dilemma of allegiance. After a confused skirmish known as 'the break of Dromore' there was panic in Belfast, where a 'lamentable cry' went up that the Irish were coming, 'sparing neither age nor sex, putting all to the sword without mercy'.[19] Hundreds fled to Scotland, and at Stranraer the town was so crowded that the women and children had to shelter under upturned boats on the shore. In the north and west Protestants flocked to the walls of Londonderry, and slowly their mood turned to resistance. Shortly after his arrival in March 1689, James advanced to Derry and laid siege to it. The governor, Robert Lundy, and the mayor were disposed to surrender on terms, as the walls were in bad repair, but the townspeople thought otherwise and the town gates were shut in the face of the Earl of Antrim's troops by thirteen apprentices. James had not sufficient men and artillery to storm the town, and determined to starve it into submission, thus beginning the famous fifteen-week siege. It was eventually relieved in July, when an English ship, the *Mountjoy*, broke the boom across the River Foyle.

James would have liked to keep the loyalty of his Protestant subjects if he could, but they were further alienated by the legislation enacted by the parliament which he summoned in Dublin in May. Predominantly Catholic, it was dominated by the Old English, who wanted only the restoration of their estates and the establishment of the Catholic faith. But James was above all, an English king, and he blocked the repeal of Poynings' Law, which would have given the Irish parliament its independence. Nor was he happy with the Act of Attainder, which indicted virtually every Protestant landowner of the New English interest.

William had sent Marshal Schomberg, a veteran of the Thirty Years War, to Ireland with an army after the relief of Derry, but he was slow to engage James's forces, and retired into quarters at Lisburn for the winter, his troops having been much depleted by sickness. He began his advance southward in the summer of 1690, now joined by King William, who had landed at Carrickfergus in June. James had decided to defend the line of the River Boyne, and there the two armies met on 1 July, a hot sunny morning. The action began at 10 a.m. when the first of William's élite Dutch Blue Guards waded across the river in a bold frontal attack. Behind them came a motley but well-disciplined army of Dutch, Danes, English, Brandenburgers, Huguenots and Ulster Protestants – not quite the Orange host that lives on in Protestant imagination – and during the afternoon they routed the smaller army of Jacobites and French. Tyrconnell and the Jacobite cavalry charged again and again to slow the Williamite advance and cover the retreat to Dublin of a king they despised. A few days later James recognised the decisive nature of his defeat and left Ireland for exile in France.

The Battle of the Boyne has been described as 'the decisive battle of modern Ireland',[20] and its significance can be seen on three levels. It was firstly an important engagement in the European war, to be set against the French naval victory at Beachy Head. Secondly, it was decisive in Ireland. By it James lost all of Ireland east of the Shannon. Louis XIV initially withdrew his troops and recalled their commander, the Count of Lauzun, but then changed his mind, sending enough help to keep the Irish war going as a useful diversion. His general, St Ruth, was killed at the critical moment in the Battle of Aughrim in July 1691, a costlier battle in terms of loss of life than the Boyne. If Aughrim occupies a less conspicuous place in popular memory, this points us to the third significance of the Boyne. It marked the end of the long tug of war that had gone on for most of the century between Catholic and Protestant for the possession of the land.

Demoralised by St Ruth's death, the Jacobite forces streamed away from Aughrim towards Limerick, where the brave and chivalrous Irish commander Patrick Sarsfield prepared for a long and determined siege in hope of the arrival of French reinforcements. But William was anxious to end the costly Irish campaign as soon as possible; Sarsfield seized the opportunity, and surrendered Limerick on terms very favourable to the Jacobites. The Treaty of Limerick, signed on 3 October 1691, really consisted of two separate treaties. By the military articles, transport was provided for all combatants who wished to go to France, and as a result 5,000 soldiers left Limerick in the French relief fleet that had just arrived, and a further 6,000 were taken in transports provided by the English government. Most of these men (and their descendants) served in the armies of France and other Catholic countries in Europe. They were the 'Wild Geese' of romantic legend, who carried with them the wrongs and sorrows of Ireland, and created a noble military record. Their valour, however, was most manifest in the ranks of England's enemies, and frequently they found themselves fighting against their own countrymen.

If the military articles were carried out to the letter, the civil articles were to be the fount of new accusations of bad faith. No religious zealot, William had readily agreed to the provision that Catholics should 'enjoy such privileges in the exercise of their religion as are consistent with the laws of Ireland or as they did enjoy in the reign of King Charles II'.[21] Security and protection were assured for all inhabitants of Limerick and other towns or areas under Jacobite control, and Jacobite landowners were secured in possession of their property. The problem was that the treaty had to be ratified by the Irish parliament, and it did not do so until 1697, by which time the new Protestant interest was well established and confident in the political power it derived from the Williamite victories. The religious tolerance embodied in the civil articles was completely ignored, and instead the Irish parliament continued to pass a whole series of penal laws against the practice of the Catholic religion and the ownership of land by Catholics. Some of these were allowed to fall into disuse in the new century, but not those concerning land ownership or rights to representation, which were steadfastly maintained and became the bedrock of political power for the 'Protestant Ascendancy', though that term was not invented until the very end of the eighteenth century.[22]

Hibernia Curiosa

Large are the treasures of oblivion . . . much more is buried
in silence than is recorded and the largest volumes are but
epitomes of what hath been.

SIR THOMAS BROWNE[1]

Ascendancy

The history of Ireland in the eighteenth century exhibits a curious imbalance. For three quarters of the century hardly anything seems to happen; then, after 1775, too much happens. It is as if the century had developed a list, and all its cargo of interesting events had slid into the last quarter. These events included, among others of lesser importance, the rise of the Volunteer movement, the achievement of legislative independence, the agitation for the reform of parliament, the failure of the Commercial Propositions, the Regency crisis, the founding of the Society of United Irishmen, the 1798 Rebellion and the Act of Union. Some have attributed this apparent inequality to Lecky's great *History*, which devoted only one of its five volumes to the period before 1760, but it was recognised long before he began his research.

We have already quoted Caesar Litton Falkiner's observation that in the eighteenth century 'the pauses are still longer, and the silence yet deeper'. He goes on to say:

> Between the events that immediately followed the Battle of the Boyne and those that closely preceded the creation of an independent legislature there intervened a space of something like ninety years. Yet, save for the brief squall that raged over Wood's halfpence, there was, throughout that lengthened period, no popular movement serious enough to threaten the repose of English ministers, much less to engross the attention of the general public of the three kingdoms. To the first sovereigns of the House of Brunswick, Ireland gave little concern through the greater part of their reigns.[2]

Nonetheless Ireland had a history between 1700 and 1775, even if it was not a history of political agitation. The days were no shorter, or less packed with incident, for the people who lived then; one is reminded again of Falkiner's words: 'it is in the examination of hidden history that the true origin of familiar events is most often revealed'.

Earnest researchers looking for evidence of radicalism in the earlier part of the century were surprised to discover not only that it existed, but that this fact was well known in the nineteenth century – historians, it seems, do not merely discover new things about the past, but forget what they already knew. Radicalism, republicanism, godlessness, rising crime and the irresponsibility of the media – all these appear in the public debate of the time. People believed that the country was going to the dogs, a sentiment vividly expressed in the engravings of Hogarth. In 1738, during a heated discussion in the House of Commons, one MP declared: 'The people of Great Britain are governed by a power that was never heard of as a supreme authority in any age or country before . . . the government of the Press.' He might have been speaking in 2001.

There were other factors at work in Ireland. The Williamite wars had secured a monopoly of power for the Protestant landowning classes; an overwhelming majority of the members of parliament were descendants of the Cromwellian Adventurers and Soldiers. In the eighteenth century Protestant meant 'Protestant by law established', a term restricted to members of the Church of Ireland – there were, of course, by now other kinds of Protestants: Quakers, Huguenots, Palatines, but above all Presbyterians, densely settled in the north-east of the island. Parliament kept a wary eye on all these groups, and especially the last, but its chief objective in the years after 1700 was to buttress its monopoly of political power by passing a comprehensive series of penal laws against Catholics. The most important of the penal laws concerned real estate, and their purpose was to prevent any increase in the area of land in Catholic ownership. No Catholic could bequeath his land by will; it had to be divided equally among his sons, and if the eldest son conformed, he inherited the estate. Rigorously enforced, the laws concerning property completed the destruction of the Catholic landed classes.

The penal laws affecting religious worship were less strenuously applied, though it is this aspect of the legislation which has given rise to the Catholic legend of a century of religious persecution, the clergy hunted down and the Mass being celebrated secretly in wild and desolate places. In fact restrictions on actual worship soon fell into disuse. 'By 1720 the worst of the penal laws were over.'[3] There was a gap between the letter of the law and its execution, and there was even collusion with friendly Protestant landlords to preserve inheritances. Two points are worth bearing in mind when considering this very emotive subject. First, it was an era when there were penal laws in all Christian countries, including England, though they were usually directed against minorities. The separation of Church and State would not begin until the century which followed. The second point is that society was still rigidly hierarchical. The penal laws, or any other action of the Irish parliament, had little relevance in the lives of ordinary working people, unless they directly inhibited their practice of the Roman Catholic faith, and the population left it to the priest and the landlord to sort things out with such higher authorities as might for the time being govern Ireland. For the landlords, and the rising mercantile class, it was a different matter. The Catholic aristocracy and gentry had much more in common with their Protestant counterparts than they had with their tenants, and felt keenly their exclusion from influence. The same was true, in a different way, of the Catholic middle class in the towns, and they would soon become an important factor in Irish politics.

The paradox was that, once it had established itself as an unassailable ruling élite, the Protestant Ascendancy took up the cause of Irish grievance against the insensitivities of English rule. The first grievance presented itself early in the century when a dispute in the courts over an estate raised the question of whether the Irish House of Lords or the English House of Lords exercised the supreme appellate jurisdiction. The Irish House reversed an appeal to the English House. The brusque response of the English government was to pass the Declaratory Act of 1720, which stated, in two sentences, first that the Kingdom of Ireland was 'subordinate unto and dependent upon the imperial Crown of Great Britain', and second, that the British House of Lords was the supreme court of appeal for Ireland.[4] The regnal title of the Act ('the Sixth of George I') became a rallying cry of the party in the Irish parliament who came to call themselves the 'Patriots'.

A few years later, when William Wood, a Wolverhampton ironmaster, was granted a patent to coin halfpence for Ireland, at colossal profit to himself, Jonathan Swift, the Dean of St Patrick's Cathedral in Dublin, published anonymously *The Drapier's Letters*, a sustained philippic against the government's misrule. In the third letter he asked why he should be a free man in England and become a slave when he crossed the Irish Sea. The fourth letter was addressed to 'the whole people of Ireland'.[5] Everyone in Dublin, including the Lord Lieutenant, knew the identity of the author, but he was never prosecuted. Even the children in the street had learned by rote from the Book of Samuel:

> And the people said unto Saul, Shall Jonathan die, who hath wrought this great salvation in Israel? God forbid: as the Lord liveth, there shall not one

hair of his head fall to the ground, for he hath wrought with God this day. So the people rescued Jonathan, that he died not.[6]

Thus did Swift earn the title he least coveted, that of 'the Hibernian patriot'.

By the mid-century those who called themselves the 'Patriot party' in the Irish House of Commons were the champions of Ireland's rights, and began a process which led ultimately to the recovery of legislative independence in 1782. It was achieved by forcing Britain's hand during the crisis of the revolt of the American colonies. The war had denuded Ireland of troops, and a citizen army of Volunteers was raised to guard the country against invasion and internal unrest. The government agreed to it with reluctance, and this wariness proved to be well founded. Officered largely by the Patriot landlords, it very rapidly became politicised, providing in the end a more representative alternative to parliament itself. Though the movement was in the main Protestant Episcopalian, the Presbyterians of Ulster flocked eagerly to the Volunteer banners and became the backbone of the northern regiments. They deeply resented their exclusion from political influence, and were no friends to the Church of Ireland, obliged as they were by law to pay tithes to that Church, and suffering irritations such as not having marriages performed by their ministers legally recognised. They sympathised with the Americans, but also with the Irish Catholics, whose situation they saw as similar to their own, if undoubtedly worse. The politics of the Catholic and Presbyterian mercantile classes began for the first time to converge, and from the activities of the more extreme and radical elements of both, the Society of United Irishmen was born in 1791. Yet neither side in this alliance fully admitted how different were the sources of their political activism, or how far apart were their essential aims. As in Northern Ireland today, there was much confusion between ends and means.

The Year of the Slaughter

Whole parishes in some places . . . almost desolate; the dead have been eaten in the fields by dogs for want of people to bury them. Whole thousands in a barony have perished, some of hunger and others of disorders occasioned by unnatural, unwholesome, and putrid diet.[7]

Want and misery in every face; the rich unable, almost, as they were willing, to relieve the poor; the roads spread with dead and dying bodies; mankind the colour of the docks and nettles which they fed on; two or three, sometimes more, in a car going to the grave for want of bearers to carry them, and many buried only in the fields and ditches where they perished.[8]

Multitudes have perished and are daily perishing ... some of fevers, some of fluxes, and some through downright cruel want, and the utmost agonies of despair. I have seen the labourer endeavouring to work at his spade, but fainting from want of food and forced to quit it. I have seen the aged father eating grass like a beast ... the helpless orphan exposed on a dunghill and none to take him in for fear of infection ... the hungry infant sucking at the breast of the already expired parent.[9]

Few readers will doubt that they can identify the event which is here described – the Great Irish Famine of 1845. But they would be wrong. All of these accounts were written in the year 1741. The famine of 1741 was the worst in Irish history. It has been estimated that almost a third of the entire population perished, so that proportionately it was worse than the famine of 1845–7. Yet it is barely mentioned in history books, and has no place at all in popular imagination. How are we to explain this?

The eighteenth century was notorious for its bad winters, and a few were of the utmost severity, not only in the British Isles but throughout the whole of Europe. Climatologists sometimes talk about the Little Ice Age, lasting from the late Middle Ages to just into the nineteenth century, a period marked by high incidence of prolonged frosts in winter. The Thames froze solid so often that it became a tradition to hold festivals on the ice, called Frost Fairs. The worst of the eighteenth-century winters was that of 1739–40. In Ireland a wet summer in 1739, followed by a wet autumn, reduced the grain harvest. The turf did not dry. Two days after Christmas a hard frost set in which lasted for seven weeks. It destroyed the potato crop overnight, and since the Irish were even then dependent on the potato, widespread distress followed. The situation was made worse by the death of very large numbers of cattle, sheep and horses. When the frost lifted, the weather remained bitterly cold. The spring was six weeks late, and the summer very chill. To general dismay frosty weather returned in the autumn, and in mid-October snow was falling heavily in Belfast.

There was a steep rise in mortality during the frost of 1740, though accurate statistics were not kept at the time. Food prices soared, and a bad harvest was anticipated because so much of the seed had been eaten by the starving population. Food riots broke out in Dublin. Plans were drawn up to try to avert the impending famine: the sheriffs were ordered to make a return of all the grain stored, soup kitchens were set up in Dublin and the other main towns, and by May 1741 women and children were receiving 'excellent soup seasoned with spices and herbs and thickened with oatmeal' on at least three days a week.[10]

By then, however, epidemics of typhus and the bloody flux (dysentery) were sweeping Ireland, carried from place to place by hordes of starving cottiers. The dysentery had begun in a jail in Monaghan in February 1740 during the frost, and had spread rapidly, becoming general towards the end of the year. When the summer of 1741 proved unusually warm, infection flared up in a population now weakened by lack of food, and began to attack the well-nourished at higher levels of society, claiming the mayor of Limerick and the judge Baron Wainwright. By June 1741 Bishop George Berkeley of Cloyne was reporting that his own family had the flux, a direct consequence in all probability of their efforts to render aid to the poor and destitute.

At the very beginning of the frost Berkeley had foreseen the consequences. On the first Sunday when he came down to breakfast without a grain of powder in his wig (flour was the main constituent of wig powder), his friends cried out in consternation 'What ails your Lordship?' 'A great deal ails me,' replied the bishop, 'for our poor are all about to be starved. We shall have a famine. We shall have a very long frost; and I am sure it has already killed all the potatoes in this kingdom; therefore the poor must depend on flour; and so no powder will I, nor shall any member of my family wear until next harvest.' During the frost, and until the summer, Berkeley gave, either in gold or in bank note, every Monday morning, twenty pounds to distribute among the poor of Cloyne, 'besides what they received daily, hourly, out of his kitchen and housekeeper's room'.[11]

Berkeley was temperamentally unable to stand by and watch people die during the epidemic which followed the famine. In America he had learned about the medicinal properties of tar-water as an antiseptic, so he began to experiment with its use among the sick. The results were so encouraging that his enthusiasm ran away with him; he came in later years to consider it a panacea, and published a long series of treatises on it.

The forgotten famine of 1740–1 was the direct consequence of the climatic catastrophe which overwhelmed the whole of Europe, twenty-one months of freak weather from December 1739 until September 1741. It followed thirty years of benign winters, and only the oldest people had a memory of very bad conditions in the 1680s. To this day it is the longest spell of extreme cold in modern European history, and in Ireland it produced *bliadhain an áir*, 'the year of the slaughter'. Nonetheless, there were other famines during the century. In 1718 Bishop William Nicolson of Derry was struck by 'the dismal marks of hunger and want' in the faces of the people in his diocese. When one of his coach horses was accidentally killed near his house, his servants were surrounded by a crowd of cottagers who cut up the carcase with axes and choppers and carried away the meat. 'We seem to be brought to the brink of famine,' wrote the bishop. 'God defend us from the pestilence.'[12] In the summer of 1726 Archbishop Hugh Boulter of Armagh reported hundreds dying of hunger. Subsequent bad harvests in the next two years caused famine in the north, beginning the stream of emigration to America which would continue for two centuries. The horror of 1741 threatened to return in 1756–7 when, after a succession of bad harvests, there were severe food shortages and bread riots.

But the experience of famine was by no means new in the eighteenth century. The past is a deep well, and the deeper the historian goes, the more astonishing evidence of replication he finds. The frequent visitation of famine through the centuries is well documented, though in earlier times the failure of harvests is most often aggravated by rebellion and war. In 1652 a Cromwellian observer said that County Clare was the saddest place imaginable, 'where people die under every hedge'.[13] In 1628 the English Privy Council was concerned about the huge numbers of Irish leaving Ireland because of 'the great dearth of cattle, and want in that kingdome'.[14] From 1600–1, when the corn harvest failed disastrously all over Ireland, the hordes of Irish beggars appearing in England, Wales and Scotland had become a serious problem, emigration from the north being at its highest during the harvest failures of 1603–5 and 1628–31.

The worst scarcity had followed in the wake of Mountjoy's scorched earth policy during the Nine Years War against Hugh O'Neill, who later claimed that 60,000 people perished as a result of it. Edmund Spenser left posterity a dreadful description of a time after the Desmond Rebellion when 'multitudes lay dead in the ditches of towns and other waste places, with their mouths all coloured green, by eating nettles, docks, and all things they could rend above ground'.

> Out of every corner of the woods and glens they came creeping forth upon their hands, for their legs could not bear them; they looked like anatomies of death, they spake like ghosts crying out of their graves; they did eat of the dead carrions, happy they, if they could find them, yes, and one another soon after, insomuch as the very carcasses they spared not to scrape out of their graves; and if they found a plot of water-cresses or shamrocks, then they flocked as to a feast for a time, yet not able long to continue therewithal; that in short space there were none almost left, and a most populous and plentiful country suddenly made void of man or beast; yet sure in all that war, there perished not many by the sword, but all by the extremity of famine which they themselves had wrought.[15]

Why then, with all this background, is the last Irish famine the only one to be remembered? The failure of the potato crop in 1845 occurred when the full light of public concern was on Ireland and its problems, in an age of rapidly developing communications, when scores of newspapers disseminated the news to every part of the globe, an age when science had effectively lifted the threat of wholesale famine from every other country in western Europe and when there was an expanding United States able and eager to receive the Famine emigrants. By the 1840s, there was in place a whole grammar and vocabulary of Irish famine which was already centuries old.

Enlightenment

The editors of a recent book of essays on *Ireland and the French Enlightenment* feel constrained to say in their introduction that 'the title of this book may raise some eyebrows . . . the concept of the Irish

Enlightenment being somewhat novel'. The idea of Ireland being largely untouched by intellectual developments taking place in Europe, they point out, is 'fairly entrenched in Ireland's national mythology'.[16] There are thousands of books written about the Age of Enlightenment, and hardly any of them have the word 'Ireland' in their indexes. It is almost as if authors inhabiting so rarefied an intellectual atmosphere dread some kind of devaluation if they mention the homeland of Sloane, Berkeley, Toland, Swift and Hutcheson. Nor do the Irish take much interest in the Enlightenment; they prefer to remember the Age of the Protestant Ascendancy, the penal laws, and the 1798 Rebellion.

No Irish history book, for example, will tell you that Swift was a close personal friend of Voltaire. The two men met in London in the early summer of 1726 through Lord Bolingbroke, and in the following year they were both guests in the house of Lord Peterborough.[17] In December of that year Swift received a letter from Voltaire in English. It was accompanied by the two essays in the same language, which Voltaire had prepared in advance of his long narrative poem, *La Henriade*, devoted to the life of Henry IV of France, the great Huguenot leader who became Catholic following his accession to the throne.

> You will be surprised in receiving an english essay from a french traveller. Pray forgive an admirer of you who ows to yr writings the love he bears to yr language, which have betrayed him into the rash attempt of writing in english.
>
> You will see by the advt. that j have some designs upon you, and j must mention you for the honour of yr country, and for the improvement of mine. Do not forbid me to grace my relation with your name. Let me indulge the satisfaction of talking to you as posterity will do ...[18]

Voltaire's purpose was to enlist Swift's help in finding subscribers for the English edition of the *Henriade*, and Swift responded warmly, arranging for an edition to be brought out in Dublin, to which he contributed a brief anonymous introduction.

Young François Marie Arouet, of good family and educated by the Jesuits at Louis-le-Grand, had written satires on some powerful people at the French court and been sent twice to the Bastille, where he lived very comfortably, continuing his writing, and adopting the pen-name Voltaire, by which he would ever afterwards be known. On 4 May 1726 he was released on the condition that he went to England, and next day he was on the coach to Calais. He arrived at Dover on a day of hazy sunshine, and was enchanted by his first impressions of England, a land of intellectual freedom and pragmatic good sense. Lord Bolingbroke introduced him to the circle of the poet Alexander Pope, which is how he first met Swift. He learned the English language with remarkable speed, and soon he was writing in English about Shakespeare and Milton.

Swift became to all intents and purposes Voltaire's agent in Ireland, and the two met again several times in London, discovering a great affinity of outlook. Voltaire was deeply impressed by *Gulliver's Travels*, which appeared at this time, and its influence can be seen in Voltaire's later work. He organised its translation into French in 1727. He never ceased to marvel, too, that a work as satirical of the shortcomings of the Christian Churches as *A Tale of a Tub* could have been written by a dean of the Church of Ireland.

Meanwhile Swift managed to recruit many prestigious subscribers for the *Henriade*, including even the Lord Lieutenant, Lord Carteret, who was Swift's friend despite the embarrassment of knowing him to be the author of *The Drapier's Letters*. Carteret ordered an entire box. So good had the advance publicity been that the work was eagerly awaited in Ireland, and we even find someone like Mrs Delany writing to a friend: 'Mr Voltaire's *Henriade* is not yet come out, 'tis writ in French which for yr sake I am sorry for.'[19]

For the rest of his long life Voltaire enjoyed a certain following in Ireland, but it was almost exclusively a Protestant one. Remarkably, not a single Catholic in either England or Ireland became a subscriber for the *Henriade*, not even Pope. King George I, however, did subscribe, and gave the author a present of 2,000 crowns, setting an example for English high society.

In Ireland Voltaire's pleas for toleration and his outspoken hatred of religious persecution touched a special nerve. On the one hand there was alarm at his deism and scepticism, but this was balanced by his impassioned humanity, which was truly non-sectarian. By the 1750s Ireland was flooded by editions of his works, the interest enhanced by his increasing notoriety.[20] His departure from the court of Frederick the Great was reported in the *Belfast News Letter* as if it were a local event.[21] The Quakers of Lisburn, upset by his description of their sect in *Lettres sur les Anglais*, met to draw up a reply to him. When he went to Geneva, his quarrels with the city fathers and his comments on Calvin's moral legacy shocked Irish Protestants, but they were reconciled to him in the 1760s by his courageous support for the Huguenots over the Calas affair.[22]

Though he never came to Ireland, Voltaire had a considerable interest in Irish history, if one skewed by some familiar French prejudices and misconceptions. He had heard the story of the Battle of the Boyne from Lauzun's own lips, and as a result wrote a rather biased account of it. He wrote also about the defence of 'Londonderi' led by 'a Presbyterian priest called Valker'.[23] He was interested, too, in Thurot's invasion of 1760 and the seizure of Carrickfergus. Above all, he was fascinated by the Irish Rebellion of 1641, which he cites over and over again as a prime example of man's inhumanity to man in the interest of religion, comparing it with St Bartholomew's Day. He also extolled the campaign to end the penal laws in Ireland as a model for increasing toleration to Protestants in France.

The Aerial Crosbie

There are people who have the misfortune to be born in the wrong century, like Mr Puckle, who invented a machine-gun in 1722, and was assured by the military experts that it had no future in warfare. Or Sebastien Mercier, the eighteenth-century Frenchman who in his novel *The Year 2440* envisaged with uncanny precision the world we already live in. The novel begins with the author meeting an elderly Englishman who detests Paris because of its narrow unhealthy streets and dissolute people. He tries to defend the city against these criticisms, and then falls asleep, as people do in this kind of novel, for nearly seven centuries.

When he reawakens in 2440 he finds the city transformed, with broad clean thoroughfares busy with fast-moving mechanical traffic. Great open squares have been made for public celebrations, and there are monuments everywhere. Large modern hospitals have taken the place of the Hôtel Dieu, and the Bastille has long ago been demolished (remember this was written in 1770). Mercier foresees dirigible airships, and travel between the planets. The telegraph and the telephone have been invented: 'There is nothing to prevent people speaking from one town to another,' he says. The Parisians of 2440 know all about the principle of evolution; mankind is millions of years old. They know about germs and microbiology. There is greater simplicity in food and dress.

Mercier does not avoid the usual pitfalls of the utopian novelist. Society has been totally reformed on the lines advocated by Rousseau. Virtue dominates conversation and human relations. The plague of war has been banished from mankind, and there is even a kind of United Nations Organisation with the Pope as Secretary-General! All citizens enjoy equal rights, and the complex and incoherent laws of the eighteenth century have been simplified and codified (thus anticipating Napoleon). The people prosper and are contented, since there are no longer extremes of wealth and poverty.

In some ways Mercier's vision is that of the defunct Soviet Union. Children are taught in school to value the hammer above the diadem. Theatres have become instruments for disseminating moral truths. Authors and artists are subject to the State censors, and the State decides what is worth keeping in public libraries. All frivolous works are destroyed, and theological books are kept under glass. The State encourages men of letters, with the sole exception of historians, since history is merely a record of the crimes and follies of mankind. The arts are highly esteemed, but only for their social utility. Paintings are judged in public contests open to all citizens and to foreigners, but wealthy connoisseurs may no longer dictate to artists. Church ceremony is reduced to the singing of hymns and vague moral exhortations. The State propagates civic virtue, and dissidents are re-educated or, if they prove invincibly obstinate, banished.[24]

Mercier's book was banned in Spain and elsewhere, not surprisingly, for nothing is more subversive than the future. It threatens the only thing that we really possess, which is the present. In our heart of hearts we can but echo the words with which Sir Boyle Roche once convulsed the Irish House of Commons: 'Why should we do anything for posterity; what has posterity ever done for us?'[25]

As it happened, Mercier was an enthusiast for balloons, documenting some of the early trials in France and helping to publicise the balloon craze which swept Europe in the 1780s and even reached Ireland. On 29 May 1786 the Whig Lord Charlemont in Dublin was writing to Dr Alexander Haliday in Belfast. Charlemont was the chosen head of the

Volunteer movement, which had in a few years transformed Irish politics, and claimed to have won the independence of the Irish parliament in 1782. Haliday was his political ally, his eyes and ears among the radical Presbyterians of Belfast, but in this letter Charlemont turns briefly aside from politics.

> Here has been just now my friend the aerial Crosbie, who, having some idea of carrying his balloon to Belfast, in order that it may from thence carry him across the Channel, swears to me that he cannot think of going thither without having the honour and pleasure of being known to Dr Haliday.[26]

Crosbie had approached Charlemont, with the encouragement of the Professor of Astronomy in Trinity College, Dublin, to seek patronage for his aeronautical schemes which seemed to most people to be mad or suicidal. Charlemont's response was good-natured and politely sceptical, though he hoped that his friend, a respected figure in northern liberal circles, might galvanise the entrepreneurs of Belfast to invest in the future. At the very least the Volunteers might give Crosbie a rousing send-off.

Haliday's reply has a contemporary ring to it. While he would be happy to do anything in his power for a gentleman of Mr Crosbie's character, he confessed he could not relish his scheme, either on his own account or on that of his fellow-citizens.

> We are at this time labouring to effectuate sundry measures of great moment and expense – the establishment of our white linen market, and completing the buildings necessary for it; the founding of an academy for education; . . . the deepening and improving of our harbour; the supporting of our poor-house, a most excellent institution, in danger of failing for want of sufficient funds. Unassisted in public treasure, we have but ourselves to trust for all this.

Haliday's objections went deeper than the absence of government funding.

> It is high time to desist from these aerial excursions, which only serve to set people a-gazing when they should be looking attentively on things within, or contiguous to themselves. These are awful times.[27]

Nothing has changed. When a rocket blasts off on a seven-year journey to photograph Saturn, the event is pushed to the end of the television news, even if it is an incredible human achievement. These are always awful times.

To his friends Crosbie exhibited all the signs of insanity. While at Trinity he paid little attention to his designated studies, but converted his rooms into a workshop, where a team of mechanics worked ceaselessly on his inventions. Six foot three inches tall, with a round ruddy countenance, and immense good nature, he was the younger son of Sir Paul Crosbie, a country gentleman in County Carlow. 'He had a smattering of all the sciences,' one of his associates recorded, 'and there was scarcely an art or a trade of which he had not some practical knowledge.'[28] His bravery and physical strength were legendary, but he was as dogged as a mule. Once he set his mind on a course of action, nothing could change his resolution to carry it out.

Crosbie was an outstanding example of a man living in another century. He cared nothing at all about politics or contemporary affairs, or indeed anything which had not to do with balloons. His brother, Sir Edward Crosbie, was a strong liberal who spoke out against social injustice; in 1798 he was tried by court martial and executed for allowing the United Irishmen to assemble on his lawn.[29] But Richard Crosbie lived only for his dream of balloons.

His dream was partially achieved, and Belfast missed its opportunity. He made two successful flights from Dublin in 1785. The first, on 19 January, ended with his landing on the North Strand. The second took place on 19 July when, at the third attempt, he ascended from the Duke of Leinster's lawn, watched by an immense crowd in Merrion Square. The event was marred by a dreadful accident. The thick parapet wall fronting the street gave way, and several spectators were killed and injured as Crosbie sailed above their heads.

> The current of wind which carried him due east soon after seemed inclined to bear him north-east and pointed his voyage towards Whitehaven. When the balloon was seventeen minutes in view it immersed in a cloud, but in four minutes after, its appearance was again testified by the numerous plaudits of the multitude. It now continued in sight, by the aid of achromatic glasses, thirty-two minutes from its ascent, when it was entirely lost to view; some rockets were sent off, and the troops of the Volunteers who attended discharged their last volleys.[30]

At this point Crosbie beheld something which no one had ever seen before, his own country and England spread out beneath him, both visible in the same instant. The maps had not lied.

> After some time he discovered several vessels crowding after him. He slowed up by slackening the ropes to the balloon; the Dunleary barge came alongside, the sailors jumped into his car, and made it fast, 'on which the aeronaut came out with the same composure and fortitude of mind which marked the whole complexion of his adventure', even when a sailor, who had injudiciously held on to the main haulyard of the balloon was hoisted screaming over a hundred feet into the air. At ten o'clock that evening Crosbie came ashore at Dunleary, and breakfasted there next morning with the Lord Lieutenant, the Duke of Rutland, and his Duchess. On his return to Dublin, the crowds carried him shoulder high to Trinity College, then to the Castle and finally to his house in North Cumberland Street.[31]

Crosbie made other inventions ancillary to his main enthusiasm, a specially designed aeronaut's suit to keep out the cold at high altitudes, and aeronauts' rations of portions of chicken packed in ice. The same kind of ingenuity was at that time being displayed by Richard Lovell Edgeworth, the father of the novelist Maria Edgeworth. An amateur engineer, he was greatly impressed by the technological achievements of the French. Living for a while in Lyons, at a time when the confluence of the Rhône and the Saône was being re-sited and a huge dam being constructed across the Rhône, he pointed out certain errors committed in the work, and was invited to assist in it. Later on, his membership of the Société d'encouragement pour l'industrie nationale brought him the friendship of men of science such as Berthollet and the Montgolfier brothers.[32]

At home in Ireland Edgeworth produced a long line of ingenious inventions: a phaeton 'so furnished with springs that each wheel would rise over any obstacle in its way'; a large umbrella for covering haystacks; a wagon divided into two parts, each with four wheels, so that the road never sustained more than half the weight of the total load; a machine for cutting turnips; a machine to measure the strength exerted by horses when drawing wagons; and a 'perambulator' for measuring roads (an odometer). He devoted much of his time to designing a 'carriage which should carry a road for itself', and so invented the caterpillar track which made the modern tank possible. He failed, however, to overcome the problem of combining strength with lightness in his track.[33]

Without doubt his most remarkable achievement was to develop an efficient system of telegraphy. Starting rather dubiously as a method of letting a man in London receive the name of the winner at Newmarket in the shortest possible time, Edgeworth's idea of building a string of semaphore signalling stations soon suggested enormous potential. As usual the military were lukewarm in their reaction, but years later, after the outbreak of war with France, interest in it revived. On 24 August 1794, Edgeworth's son Lovell sent and received four messages across the thirteen miles of water dividing Scotland from Ireland. In 1796, with a United Irish insurrection looming, and fears of a French invasion, Edgeworth proposed a system of fourteen or fifteen signalling stations to convey intelligence between Cork and Dublin. The government toyed with the project, but ultimately rejected it. Early in the next century the threat of invasion was renewed, and this time the government approached Edgeworth and commissioned him to build a telegraph from Dublin to Galway, a distance of 125 miles. He devoted two years of labour to it, and when it was complete he showed the Lord Lieutenant that he could send a message from Dublin to Galway in eight minutes.[34] It was a remarkable achievement.

Liberty and the Hour

We were deceived not in liberty but in the hour. We believed we were in Rome, but we found ourselves in Paris.

PIERRE VERGNIAUD[1]

The First Republicans

In 1787 the Duke of Rutland, making his viceregal tour of Ireland, observed that 'the province of Ulster is filled with Dissenters, who are in general very factious – great levellers and republicans ... The dissenting ministers are for the most part very seditious, and have great sway over their flocks.'[2] This was an opinion shared by John Beresford in 1798: 'the Dissenters are another set of enemies to the British government. They are greatly under the influence of their clergy, and are taught from their cradles to be republicans, but their religion, which is as fierce as their politics, forbids them to unite with the Catholics.'[3]

Where does this republicanism come from? Some thirty years later we find William Hazlitt writing tongue-in-cheek that 'these same dissenting ministers throughout the country (I mean the descendants of the old Puritans) are to this hour a sort of Fifth-monarchy men, very turbulent fellows, in my opinion altogether incorrigible, and according to the suggestions of others, should be hanged out of the way without judge or jury for the safety of church and state'.[4]

Hazlitt knew whereof he spoke. His father, the Reverend William Hazlitt, was one of these Dissenting ministers ('the *ultima Thule* of the sanguine visionary temperament in politics'[5]), a pupil of Hutcheson at Glasgow, and the son of a County Antrim Presbyterian. He had been a Unitarian minister in County Cork, in East Anglia and in Boston, Massachusetts, before settling down as pastor of the Dissenting congregation at Wem in Shropshire.[6]

There are, buried in these quotations, words which provide valuable clues – 'levellers', 'republicans', 'Fifth-monarchy men'. They take us back to the English Civil War, to 1647 and those tremendous debates at Putney when the army of parliament drew up blueprints for universal manhood suffrage, equal electoral districts, biennial parliaments, the abolition of the monarchy and the House of Lords, freedom of conscience, the right of private soldiers to be consulted by their officers, equality before the law and the redistribution of property. It was, for a brief moment, a gap in the curtain, a time warp before the seventeenth century closed in again. Every man born in England, argued Colonel Thomas Rainsborough, 'the poorest he ... as the greatest he', ought to have a voice in choosing those who made the laws under which he was to live and die.[7] Levellers, agitators, new agents, Fifth-monarchy men – the army split into factions, and every voice was heard, from communist to religious fanatic. The terrible gulf between theory and practicality was plain for all to see, and Cromwell certainly saw it.

Nevertheless, on 19 May 1649 an Act of Parliament decreed that England should henceforth be governed 'as a Commonwealth, or a Free State, by the supreme authority of this nation'. For the next decade Ireland, too, would be governed as a republic. How strange that the birth of Irish republicanism should be attended by the unlikely figure of Oliver Cromwell.

This way of looking at the constitution did not disappear in 1660. It survived the Restoration and the Whig Revolution of 1688, and its adherents emerged in the eighteenth century as the 'real Whigs' or Commonwealthmen, not to be confused with the mainstream Whigs. Such essential republicanism was part of an international underground which was seen as a threat to established authority in many countries, a curious mixture of admiration for ancient Roman virtue and Calvin's Geneva, and formed in time an intellectual network whose influence could be perceived from the Back Bay in Boston to the Netherlands and the Protestant cantons of Switzerland. For various reasons it does not figure prominently in the history books; it was subversive in both political and religious terms, throwing up characters who could not resist controversy.

Technically the Presbyterians of the Civil War period had taken a very different political stance from the republicans. It was indeed the protest of the Presbytery of Belfast against the execution of King Charles I in 1649 which drew forth Milton's famous outburst: 'Belfast, a barbarous nook in Ireland', a place 'whose obscurity never before came to our hearing'.[8] But a less than deferential view of kings, and all unelected governments, unless they proceeded on acceptable moral principles, was the very definition of Presbyterianism. The relationship between the governors and the governed was always contractual.

There is a strong similarity between the rhetoric of the first United Irishmen and the teaching of the philosopher Francis Hutcheson, who was an Ulsterman, born at Carryduff, County Down, in 1694. In 1729 he was appointed Professor of Moral Philosophy in Glasgow University. The political content of Hutcheson's teaching was startlingly modern. He taught that slavery in any form was a totally unnatural state, and ought not to descend to another generation. He endorsed the right of resistance to private and public tyranny; servants might leave unjust masters; wives had rights against husbands, children against parents. The criterion of virtue in any delegation of power was the well-being of the whole people, and, of any failure to achieve this, the people must be the judge. Government must be so planned as to prevent mischief, even if it fell into bad hands. A popular elected assembly, and a senate with a limited term, would provide security against tyranny – essentially a republican form of government. He supported the idea of a ballot and frequent elections, and the simplification of the laws. Sixty years later most of these desiderata would appear in the columns of the United Irish newspaper, the *Northern Star*.

Hutcheson's influence has been remarkably wide. He was not in the front rank of original thinkers, but he had the gift of inspiring his pupils, like Adam Smith, for example, who transformed economic theory. Later his work had an extraordinary popularity in France, where it was taken up by Diderot and the Encyclopaedists. In the 1720s he had been the natural leader of a group of young Ulster Presbyterians drawn together by their experience as undergraduates at Glasgow, and his closest friend was the Reverend Thomas Drennan, the minister of Belfast First Presbyterian congregation, and the father of Dr William Drennan, who more than anyone can claim to be the United Irishmen's ideologue.

For William Drennan the legacy was personal, congregational, tribal and intellectual; and it is here, curiously enough, that the seed of the Society of United Irishmen was sown. All these elements were in his consciousness when, on 21 May 1791, he wrote to his brother-in-law, Sam McTier: 'I should much desire that a Society were instituted in this city, having much of the secrecy and somewhat of the ceremonial of Freemasonry.' It was to be 'A benevolent conspiracy – a plot for the people – no Whig party – no party title – the Brotherhood its name – the Rights of Men and the Greatest Happiness of the Greatest Number its end – its general end Real Independence to Ireland, and Republicanism its particular purpose – its business by every means to accomplish these ends as speedily as the prejudices and bigotry of the land we live in would permit.' And he adds that one of the means would be communication with leading men in France, in England and in America so as to cement the scattered and shifting sand of republicanism into a body, a 'stable unseen power'.[9]

There was also, of course, a tremendous external influence at work here.

Drennan was writing two years after the outbreak of the French Revolution, while it was still taking shape. The French Revolution was not like any other revolution which had occurred in the eighteenth century. The error of assuming that it was just another national uprising misled the rulers of Europe at the time, and misleads many people still, though when Chou En-Lai was asked what he thought the result of the French Revolution was, he replied that it was too early to say. The nearest event we can compare it with is the Reformation. Like the Reformation it was, to quote the French historian Albert Sorel, 'abstract in principle and cosmopolitan in action. It rose from universal ideas and so could appeal to all peoples. It brought together nations which had been divided, divided those which had been united.'[10] The cosmopolitan nature of the French Revolution's appeal should not be overlooked, or confused with what came later. 'Everyone desired absolutely to be one with mankind', wrote Goethe, and Robbie Burns sang that 'man to man the world o'er, shall brithers be for a' that'. When Wordsworth wrote in *The Prelude* 'I became a Patriot' he did not mean 'I became a Frenchman.'

Fifty years ago an American historian, R.R. Palmer, published a two-volume study called *The Age of Democratic Revolution*, in which he propounded the theory that everywhere in the Atlantic world during the last two decades of the eighteenth century the mercantile middle classes became sufficiently numerous and powerful to challenge the traditional landowning interests over political representation in government. The difficulty with general theories in history is that they tend to become beds of Procrustes; if an arm or a foot sticks out inconveniently, you simply lop it off to fit the scheme. But the idea of an Atlantic Revolution has much validity. Palmer studied political agitation in the countries concerned and found a pattern. The 1780s were a period of challenge (the subject of his first volume), and the 1790s, after a spell of *reculer pour mieux sauter*, saw the actual insurrections (the subject of his second volume). Ireland fits into this pattern very neatly, and reflects the downward social shift which Palmer found elsewhere.

Looked at in this light, the French Revolution appears merely as the *decumanus fluctus*, an extra large wave on the incoming tide of democracy. But in time the tide turns, and, as it recedes, some ancient and ugly reefs begin to reappear. They have never gone away. The French Revolution degenerated into bloodshed and tyranny, and began to use the international appeal of its ideas simply as an instrument of French foreign policy and espionage, exactly as the Soviet Union was to do in the twentieth century.

There is a fairly general perception that the United Irish movement, like the French Revolution itself, owed much to the rationalism of the eighteenth century, that its leaders were typical men of the Enlightenment. Wolfe Tone is often so described. It might be, however, that they were more typical of the cultural reaction to it, what we have come to think of in literature, art and music as the Romantic movement. Wolfe Tone, Lord Edward Fitzgerald, Archibald Hamilton Rowan, and James Napper Tandy are Byronic figures, seen against a stormy sky or on the field of battle, Dantons who will either save their country or go gloriously to the guillotine. And among the most seductive potions in the Romantic alchemy was nationalism, the antithesis of the cosmopolitan ideal.

Drennan, being Presbyterian, had less flair for attitudes, and personally no desire to be a martyr, but he was brimful of the Romantic ideals. His poetry is cluttered with the props of Romanticism – moonlight, ruins, Ancient Druids. With Drennan you can actually see the moment when nationalism becomes dominant. In the first of the *Letters of Orellana* to his fellow-countrymen, he is really addressing himself:

> Your boyhood and your youth were led astray by false associations, and blinded by the refined delusion of history; you claimed relationship with the Saxon *Alfred*, with *Hampden*; Sidney, who shook the gallows with his undaunted tread, was, *to be sure*, one of your great progenitors! 'Tis all a fairy tale of infancy. You are all *native Irish*, under the controul of an *English pale*.[11]

These words were written in 1784, five years before the storming of the Bastille, so neither his republicanism nor his nationalism derives initially from the French Revolution. He had thrown himself heart and soul into the movement for the reform of the Irish parliament, associated with the Volunteers. The Volunteers of Belfast and the north-east, largely Presbyterian, had been at the cutting edge of that campaign, and had shared in the heady victory of winning independence for the Irish parliament. But by 1784 the reform movement was beginning to falter, leaving unresolved the issues of representation and the restoration of political rights to Catholics. Drennan was in despair, but the outbreak of the French Revolution had an electrifying effect, and the Volunteers were revived as a national guard on the French model.

Drennan's idea for a secret society was put into operation by a dozen of the most radical of the Belfast Volunteers in October 1791. They were all Presbyterian, and two were sons of the manse. Drennan drew up their Test, a very Presbyterian instrument, and it was only then that they invited Wolfe Tone to come to Belfast and help frame their resolutions. However, it was Tone who suggested changing the name from 'the Irish Brotherhood' to 'the United Irishmen'. A second society was formed in Dublin, on a much wider religious base, but, contrary to popular belief, the association did not rapidly extend over Ireland. Apart from the societies in Belfast and Dublin, and one or two in Antrim and Down, few can be traced. We are talking, of course, of the constitutional phase of the movement. After war was declared against France in 1793, the United Irishmen became by definition potential traitors, and the whole movement went underground, its members subject to prosecution for sedition. From 1795 it was, in fact, succeeded by a widespread popular radical association. The 'New System', as it was called, was organised on military lines, with provincial, county and baronial committees and ultimately a national executive. Each United Irish regiment had a 'colonel', and the commanding officer in each county was an 'adjutant-general'. This clandestine army had its political wing in the United Irish clubs, but its purpose was to prepare for insurrection, coinciding, it was hoped, with an invasion by the French.

Drennan, after being tried for seditious libel in 1794 and acquitted, had nothing more to do with the movement. Tone was threatened with prosecution for treason in 1795, after injudicious contacts with a French spy, but was allowed to go to America, from where he made his way back to France, and worked tirelessly to persuade the successive Republican governments to sanction an invasion. The outbreak of the Rebellion in Ireland in May 1798 took him by surprise, and particularly in one aspect.

> In all this business I do not hear one syllable about the north, which astonishes me more than I can express. Are they afraid? Have they changed their opinions? What can be the cause of their passive submission at this moment, so little suited to their former zeal and energy?[12]

In truth great changes had occurred in Presbyterian radicalism since 1791, which are not sufficiently allowed for in the popular view of 1798, to such an extent that Bishop Thomas Percy of Dromore could reassure his wife on the eve of the Rebellion that 'a wonderful change has taken place among republicans in the north, especially in and near Belfast', and his vicar-general went so far as to predict that the northern Dissenter would now be 'quietly a spectator of that destructive flame which he himself originally kindled up'.[13] Though some of the middle-class leaders, like Samuel Neilson and Robert Simms, remained in the movement, many others slid away, and some of the Belfast businessmen defected when they found which side their bread was buttered on. Their enthusiasm for the French Revolution waned as the shadow of the guillotine loomed over it. It cooled altogether when the French overthrew the Dutch constitution, invaded the Protestant cantons of Switzerland, and finally threatened war against the infant United States.

Moreover, contrary to the generally held belief, sectarian animosity did not die away in the decade of the United Irishmen – that was merely the ideal which they expressed. In reality it flared up again with renewed intensity. One might say that in 1795 the eighteenth century ended, and the seventeenth century began all over again. In that year the long-smothered war in County Armagh between the Protestant Peep O'Day Boys and the Catholic Defenders burst into flame and led to the formation of the Orange societies. The United Irishmen tried to use this as propaganda, and successfully recruited many Defenders into their ranks, but they further alienated their co-religionists, and at the same time provided a weapon that was to be used in the suppression of the Rebellion. It is conveniently overlooked that as early as 1792, Wolfe Tone and Neilson went to Rathfriland in County Down to help the parish priest and the Presbyterian minister mediate a truce after serious sectarian disturbances there. Tone dismissed Rathfriland as an inconvenience which would not stop 'the growing liberty of Ireland', but before their second visit they were warned that their lives might be in danger, and so brought with them four cases of pistols. They met with considerable hostility, and the town's only inn refused them accommodation. They were obliged to go off to Rostrevor for a holiday instead.[14] 'It was,' writes Marianne Elliott, 'typical of Tone's romantic attachment to his belief that the future for a more liberal Ireland lay with the advanced thinkers in the north.'[15]

Catherine the Great explained the matter succinctly to Diderot and the *philosophes* she so admired. 'With your fine principles you can make beautiful books, but they don't work out in practice. You forget the difference in our positions. You only work on paper, which will put up with anything; while I, a poor Empress, have to work on men's skins, which are ticklish and easily irritated.' And she asked, embarrassingly, 'Is it really certain that humanity is capable of perfection?'[16]

Thanks to the French Revolution a *Zeitgeist* was created in the 1790s which eventually permeated society at every level. It dictated fashion, from clothes and cropped hairstyles to speech and locution. The ideals of liberty, equality and fraternity, through the works of Tom Paine, political pamphlets, newspapers, the weaver poets and reading clubs, moved down through the levels of society – nowhere more perhaps than in the Scottish-influenced counties of Antrim and Down. The insurgents of 1798 were not, however, the same people as the urban radicals of 1791. The agenda had begun to change; already they were being influenced by another revolution altogether.

It was prefigured in 1792 when Tone had been conducted round the bleach-green of William Sinclair near Belfast, but had not realised the significance of what he was seeing. 'A noble concern; extensive machinery. Sinclair's improvements laughed at by his neighbours, who said he was mad . . . Almost all the work is now done by machinery; done thirty years ago by hand, and all improvement regularly resisted by the people.'[17] The social base of the United Irish movement had been widened by the recruitment of artisans and rural workers. By 1798 the demand for the rights of man is being replaced by the demand for the rights of workers, and not long afterwards, the first trades unions appear. James Hope, a leading United Irishman and a socialist before his time, is as critical of employers as he is of landlords.

The political mobilisation of artisans and rural workers, for the first time in Irish history, had created a very formidable insurrectionary movement by 1796, and here we see the importance of timing in the insurrections of 1798.

The Leaves of the Shamrock

It has come to be almost universally accepted that the great Rebellion of 1798 was solely the work of the United Irishmen. At the most popular, and most political, level of Irish history, the story runs like this. The

Rebellion was led by Wolfe Tone, who had founded the Society of United Irishmen in Belfast in 1791. This event marked the birth of Irish republicanism. Inspired by the French Revolution, Protestants and Catholics laid aside the mutual hostility of centuries and united in the common cause of nationalism and independence, a cause which has triumphed in the modern Irish Republic. But Tone was not the first United Irishman, and he did not lead the Rebellion of 1798. Moreover the politics of 1791 need to be carefully separated from those of 1798.

A Hercule Poirot, called to the scene of the crime, and hearing such an account from his assistant, might say: 'Ah! But observe, my dear Hastings, we have here not one insurrection but three, in quite different parts of the country, with quite different characteristics, and not at the same time. And then, to quote my distinguished colleague Sherlock Holmes, there is the curious incident of the dog in the night time.' Let us look briefly at the timetable. The intervals are very important, because they enabled the government to retain control throughout the entire period of danger. The first serious rising began on 26 May 1798, and was largely confined to the counties of Wexford and Wicklow, an area in which it was believed that there had been little United Irish organisation. It was led initially by two Catholic curates, Father John Murphy of Boulavogue and Father Michael Murphy of Ballycarnew, both of whom had, a few weeks earlier, pledged their loyalty to 'His Sacred Majesty, King George III', and joined in offering a reward for the apprehension of 'wicked and designing people' who spread rumours that Catholics were planning a revolt.[18] Rumour was indeed the chief cause of what followed, for the country people came to believe that hordes of loyalists and Orangemen were about to descend on them. The Wexford rebellion quickly developed a sectarian character. On 5 June over a hundred Protestants were burned to death in a barn at Scullabogue, and when a republic was set up in Wexford town, loyalists were summarily tried and executed on the bridge spanning the River Slaney. These events ran completely counter to the ideals of the United Irishmen, and had a devastating effect on Protestant opinion throughout Ireland. If, as has been recently suggested, there was in fact a United Irish command structure in place, it had clearly little control over events.[19]

For two whole weeks, while rebellion raged in Wexford, Wicklow and parts of other counties, the north, which had been the centre and soul of the United Irish movement, remained sullenly calm, to the astonishment and relief of the government. Then on 7 June County Antrim broke out in rebellion, followed a few days later by County Down. Here the insurgents were overwhelmingly Presbyterian. We now know that the middle-aged leadership had refused to sanction a rising without the assistance of a French invasion, and it was in these circumstances that younger men like Henry Joy McCracken and Henry Munro were forced into taking command. The revolt was checked on the first afternoon when McCracken's forces were routed at Antrim town, and the vast army of insurgents which had gathered on Donegore Hill melted away. For the next three days the town of Ballymena was in rebel hands, before accepting the amnesty offered by Colonel Clavering. In Down the rebels were initially more successful. On 9 June they ambushed a detachment of the York Fencibles at Saintfield. The victory, the only one in the northern rebellion, put great heart into the men of the Ards Peninsula, who moved westwards round Strangford Lough to reinforce rebels who had gathered in the centre of the county. Henry Munro established his headquarters on Ednavady Hill, and the whole rebellion ended bloodily with his defeat at Ballynahinch on 13 June.

The northern revolt was of a much less serious character than that in Wexford. On the day after he gave the signal for the rising, Father John Murphy and the rebels under his command had all but annihilated the North Cork militia sent against them, and had gained control of the county, including the towns of Wexford and Enniscorthy. But their failure to take New Ross on 5 June, despite enormous slaughter, doomed the insurrection to ultimate defeat. Nevertheless, it was not until 21 June that the main rebel stronghold at Vinegar Hill was stormed and the rebellion ended.

Both these rebellions had been crushed, and something like peace restored by the late summer, when the third insurrection broke out in County Mayo, in the far west. It was provoked by the arrival of the French, who came too late and landed on the wrong side of Ireland. The French troops inflicted a sharp defeat on General Lake and the British at Castlebar before beginning their advance into the heart of Ireland, at the head of a host of country folk in arms. They were forced to surrender on terms at Ballinamuck, County Longford, on 8 September. All three insurrections propagated a standard United Irish ideology, and made copious use of the terms made fashionable by the French Revolution – Republic, Year of Liberty, Committee of Public Safety – but they were essentially rebellions of quite different sections of the population, whose aims differed, and who were to some extent hostile to one another.

The Presbyterian rebels in Antrim were, before they rose, already in-censed against the rebels responsible for the massacre at Scullabogue, and the Wexford rebels regarded all Protestants as Orangemen who had harried and slaughtered Catholics. Most of the simple and devout country people who followed General Humbert's banner in County Mayo would have regarded anything deriving from Protestant politics as impious by definition. To their credit they shed very little blood except on the field of battle, though later they were punished just as savagely as those who had.

Irish radicals in the late eighteenth century were subject to the same influences as people of like mind elsewhere, but, as Elie Halévy long ago demonstrated, ideas exert their chief political influence after they have hardened into dogmas, and this occurs through their application to real interests in definite circumstances. The ideas of the United Irishmen are a classic example of this. In Ireland the consequences were inevitably dif-ferent from those which ensued in England, or France, or Poland. The ideas took root in Irish ground, and produced an Irish harvest. It might be said, however, that at this period Ireland was more in step with the thinking of western Europe than was generally the case, though this is true only on certain levels.

The sources of political inspiration for the Irish educated classes had become less indigenous as the century progressed. The 'national' com-plaints of Molyneux and Swift were augmented by those of Rousseau and Paine. It was not so much because Ireland was more provincial in the earlier part of the century. Recent closer research into the import and sale of books in Ireland has shown that this could not be said of the educated section of Irish society;[20] but by 1790 the thinking of the *philosophes* was known to a wider and more heterogeneous audience in Ireland. The result was an extension of the conception of reform. In the words of a well-worn examination question, the United Irishmen were (initially at least) more interested in the rights of man than the rights of Ireland.

Far from wishing to bring about the kind of confessional nationalism which today divides rather than unites Ireland, the United Irishmen ar-dently hoped for a lessening of clerical influence over the masses. They had convinced themselves by their analysis of Irish society that this was actually happening, and they desired to accelerate the process. An es-sential part of Wolfe Tone's political mission was to liberate the Irish majority from the thraldom of the Catholic Church. Even before the

French Revolution, Irish francophiles had absorbed some of the prejudices of the French Enlightenment. They believed that to be happy, men had only to be rational, and that religion itself had to be capable of a rational explanation. We have since discovered that men are not, after all, rational beings, and one of the achievements of twentieth-century philosophers and scientists was to explain the failure of the rationalism of the Enlightenment. It was, nevertheless, a brave and impressive attempt to make the universe explicable, and the effort of a post-Freudian society to base its conduct on the irrational has not been a conspicuous success.

On the more practical front the French Revolution led to a re-examination of political principles. First there was the question of Ireland's peculiar constitutional position, tied to England and sharing the monarchy, for in strict constitutional theory Ireland had its own sovereign, though the monarch was usually the same person. Ireland could not thus become a republic on the French model unless Britain became one also. One can scarcely doubt, however, that if Britain had followed France and become a republic, Catholic Ireland would have clung to the monarchy as the very badge of national distinctiveness, which brings us back to the anomalous situation at the end of the seventeenth century. Ireland would have been Jacobite rather than Jacobin. This was the essence of Edmund Burke's argument, that every effort should be made to conciliate Irish Catholics and steer them away from the dangerous United Irishmen.

For the first United Irishmen, mostly middle-class Belfast Presbyterians, republicanism was largely a theoretical matter, and did not necessarily imply separation from the mother country. In Ireland, however, it became inextricably bound up with nationalism, and has remained so ever since. It is hard now to imagine an Irish republican unionist, though in other countries and other circumstances, unionism would not of itself imply monarchism. This is interesting, because it means that in the history of Irish republicanism, national feeling prevailed over the instinctive Catholic distaste for republican principles.

In England patriotism acted as a counterweight to democratic fervour, whereas in Ireland patriotism and radicalism to some extent coincided. English radicals who looked favourably on the French Revolution had not to deal with the complications of the Catholic question and the Ascendancy. Pitt the Younger had defined the English aristocracy as 'the true poise of the Constitution', and Macaulay was to call it 'the most democratic' in the world.[21] But in Ireland the ruling caste was not of the same religion as those ruled; it was alien because of the perception that it had been created artificially in place of an old, and true, aristocracy, and this simple fact became the core of the land question.

On the other hand radicalism in Ireland tended to be more purely political and less social than in Britain. Eighteenth-century radicalism perished in 1798 at Antrim and Ballynahinch, and trade unionism took root in the first of Belfast's textile mills in the early decades of the nineteenth century. The bulk of Ireland's rural labouring population were never behind the ideals of the original United Irishmen, but they were behind the 1798 insurrection. They were primarily interested in land and religion, and the United Irish radicals were not able to appeal to them satisfactorily in these areas. The United Irish movement was in no sense socialist, and it was not until the nineteenth century, and indeed late in the century, that the Irish rural community was shown that land could become politics. As far as Catholic emancipation was concerned, the issue was focussed on representation, and of benefit only to those further up the social scale. For the commercial middle class in Ireland each of the famous watchwords of the French Revolution had a special resonance. 'Liberty' appealed directly to the old complaint about Ireland's constitutional rights; 'Equality' was what both Catholic and Dissenter sought from the Ascendancy; 'Fraternity' appealed to the desire that Irishmen and Irishwomen of all religious persuasions should unite in the best interests of the country. The main demands of the United Irishmen were in a sense the restatement of these ideals – independence, parliamentary reform and Catholic emancipation.

Many of the differences between Britain and Ireland were illustrated by the situation of the Irish Whigs. The reform movement led by Grattan and his supporters drew its strength from the English Revolution of 1688, but that event had a different significance for Ireland. The Whigs' difficulty was that their principles were unfitted for local application, and left them vulnerable to criticism and ridicule from radicals.[22] Wolfe Tone said that the Whigs dreaded the people as much as the Castle did.

Radicalism in Britain, though crushed after 1793 because of the outbreak of war with revolutionary France, re-emerged after 1800 in much the same form, and with many of the same objectives. In Ireland, however, the 1798 Rebellion made a sharp break; thereafter Irish radicalism took a different turn. One can see this clearly by comparing the content of the *Belfast Monthly Magazine* (1808–15) which Drennan helped to edit, with the content of Drennan's radicalism before 1798. The Irish radicals remained in business only by carefully straining out of their programme every element which had the prison taint of 1798 about it. The conduct of the Royal Family, particularly of George IV and his brothers, replaced the great national issues. Only Catholic emancipation survived the Union as a 'Protestant radical' issue.[23]

People in the eighteenth century, like people today, were not disposed to look very far ahead. Apart from a few intrepid futurologists like Mercier, Crosbie and Edgeworth they were content to devote most of their energies to contemporary politics however evanescent, which usually meant seeking solutions to problems which were already stale, and likely to be solved by processes other than political ones. Political activists, like admirals and generals, often went on preparing for campaigns which had already been fought. And the same was true of governments. The rapid changes which occurred in political and social organisation in the last decade of the eighteenth century trapped Irish republicanism in a curious time warp. In one sense the republican philosophy was already out of date by 1798, the year which is supposed to mark its birth. The problem was to some extent encountered by all the radicals of the time, and was neatly expressed by the Girondin leader Pierre Vergniaud. 'We were deceived not in liberty but in the hour. We believed we were in Rome, but we found ourselves in Paris.'[24] Faced by the complex problems of contemporary society, more evident in France than elsewhere, the radical brought to them an insight mostly derived from his classical education. The rules for ancient Greece and Rome proved to be inadequate, just as the ideals of the French Revolution are inadequate for the political and social problems of today.

Why, Soldiers, Why?

Virginia Woolf said that writing biography was like watching fish in a tank: they think that they have complete freedom of action, but we know otherwise, because we know how the story ends. Wolfe Tone is an outstanding example of this. It would be possible to write an interesting biography of Tone with Irish politics forming only the background. It would tell the story of an insouciant young Trinity graduate whose abiding ambition was to wear the scarlet uniform of a British army officer, and whose imagination was fired by the published account of Captain Cook's discovery of the Hawaiian Islands. Later he drew up an elaborate memorandum urging the British government to expand the Empire by establishing a colony of armed settlers there. In his teens he fell hopelessly in love with the wife of Richard Martin, the animal rights campaigner. Eliza Martin was an actress, and inspired in Tone a lifelong passion for the theatre. In 1783, at the age of twenty, he appeared with her in a double-bill performance in Galway of John Home's tragedy *Douglas* and Isaac Jackman's farce *All the World's a Stage*, in which he played the part of a comic butler who bungles an attempt to cut his own throat.[25] The affair, which seems to have been innocent, ended abruptly; just as well, perhaps, since Martin was an accomplished duellist. Some years later, Martin brought a successful 'criminal conversation' case against one Petrie, a less innocent lover of Mrs Martin's. On the rebound Tone eloped with the sixteen-year-old daughter of a Dublin woollen draper, and thereafter, though further amours are hinted at in his *Journals*, he appears to have been a devoted husband and family man.

To a large extent these early influences determined the rest of his short career – an interest in politics which began with the debates in Trinity's Historical Society, a passion for all things military, love of the theatre, an ideal of romantic love and heroism. In some ways his involvement with the Catholic Committee and the United Irishmen after 1790 seems almost a digression. At the heart of it is the disappointment of a young man of parts who feels, like Swift (one of his idols), that he is treated as a second-class citizen just because he is Irish; he is the quintessential 'colonial outsider'.[26] One way or another, the national apotheosis has obliterated the memory of the living man, and even the evidence of his own memoirs is set aside or ignored.

Not only did Tone *not* lead the 1798 Rebellion, but he chose the very day of its breaking out to give up all hope of it. To understand why, you must remember that Tone had been toiling for months in Paris to influence this or that member of the French Directory in favour of a French expedition to Ireland. Bonaparte received him very graciously and gave him to understand that a combined naval and military expedition to invade England was one of his first priorities. But it was a ruse.

Bonaparte's eyes were already fixed on Britain's Indian empire.

At the end of April 1798 Tone learned that his brother William, whom he had not seen for six years, was second-in-command of the troops of the Mahratta Confederacy in India. Soon afterwards he heard the rumour that the Toulon Fleet's destination was to be the East, and not the British Isles after all. He was by now thoroughly disillusioned by the intrigues against him by the other emissaries of the United Irishmen in Paris. On 26 May 1798, the day that Wexford blazed up in rebellion, he wrote to offer Bonaparte his services in India.[27] How different Tone's treatment in the history books might be had he died at the beginning of 1798 and not the end.

One cannot proceed very far with Tone's memoirs without coming upon his favourite quotation. At every set-back, every check to that ebullient spirit, he shrugs his shoulders and sighs:

> 'Tis but in vain
> For soldiers to complain

He was fond of playful allusions, but this one stands out, and one is driven to wonder why it specially appealed to him.[28] Had Tone been an American patriot, we should no doubt have shelves full of editions anotated by teams of scholars, in which every word he quoted was traced to its source. Such scholars are like owls, as Lichtenberg observed, good at catching mice in the dark, even if they smash into church steeples in daylight.[29] But Irish historians have been, until recently, remarkably incurious about what Tone read. It was enough that he uttered the deathless words about uniting Protestant, Catholic and Dissenter to make Ireland free.

Marianne Elliott, in her 1989 biography, usefully identifies many of the allusions, but not this one. It is doubtful indeed whether one could easily come upon it except by serendipity. Suppose that one were browsing through the *Journal of the Society of Army Historical Research* for October 1927, for an entirely different piece of research, and the familiar quotation just caught the corner of one's eye. A stray antiquarian piece, some notes on an old song, the words of which are believed to be in a manuscript book of poetry in the Advocates' Library in Edinburgh, dated 1712, under the title of 'The Duke of Berwick's March', or, alternatively, 'Why, Soldiers, Why?' Alas! The librarian of the National Library of Scotland could not trace it in October 1927. So our earnest inquirer tracks it down in

William Chappell's *Popular Music of the Olden Time* (London, 1855–8), where it is called 'How Stands the Glass Around?' Chappell notes that it is commonly called General Wolfe's song, and is said to have been written by the young James Wolfe on the night before he commanded the English forces against the French in the Battle of Quebec in 1759, during which he was killed. Wolfe Tone's interest becomes crystal clear,[30] but this tradition of the origins of the tune is sufficiently disproved by a copy of it, under the title 'Why, Soldiers, Why?', in *The Patron, or the Statesman's Opera*, performed at the New Theatre in the Haymarket in 1729. And we already have an earlier date in 1712.[31]

Here are the words and music.

Why, soldiers, why
Should we be melancholy, boys?
Why, soldiers, why?
Whose business 'tis to die!
What! sighing? fie!
Damn fear, drink on, be jolly boys!
'Tis he, you, or I;
Cold, hot, wet, or dry,
We're always bound to follow, boys,
And scorn to fly.

'Tis but in vain,
(I mean not to upbraid you, boys).
'Tis but in vain,
For soldiers to complain:
Should next campaign
Send us to Him who made us, boys,
We're free from pain;
But should we remain,
A bottle and kind landlady
Cures all again.

To an extraordinary degree Tone exemplified the characteristic ambiguity of the Irish attitude to soldiering, which for centuries has led to Irishmen fighting other Irishmen, and continues to this day. Facing captivity, and certain death, the blue uniform of France placed him securely in the honourable tradition of the Wild Geese, but he was not really in their ranks. The earliest and dearest ambition of his heart was to wear, like his friend Thomas Russell, and Russell's father, the red uniform of England. As for so many others, Ireland got in the way. Incidentally, 'Why, Soldiers, Why?' had another title in the eighteenth century. It was called 'A Soldier's Song'.

The Restless Nation

Ireland is a little country which raises all the great questions.

GUSTAVE DE BEAUMONT[1]

The Fatal Union

'Do not make an union with us, Sir', Dr Johnson advised an Irish gentleman in 1779. 'We should unite with you only to rob you. We should have robbed the Scotch, if they had had anything of which we could have robbed them.' The date is interesting, confirming Boswell's gloss that the project of a legislative union between Great Britain and Ireland was one 'which artful politicians have often had in view'.[2] It was in fact first raised in the Irish parliament not long after the Union with Scotland of 1707, when Irish MPs were very much in favour of it, but their petition was turned down by England. Mooted again several times in the 1750s, it aroused such fierce Irish opposition that it was not pursued. Only in the aftermath of the 1798 Rebellion, when Irish politics seemed bankrupt, was Pitt the Younger able to press forward with its enactment, no longer as something desirable, but as an absolute necessity.

Posterity's view of the Act of Union has been largely that of Dr Johnson. On the surface it would seem to be an odd one. Far from 'robbing' Ireland, Britain has been obliged since 1800 to pour wealth and resources into that country on an astronomical scale, and to this hour it continues to spend billions of pounds in the protection of Northern Ireland from terrorist violence, billions which the North can never hope to repay. This does not mean, of course, that even the British part of the population there think that the money is being well spent. In English eyes, Ireland has been, at least since Tudor times, a kind of bottomless sink into which money disappears as if by magic.

The robbery implied is not therefore the obvious one of wealth or natural resources, though this has not deterred nationalists from repeatedly levelling the charge. It is of a more abstract nature. By the Union Ireland lost its independent parliament, its genius was stifled, its people degraded, and its national potential thwarted and diminished for 120 years. 'The Act of Union,' wrote Arthur Griffith in 1902, 'was at the time of its passage, and always has been since declared by independent Irish lawyers and statesmen to be a nullity, a usurpation and a fraud.'[3] The refusal of George III to go along with Pitt's master-plan, and honour the implicit understanding that the Union would be accompanied by Catholic emancipation, sealed its fate. Henceforth the Act was regarded as a kind of national swindle.

It is therefore very difficult, and perhaps impossible, for us ever to see the Union in its proper historical context. We are aware not only that it failed, but that it seemed doomed to fail from the outset. We cannot now see clearly why Pitt and his ministers hoped that it would succeed. In the short term the only one of its objectives to be achieved was the strengthening of the defence of the British Isles during the most critical stage of the Napoleonic Wars; in the long run it was ended by violent revolution and at the cost of much bloodshed. In the words of Oliver MacDonagh, the Act of Union was 'an act of miscalculations'. 'What was meant to issue in a compound of government, produced an unending series of explosions.'[4]

There is no evidence that Pitt had long nourished a determination to suppress the Irish parliament. His lack of interest in Ireland was notorious, and he was content to leave its government to the ruling Irish junta in Dublin Castle for as long as they conducted it efficiently and without too blatant an abuse of power. However, the successive crises of 1782 (parliamentary independence), 1785 (the rejection of the Commercial Propositions) and 1788–9 (the dispute over the Regency) had indicated the danger inherent in the continuation of this policy. All the problems were compounded, and the political landscape transformed, when Britain went to war with revolutionary France in 1793. The Fitzwilliam fiasco in 1795 forced Pitt to consider Union as an alternative to the prevailing system. The French attempt to invade Ireland at Christmas 1796, followed by the imminent threat of a United Irish rising in 1797 and the reality of the naval mutinies at Spithead and the Nore in England, all at a time when Britain's back was to the wall, made the Union virtually inevitable. When the Irish insurrection finally came a year later it was less dangerous than it would have been in 1797, yet it was the most formidable of all Irish rebellions and cost 30,000 lives. In such perilous circumstances it seemed to Pitt that a legislative union with Ireland might be able to contain and reduce the sectarian, political and economic problems with which the Irish parliament and office holders had failed to cope. It could scarcely do worse, and if the opportunity were seized to grant Catholic emancipation at the same time, it would secure the Catholic population against Jacobinism and disloyalty (as Edmund Burke had always argued), while offering the Protestants safety as part of a larger British population.

We have continually to remind ourselves, therefore, that the failure of the Union was not in fact inevitable. Such arrangements work well if they are to the benefit of both parties, and Pitt clearly had this in mind when he quoted in the Commons Vergil's lines:

paribus se legibus ambae Invictae gentes aeterna in foedera mittant[5]

('let the two peoples, both unconquered, agree to a perpetual compact with equal laws'). Against this, one might say at once that Ireland as the weaker and poorer partner was bound to come off worst; but this was true only if the relationship was seen always as one of struggle and re-crimination. The Union with Scotland worked reasonably well *on the whole*, though fewer and fewer Scots people are prepared to admit this. If a union is seen in terms of co-operation and economic benefit, rather than (for want of a better word) in narrowly tribal terms, and between nations which have basically the same beliefs and the same end in mind, then the weaker partner is undoubtedly the more fortunate. But mind-sets change, and the contemporary fashion in Scotland takes a very different view. Elements of both the Scottish and Welsh population have, in their re-sentment of the English, imitated the nationalist rhetoric of the Irish; but the fact remains that at no time since 1707 has Scottish dislike of England reached the murderous intensity that is shown in Ireland. It is not underpinned by bitter religious hatred.

In the case of the Act of Union with Ireland, it is perfectly legitimate to ask which country has suffered more, though the question is in fact never asked. In general English people are too busy apologising to the Irish for past history ever to consider the wrongs which Ireland has inflicted on England, and that is the way Ireland would like to keep it. But one might fairly ask this question. Would a single member of the Westminster par-liament have voted for the Union if he had had the gift of prophecy? Would he have voted for it if he had been able to foresee its baneful effect on parliament alone? Given that the Union in some sense failed at the outset, and that the failure became more and more obvious as the country progressed, another question then arises. Why did England, while con-ceding so much to Irish demands, refuse to repeal the Act itself until well into the twentieth century, and then only in response to a vicious guerrilla war and widespread violence? To this question we shall return.

So much has been written about the Union that we are in danger of overlooking the fact that the problems posed by Anglo-Irish relations were acute for centuries before 1800, and have remained acute since 1920. We are in danger of thinking that Ireland had no other history since the eighteenth century than the doleful story of the *mésentente*. The torrent of polemical writing in the nineteenth century created a picture of a nation in bondage, a people sullenly acquiescent under an alien government, waiting for liberation, planning rebellion and civil disobedience, while in the twentieth century it was redefined as a process of decolonisation. P.S. O'Hegarty called his *History of Ireland under the Union* (1952) the story of a people coming out of captivity. It is easy, therefore, to think of a static political situation, of what A.V. Dicey, the brilliant English jurist, called 'the artificial suppression of revolution'.[6] He argued that under the Union Ireland was prevented from curing its evils by revolution, which was occasionally a successful remedy.

Even the most cursory study of the period shows that Irish political history was anything but static. Far from being frozen in a political trance, Ireland changed continuously and fundamentally. Its society and institutions underwent a whole series of revolutions, each of which was ultimately more significant than the few abortive armed risings which occurred between 1800 and 1916, and these revolutions were made possible by the Union, not held back by it. One might go further and assert that it was the dynamic force in most of them.

To put the same point in another way, the ideal which inspired those attempts at the violent overthrow of English government in Ireland was only one of the factors which moulded modern Ireland, and not necessarily, as we have been conditioned to believe, the most important one. The 'national struggle' to achieve independence, which is often approached anachronistically from the present, has subsumed all other aspects of national life. The basic principles on which the case for Irish total independence rested were, in some ways, already dubious in the eighteenth century. In the nineteenth, they became even less sound. Take, for example, the economy. The idea that England had always stifled the economic prosperity of Ireland is one of great antiquity and astonishing resilience. It was old when Swift took it up in 1720, and it is still strenuously argued in nationalist areas of Belfast and Derry, while the Republic of Ireland itself co-operates very profitably with the commerce of Britain. It is not of course to be denied that for three centuries before 1800 England did put its selfish commercial interests first by placing restrictions on Irish trade, and that these were passionately resented, as they were in America, but they were succeeded in the nineteenth century by massive aid to Ireland's economy. What is not so clear is the extent to which Ireland could have prospered on its own.

For the present discussion we need not go further back than Wolfe Tone, who allowed himself to be persuaded by one Thomas Digges that 'if Ireland were free, and well governed, being that she is unencumbered with debt, she would in arts, commerce and manufacture, spring up like an air balloon, and leave England behind her at an immense distance. There is no computing the rapidity with which she would rise.'[7] Digges was, it subsequently developed, an economist of the sharper kind. He was arrested for stealing from one United Irish leader, Samuel Neilson, and he impoverished another, Thomas Russell, who imprudently went bail for him. The optimism he expressed has not weakened with time, and the current fashion is to attack economic 'imperialism' for the controls relinquished with the Union.

The traditional view of Ireland's economy in the nineteenth century is that the Union was responsible for the decline of Irish prosperity everywhere except in the north-east, where Belfast and the Lagan valley were integrated with the industrial complex of the north of England. Irish manufacturers were exposed to the competition of the richest industrial country in the world, and Westminster legislated in favour of British factory owners. The monetary difficulties of Ireland were accentuated, and even caused, by the export of capital from the country in the form of rents paid to absentee landlords. As so often happens in human affairs, what is highly visible and simple to understand is accepted as an explanation, and becomes a focus for hatred.

Modern economic historians do not accept the explanation. They point out that Ireland's economy was much more independent of political and religious factors than we have been led to believe, and they show how such an erroneous view could be arrived at. Until comparatively recently the economic history of Ireland was written largely from economic tracts of the seventeenth, eighteenth and nineteenth centuries, and these were mainly political in purpose. Historians accepted what people *said* were the causes of economic weakness and decay. Now they base their conclusions much more on the painstaking direct analysis of every scrap of statistical evidence which has survived. It is in areas like these where the historian as accountant comes in to his own.

'Because decline followed the Union,' writes L.M. Cullen, 'it was supposed that it was caused by the Union.'

This necessarily pre-supposed that economic change and the Union approximately co-incided. This was not in fact true; the correlation between the withdrawal of protection in the first quarter of the century and industrial decline is poor enough. Much industry in factory and in a domestic setting alike survived into the 1840s and even later. The retardation in decline in the first forty years of the century and acceleration subsequently appear to contradict the thesis that the seeds of economic decline lay in the Act of Union itself. However, O'Connell's agitation for the repeal of the Union identified what was described as the 'commercial injustices' of the Union as the cause of the economic difficulties with which the country had to cope in the nineteenth century.[8]

There were, after all, two broad kinds of influence at work, each of which was more powerful than the legislation flowing from Westminster. On the one hand were the factors of geography. Ireland possessed none of the resources then considered necessary for industrialisation – in particular it lacked coal. Nor was it fortunate enough to be situated at a crossroads of commerce in Europe. Secondly, and until recently much less considered, there was the congruity of economic trends in rural communities of the same kind throughout Europe. The phenomenal growth of population between the middle of the eighteenth century and the Famine, which has given rise to such brisk argument among economic historians, was not peculiar to Ireland, and the demographic decline which was so dramatic in Ireland thereafter was not *solely* because of the Famine. Even if famine had not supervened, Cullen tells us, a decline in population would have occurred, since emigration was sharply rising. Again, the great technological improvement in transport, in particular the spread of the railways, affected other communities in similarly unpredictable ways.

At the beginning of the nineteenth century Irish people were confident that their country was on the brink of an industrial revolution, the early signs of which had already appeared before 1800. When it did not develop in the form which they had anticipated, the disappointment was keen. The revolution did in fact occur later in the century, but in a form which served to accentuate one of the oldest of Ireland's problems, for the only area to be industrialised intensively was the Lagan valley, an area largely populated by Protestants of Scottish descent.

This element of the population, from which the Society of United Irishmen had drawn its first members, had increasingly sound economic reasons for supporting the Union, reasons which were in some ways different from those which caused Protestants in other parts of Ireland to adhere to the Union. Industrialisation gave a double twist to the sectarian division, for it created within the predominantly Presbyterian town of Belfast several large Catholic enclaves, and thus produced the conditions for the periodic riots, of a very ugly kind, which are such a baneful characteristic of Belfast's history.

The Liberator

One might be tempted to consider the whole period from 1800 in an economic determinist way, if only to counteract the familiar political history, but Ireland is notoriously intractable in this kind of analysis, a fact which explains why the commentaries of Marx and Engels seem so wide of the mark. For in Ireland politics and personality *do* manage to transcend vulgar economic compulsions. There could be no better example of this than the extraordinary influence on Irish history of Daniel O'Connell.

So great was this influence that the first half of the nineteenth century becomes an enormous plateau, dominated by his personality. Yet by the middle of the twentieth century O'Connell's nationalism has been long out of fashion. Like Butt and Redmond, he was a subject for PhD theses, but not for popular history. This was a strange irony, for it was he who made Irish nationalism popular in the exact sense of the word. O'Connell, who turned his back on revolution as a means of ending the Union, brought about the first, and perhaps the greatest, of the revolutions of the period: Catholic emancipation. The initial and most obvious failure of the Union was that it did not establish equal rights for Catholics. For the first twenty years of the century, the campaign for Catholic emancipation was necessarily carried on by Protestant members of the Westminster parliament, particularly Henry Grattan. But Catholic support for the campaign was patchy, and Catholic opinion was divided on strategy. Organised political activity was confined largely to the surviving Catholic aristocracy (who had launched the campaign as far back as 1760), the landed gentry, and the middle-class lawyers and merchants in the city of Dublin. So circumspect was their approach that a petition to parliament for the removal of Catholic disabilities was brought forward in 1805 only after much opposition in Catholic ranks.

That petition, however, brought into politics a young barrister who specialised in criminal cases, and who was already becoming popular because every successful defence in such cases was regarded as a blow against the government. O'Connell was the son of a Catholic landlord in County Kerry. His family had a tradition of military service; his uncle, also called Daniel O'Connell, had commanded one of the crack regiments of Louis XVI's army on the outbreak of the French Revolution. The young Daniel O'Connell was himself sent to school at St-Omer in the north of France in 1791, and his experience of revolutionary France was an important factor in shaping his lifelong abhorrence of the use of violence for political ends. He evinced a dislike and fear of the French revolutionaries, which was not surprising since the Irish colleges and the Wild Geese – of which his uncle was one – with their monarchist tradition were objects of great suspicion in revolutionary France. When he returned to Ireland he briefly became a United Irishman, but soon came to regard them also with revulsion. This instinct persisted throughout his career, and made him adhere firmly to the methods of constitutional nationalism.

While O'Connell represented a pious and conservative side of the Catholic tradition, and while he had seen enough of revolutionary violence to repudiate it, he did, as a student at the Inns of Court in London, come under the influence of some of the radical thinkers. The lingering rays of the Enlightenment, and his reading of Paine and the English utilitarians, made him a radical in politics. There were many problems to be addressed in the Ireland of his time. Local government cried out for reform, and there was no really effective machinery to provide relief for the destitute. Both Catholics and Protestants resented having to pay tithes to the Established Church. Above all there was the question of Catholic emancipation.

It has come to be called that, though in fact the dismantling of the penal laws against Catholics had begun as far back as 1770, and by 1793 all but a handful of the disabilities on Catholics had been swept away by Hobart's Act of that year. However, among the few which remained was the prohibition on any Catholic taking a seat in parliament, and, as Wolfe Tone had pointed out, much of the new equality was meaningless without the right of representation. It was on this grievance that Catholic attention was now concentrated.

The transfer of the emancipation debate from the Irish parliament to Westminster altered its character. In Ireland it had always been argued that emancipation would lead to the overthrow of the Established Church, the land settlement and the existence of the 'Protestant nation'. This is in fact precisely what it did do ultimately. English opinion, however, was opposed to emancipation on rather different grounds – that Catholics (including English Catholics) could not really be completely loyal British subjects because of their allegiance to the papacy. This was the legacy of English history in the sixteenth and seventeenth centuries, and the residual feeling was still strong.

To allay these fears Grattan had in 1806 proposed that emancipation should be accompanied by a measure of government control, allowing the Crown to veto the appointment of any Catholic bishop whom it considered suspect. The veto aroused unexpectedly strong opposition in Ireland. The Catholic bishops bowed to the pressure of popular feeling and rejected the formula, whereupon the Bill was withdrawn. From this point the aristocratic influence on the emancipation movement declined. A new Catholic committee was set up in 1810, and in 1811 it took the name of the Catholic Board. The combination of middle-class and clerical influence in its affairs was very significant for the future. The Catholic Board was dissolved in 1814, when Sir Robert Peel was Chief Secretary, and the emancipation campaign declined. Within a few years, however, a more liberal atmosphere developed and in 1819, the year before his death, Grattan introduced his last Emancipation Bill in the House of Commons. It was defeated by only two votes. In 1823 the Catholic Association was formed to campaign for Catholic emancipation; it consisted largely of merchants, professionals and landowners. The following year O'Connell remodelled the association, and changed its constitution in a way which was to prove a turning-point in Irish history. Those who could not afford the annual subscription of one guinea were allowed to become associate members by paying just one penny a month. This simple but ingenious move had astonishing results. The whole face of the agitation was changed. Almost by accident O'Connell had discovered how to tap the reservoir of Ireland's Catholic poor, and, as an indirect consequence, nationalism was set on a new and populist road, which it has kept to ever since.

Harvesting the subscription posed a logistical problem, but this was solved by the parish clergy volunteering to collect the 'Catholic rent', as it soon became known. In no time at all a thousand pounds a week was pouring in to the association's funds. O'Connell had achieved something which would have been quite impossible during the previous century; he had united Catholics of all social levels with the parish priests in a single political purpose. It took some time for old penal attitudes to wear off, as ordinary Catholics discovered the power of numbers in asserting their demands. If there was at first no very clear idea of who exactly would benefit, there was a growing feeling that the Catholic faith would remain degraded until secular emancipation was won.

O'Connell had created a formidable political machine, and he was now ready to test its strength. He addressed the government with calculated defiance, keeping well within the law but not troubling to disguise the underlying threat of civil disorder on a wide scale. His aim, in a series of increasingly violent speeches, was both to frighten the government and to remove the ingrained sense of inferiority created by the penal laws. The government in turn prosecuted him (unsuccessfully) for incitement to rebellion, and then, very reluctantly, suppressed the Catholic Association in 1825. O'Connell immediately re-established it under another name. The Catholic rent was still collected, and the campaign went on as before.

Its success owed much to the fact that it coincided with a building up of pressure in Britain for the democratisation of the franchise. In 1828 George IV had appointed the Duke of Wellington, the victor of Waterloo and a national hero, as Prime Minister at the head of a Conservative adminis-tration, with Sir Robert Peel as Home Secretary. In the tempestuous days when George IV had been Prince Regent, Peel had been courted by the radicals and had been favourable to the idea of Catholic emancipation, but he had now set his face against it, and the clear understanding behind these appointments was that both men were resolutely opposed to it. The rest of the Cabinet, however, were divided on the issue. When Wellington appointed William Vessey Fitzgerald, one of the members for County Clare, as President of the Board of Trade, O'Connell saw his opportunity and determined on a bold experiment.

The rules of parliament obliged Fitzgerald to seek re-election, and O'Connell came forward as a rival candidate. If elected, he would not be able as a Catholic to take his seat. As it happened, Fitzgerald was a very popular Protestant landlord and a keen supporter of Catholic emancipa-tion, but there could be no doubt about the outcome. O'Connell was duly elected. Catholics now became aware of their electoral strength, and huge demonstrations were held in various parts of the country, peaceful in organisation but menacing in their implications.

Because the ministry and the Tory party were so divided, Peel advised Wellington to yield. Not without difficulty, George IV was persuaded to their opinion, and in March 1829 the Roman Catholic Relief Bill passed through parliament. The concession was still hedged with qualifications – no Catholic could become Regent, Lord Lieutenant or Lord Chancellor, and although MPs were no longer obliged to take the Oath of Supremacy, they had to take a long oath of loyalty to the Crown. The army of forty-shilling freeholders who had won the victory were promptly disenfranchised in favour of a £10 property franchise. Nevertheless the main point had been gained; henceforth Catholic MPs would sit at Westminster.

It should not be forgotten that the legislation was an important advance in civil rights for British Catholics, but its paramount significance was in relation to Ireland. The actual date of Catholic emancipation is not, in itself, significant, except that it came so late. That it occurred in 1829 rather than in 1795 or 1800 was the fortuitous consequence of a series of political accidents, 'the interplay of the contingent and unforeseen'.[9] But its implications were supremely important. In the House of Lords, the Protestant Archbishop of Armagh, Lord George Beresford, in opposing the Bill, accurately forecast the consequences of its passing. What was involved was not the sharing of political power, he said, but its transfer.[10] It was to lead inexorably to the disestablishment of the Church of Ireland, and then to the fall of the landlords. It meant the end of the 'Protestant Ascendancy', and consequently of the 'Protestant nation'.

The methods by which it was achieved were as significant as the revolution itself. The organisation of mass support through the Catholic Association, the uniting of Catholics of all social ranks and the direct involvement of the Catholic clergy in the political campaign were all to some degree new departures in Irish history. The other side of the coin was that O'Connell, by his success, alienated Protestant sympathy for his radical causes, and this, too, was a revolution of great consequence. Never since has any leader of popular Irish nationalism been able to attract the support of Protestants in the north-east.

Catholic emancipation brought into existence the Catholic nation, with a distinct identity and national purpose. It took the place of the Protestant nation of the eighteenth century, with of course far greater justification in numerical and democratic terms, but by the end of the period of the Union it was to show itself, in a somewhat different fashion, to be every bit as exclusive as the previous tenant of the house of nationhood. The tragedy was, and still is, that neither has been able so far to win the allegiance of the whole of the Irish people. Changes in Protestant attitudes to the Union had taken place. Once it was realised that the Union was not going to be accompanied by Catholic emancipation, all those elements which had so vehemently opposed it in 1799, including the infant Orange Order, became not only reconciled to it but prepared to support and defend it to the full.

The Union was intended to be a kind of deal or trade-off. By allaying the fears of Protestants that they would ever be in a religious minority in the state they belonged to, the British government hoped that its hands would be freed to take a more liberal attitude towards its Irish Catholic subjects. This compromise underlies the relationship with Northern Ireland to this day, and explains why English Protestants do not see eye to eye with their Ulster co-religionists on this question. One of the purposes of the Act of Union was to offer a number of guarantees to Irish Protestants. The first was their continued monopoly in, or at least control of, local government and the public service, the professions and higher education, and land ownership and the instruments of order. Another guarantee was the maintenance of the privileges and finances of the Established Church. A third was that all the ultimate decisions in Irish government would continue to be made in London, consonant with the beliefs and outlook of the Protestant majority in the United Kingdom as a whole.[11]

The history of Ireland since 1829 has been largely the story of the breaking of these guarantees by successive British governments. The continuing paradox was that the terms of the Union were broken first on the British side, and not on the Irish. That explains why, as time went on, Episcopalians and Nonconformists, once bitter opponents, closed their ranks and began to regard the Union as the bulwark of their endangered situation, and why ultimately the Union came to fulfil a purpose quite different from that which was originally intended.

After a brief experiment in 'testing the Union', O'Connell co-operated with the Whig governments in the 1830s in the hope of persuading them to introduce sweeping reforms in Ireland, but the genie of Irish popular violence was out of the bottle, and conditions in Ireland became more chaotic than ever. In 1840, rightly surmising that the Whigs would not remain in office for much longer, O'Connell launched his campaign for the repeal of the Act of Union. He did not demand the independence of Ireland, but the restoration of a parliament in Dublin. Home Rule on O'Connell's terms, however, meant something radically different from the parliamentary independence which had been extinguished in 1800, and as early as 1833 the historian Thomas Babington Macaulay had pointed out in the House of Commons that O'Connell's reasons for a parliament in Dublin could be invoked for one in Londonderry, then regarded as a Protestant stronghold in the north.[12]

During 1842–3 the repeal campaign, by reviving the methods which had achieved Catholic emancipation and adding the new tactic of mass rallies known as monster meetings, gained momentum. But this time O'Connell faced a British government which was united on the issue and had the overwhelming support of parliament. The circumstances were different from those of 1829, and he was forced to give way, calling off the monster meeting which had been summoned to assemble at Clontarf in October 1843. The government held firm and was prepared to put troops on the roads and in the fields. Obliged to choose between letting loose the civil war he had so successfully held *in terrorem* over the government's head and living up to his principles of non-violence, he took the honourable course. By so doing, however, he slipped down several notches in the pantheon of Ireland's patriot heroes and martyrs. Today he is remembered as the Liberator, but not as the Repealer; yet he is the architect of the modern Republic of Ireland, and, some would argue, of partition.

The real consequences of the repeal movement were not those O'Connell had anticipated. It provoked into existence the Young Irelanders, a group of young educated men, Catholic and Protestant, who worked out an intellectual ideal of Irish nationality, irrespective of descent or creed, which formed the basis, in theory at least, for much nationalist thinking in the future. Their nationalism was imbued with Romanticism, responding once again to European influences, mainly literary, and it contained an element of revolutionary violence, for their heroes were the United Irishmen and the rebels of 1798. On this, and on many other issues, including the vexed question of a new non-sectarian university in Ireland, they came into sharp collision with O'Connell. His support for the Catholic bishops in their condemnation of the 'Godless colleges' revealed him in their eyes as a bigot. However, just as it is unfair to O'Connell to suggest that his personal view of nationhood was sectarian, it is unrealistic to suppose that their ideas could have triumphed in practice. As with the United Irishmen, we tend to take what was said for what was actually achieved. It is the perennial Irish failing.

Famine

However we regard it the Famine must appear as a watershed in the Union period. It, too, was a revolution, but not one brought about by any human agency. Academic historians now hesitate to blame England, or the Irish landlords, or any single specific source for the magnitude of the disaster. As we have seen, famine was not just an event of the nineteenth century, but a constant in Irish history, and it already had a language of its own. What happened after 1845 was a natural catastrophe, magnified by human frailty, short-sightedness and at times cold indifference, but these are not simple absolutes applicable to whole nations or even whole groups and classes of people. Alongside them, and interacting with them, were strength, far-sightedness, warm compassion and sacrifice. The attitude of the Tories when they were in government in 1845 was, in fact, more liberal and compassionate than was that of the Whigs who succeeded them in office the following year.

The way in which the Famine has been remembered has caused the scale and dedication of the relief efforts to be forgotten. Quite apart from the public attempts to mitigate the disaster, there were impressive contributions by voluntary charities. Lionel de Rothschild, heading the efforts of the Jewish community, helped to set up the British Association for Relief in Ireland, negotiated a Famine loan of £8 million, and diverted his own ships to Irish ports with cargoes of grain he had paid for himself.[13] The census report for 1851 recorded that the Society of Friends (the Quakers) in the United Kingdom 'were foremost in the field of benevolent action, and the British Association was the most prompt in its measures of charity'.[14]

Subsequently the lack of vision and humanity was *all* that was remembered, and remembered with ever-increasing bitterness. Many nations (most, indeed) have the gift of forgetting their worst experiences, but not Ireland. The Famine memory has strengthened rather than weakened, until it has poisoned almost every aspect of Anglo-Irish relations. England had many enemies who immediately supported the Irish recriminations; England was hated and envied in Europe for all kinds of commercial and political reasons, but no European nation regarded the English as a specially cruel or illiberal people. There was a good deal of evidence to the contrary, as far as oppressed small nations were concerned – the paradox was indeed commented upon at the time – and England was, and continued to be, a refuge for dissidents from countries who deplored its democratic indolence. For the Irish, however, the Famine was a crime against humanity which could be laid at the door of the perpetrators of the sack of Drogheda, the land confiscations, the brutal suppression of the 1798 Rebellion, and the yoke of the Union, and the English educated classes have not been slow to accept the gravamina of these charges, to acknowledge their guilt, and even apologise for it, to the further confusion of Anglo-Irish relations.

The recognition of these facts in no way dilutes the horror of the Famine. It was the last famine in western Europe, and the immediate suffering is a matter of copious record. It is flagged in European history by the halving of the population, through various causes, in the years which followed. From 8.5 million in 1841, the population of Ireland dropped to just over half of that a hundred years later. Today the population of the island, including both jurisdictions, is still just over 5 million, of which 1.5 million live in Northern Ireland. In the same period the population graphs of Scotland and Wales show a gentle upward curve, and England a very steep one, but for Ireland the rising curve falters at 1845, and falls almost perpendicularly for the next twenty years.

The aggregation of circumstances which history calls the Irish Famine is not, however, a single catastrophic event in 1845. It was an accumulating disaster which sent shock waves through Irish society for two decades and more. Blight continued to affect the potato crop for the next five years. The major cause of death was not starvation, as is so often believed, but the terrible epidemic diseases which swiftly followed in the wake of food shortages and malnutrition – typhus, relapsing fever, dysentery and, in 1849, cholera. No part of the country escaped, as the movement of the destitute towards the towns and workhouses carried disease from county to county. Mortality was highest in the towns, where the fevers ravaged the workhouses. The east suffered less than the west, and the north-east suffered least, but nowhere escaped.

The Famine destroyed the unstable Irish economy which had developed during the Napoleonic Wars. The dramatic fall in population altered the framework of Irish society. Between 1845 and 1851 the population fell by 2 million. Of these, approximately half perished from malnutrition or disease, and half emigrated to Britain or North America. In rural society the cottier class almost disappeared. On the political level the whole Irish question was given a new dimension by the Irish in the United States, Australia and elsewhere.

Despite these seismic waves moving through the Irish nation, politics as such seemed inert. As so often, the surface impression was misleading, for the character of the agitation which resurfaced after 1870 was profoundly influenced by the upheavals of the 1840s. Above all, the land question came to the forefront of Irish politics, and stayed there until the end of the century. The assault on the Union was renewed on two fronts. In 1858 a number of men who had been involved in the abortive Young Ireland uprising of 1848 founded the Irish Republican Brotherhood in Dublin. While accepting Thomas Davies's non-sectarian definition of nationality, they believed that Britain would never concede Irish independence unless forced to do so by violent revolution. They also realised that the Irish emigrant communities which had developed in the United States since the Famine provided an opportunity to widen the assault on Britain; consequently the Fenian Brotherhood was also founded in New York at this time. So began a recurrent theme of modern Irish history: the United States as a reservoir of money, men and grievance against Britain which could be tapped in the cause of Irish nationalism.

Today we see the Fenians as the men who passed on the torch of republicanism from the United Irishmen to the insurgents of 1916, and passed it on without examining the flame too closely. Ignoring all other issues, including to a large extent land reform, they concentrated on the theme of physical force. When finally they attempted their coup in 1867, the government knew all it needed to know about them, and most of the leaders were already in prison. The Fenians, like the Young Irelanders, were never more than a minority in nationalist politics, but once again their ideas, and perhaps more their actions, profoundly affected the shape of Irish history.

Home Rule

For the immediate future Irish hopes lay with the Home Rule movement, which had been founded in 1870 by a Protestant lawyer, Isaac Butt. Originally conceived as a moderate force campaigning for a federalist system of Irish self-government, the Home Rule movement developed from the late 1870s into a national pressure group, headed by the Irish MPs at Westminster, who increasingly turned to obstructing parliamentary business in order to focus attention on Ireland's grievances. Butt was replaced as leader by Charles Stewart Parnell, a Protestant landlord from County Wicklow, and a political leader of great skill. In 1879 the crucial connection between the 'national question' and the 'land question' was struck in the 'New Departure'. This fusion of Parnell's Home Rule parliamentary party, Michael Davitt's land agitation against the landlords, and the revolutionary oath-bound America-based Fenian Brotherhood proved a powerful combination.

Davitt's Land League had the support of the Catholic clergy, and the so-called 'land war' of 1879–82 was the biggest mass movement in modern Ireland, paralysing the legal system in the west, and at one point virtually assuming the functions of a government. Both the seriousness of the land war and the extent to which it foreshadowed the events of 1919–23 are somewhat underplayed in history textbooks, at least in their revolutionary aspects. To a considerable degree the disorders of the land war dictated the form and pattern of the 'troubles' of the twentieth century.

Even before the land agitation reached its height, William Ewart Gladstone, then in Opposition, had embarked on his campaign to do justice to Ireland. From the days of his first Liberal ministry in 1868–74 Gladstone always made it clear that the moral content of public policy was paramount. It was his peculiar contribution to Irish history that he presided over a revolution in government thinking on Ireland with which he was not personally in sympathy, obeying, as he saw it, a higher moral dictate. A devout Anglican who in 1839 had written a book to defend the principle of Church establishment, he nevertheless disestablished the Church of Ireland in 1869. A landowner who carefully instructed his son in the rights and duties of proprietors, he deliberately undermined the legal rights of Irish landowners by the Land Acts of 1870 and 1881. Finally, a British patriot (though never an uncritical one), he resolved to split the United Kingdom itself by attempting to repeal the Act of Union in 1886 and again in 1893, but each time failing to carry parliament with him.

Gladstone had come to realise, from a long study of the subject, that all those principles and institutions which he cherished most in the English political system simply did not work in Ireland. The consequences of this revolution, even if it was but the logical outcome of 1829, were so staggering that they were not fully appreciated by contemporaries. Gladstone's assertion in 1868 that his mission was 'to pacify Ireland' has created the impression that the rest of his career was devoted to that mission. This view was popularised by J.L. Hammond's classic *Gladstone and the Irish Nation* (1938), which has greatly coloured the history textbooks. In fact this is a distorted perspective, based on a very simple idea of what politics is about. It has been cogently argued that Gladstone's Irish policy, and especially his conversion to Home Rule, must be seen as the practical and day-to-day response of a Prime Minister to party pressures and the strength of domestic and foreign opinion, rather than a grand design.[15] Now that all his correspondence is in print, there is a good deal of evidence to suggest that this was so.

It is worth noticing also that Gladstone did not follow his intuition that Ireland was 'different' into the convoluted recesses of the Ulster problem. He seemed, indeed, to have an uncharacteristic blind spot there; even John Morley, his Chief Secretary for Ireland, declared that he gave the question no real thought. This was undoubtedly an unfair exaggeration, but it was heartily endorsed by a deputation of Belfast businessmen who waited on him at No. 10 in 1886. One of them came away declaring that the Prime Minister was clearly insane.[16]

Neglect of thorough research into a problem facing him was not a habit of Gladstone's. Famously, he stands apart from most other prime ministers in this respect, and there is evidence that he did strive to understand the roots of the 'Ulster' objection to Home Rule. Introducing the Government of Ireland Bill 1886 (to give it its proper title) he was, not surprisingly, anxious to minimise the threats of massive resistance, even by force of arms, dismissing them as 'momentary ebullitions, which will pass away with the fears from which they spring'.[17] On the defeat of the Bill, Belfast was in flames, the precursor of many near-civil-war situations that have occurred since then. Some 115 years later the ebullitions are still with us, which tends to confirm Tolstoy's view that great men are not really the makers of history, but its victims.

After the failure of Gladstone's second Home Rule Bill in 1893 the transfer of authority in Ireland into Irish hands was really completed by the legislation of Conservative governments between 1895 and 1905, as they attempted to 'kill Home Rule by kindness'. The strategy was to separate Home Rule from the land campaign. It failed because it turned out that the Irish wanted, not the substance of Home Rule, but the letter. As George Bernard Shaw was to point out, self-determination is not for the good of people, it is for their satisfaction. It was just at this time that the 'new nationalism' was born, leading ultimately to the last of the revolutions of the Union period, and the only one which goes by that name in the history books, and in the national consciousness.

Revolution

It is reasonable to fear that the Revolution, like Saturn,
might devour its children one by one.

PIERRE VERGNIAUD[1]

Interlude

O ne of the fascinations of historical research is to seek explanations for those apparently complete changes which overtake an entire population in the course of a few years. Certain rhythms in history are obvious. Sons disown the mental baggage of fathers, and grandsons reclaim it. The pendulum of popular opinion swings far in one direction, and inexorably retraces its path. Revolutions begin, not when things are at their worst, but when they are getting better, and they usually end with the return to power of the classes and concepts against which they are directed. The view of Ireland which is held by people who are not Irish is that nothing ever changes there; attitudes and prejudices are ingrained. This is obviously true at one level, but it is not entirely borne out by Irish history. Irish opinion can be surprisingly malleable.

It is impossible to assign one simple reason for the dramatic change which occurred in Ireland between the death of Parnell in 1891 and the 1916 Rising. In retrospect we are aware that the former event seems to end an era. Parnell was a comparatively young man when he died (he was only forty-five), but Dublin wept for 'poor oul' Parnell'.[2] The deeper effects of Parnell's fall were not immediately apparent. The formal shell of politics continued in existence for twenty-five years, but under the shell many changes were taking place. Popular movements were springing up which had aims different from, and even antagonistic to, those of the Irish Parliamentary Party. The new forces were no more immutable nor indestructible than those which they replaced, but in time they were to provide nationalist Ireland with new orthodoxies.

At the time no one could see the ways in which they would change the shape of the 'Irish question' in the twentieth century. Though the reasons for this change are complex, and to some extent still obscure, some of them can readily be identified. In the first place Irish society was undergoing (though very gradually when compared to other western societies) the process which historians have come to call 'modernisation'. It is an unsatisfying and treacherous term, since it involves some rudimentary misunderstanding of the meaning of the word 'modern', a word which has no validity whatever when used historically. That which is modern becomes history with each passing second. But in so far as 'modernisation' indicates certain kinds of social and political change as a result of industrial or scientific revolutions – advances in technology, democracy, literacy and political organisation – it is a useful enough term for historians. With fashionable usage, however, it hardens into a concept or even dogma, and this in turn is used as a measure of a nation's development, as if time had decided to stand still.

What it means in Ireland can best be seen if we compare Irish society in 1900 with what it had been at the time of the Union. For one thing, society in 1900 was markedly more egalitarian. The effect of Catholic emancipation, the disestablishment of the Church of Ireland, land legislation, and the undermining of the Ascendancy was to create a society which was less preoccupied with class than was English society. It could be argued, of course, that divisions of class had been replaced by those of religion. Irish society was more politically awakened than it had been in the first half of the century. Contrary to popular belief, it had always been comparatively literate, and it was now served by a plethora of national and provincial newspapers.

Emigration to America, though rooted in hardship, ultimately widened Irish horizons, creating an Irish empire overseas, and tapping into a vast reservoir of anti-British sentiment. The coming of the railway, and later the motor car, to Ireland transformed communications and stimulated commerce. By 1900 Ireland, which had suffered much, was in the fortunate position of enjoying all the harvest of the Industrial Revolution without having to undergo the horrors of the satanic mills. While the country could not be said to be in the van of Europe's technical and scientific progress, most of its blessings were to reach Ireland in time.

Many of these blessings came from the hand of the oppressor, but earned him no praise. Far from expressing any gratitude, the Irish continued to accuse him of having brought about the Famine as a deliberate act of policy. The most obvious effect of commercial and technical progress was, in the eyes of some Irish people, to accelerate the pace of anglicisation. What England had failed to achieve with its soldiers, it would attempt with an army of commercial travellers. As a matter of fact it is doubtful that this was actually the case. By the late nineteenth century the process was as complete as it was ever likely to be. What modernisation did was to make it more obvious, or perhaps to set up some kind of friction between modernity as such and the continuing veneration for a peculiarly strong Irish heritage and history, something which is clearly seen to be happening today. A century later, Ireland still balances uneasily between enjoying all the technical wonders of the global village and wallowing in the sentiment of a rich cultural past of a rain-soaked island cut off from the contamination of the world.

However this may be, Irish nationalists in the last quarter of the nineteenth century felt that Ireland was becoming more English in culture, and that the old, distinctive Irish culture (meaning largely the Gaelic version of it) was rapidly attenuating. The new cultural influences which came into play in the south and west of Ireland were a deliberate defiance of this anglicisation.

All states need a focus, a metropolis or central locality, which in time acts as a standard of the national culture. The British state, as distinct from the country known as England, has really existed only since the eighteenth century. London and the Home Counties became by chance the focus and standard for the whole of the British Isles, the national centre of wealth, political power and *English* culture. As old local bonds were weakened by modernisation, the magnetic pull of London increased, and 'British' was stamped on every product which poured into village shops from the Hebrides to Connemara. Moreover, after 1880 London was also the heart of the most powerful and wealthy empire on the face of the globe. If this brought great material benefits to Ireland, rarely acknowledged, it is also true that Irish soldiers were in the forefront of every one of Britain's imperial wars. Irish opinion on the Empire was schizophrenic. While some Irishmen felt themselves to be at the very centre of the Empire, others considered themselves as virtual slaves in England's oldest, and most abused, colony. It was by no means uncommon for both of these sentiments to be entertained simultaneously. This duality is still strong, and is one reason why Irish nationalists seem in English eyes so much more interesting than Irish unionists.

Many of the Irish MPs at the time had no special enthusiasm for arresting or rejecting the anglicising process. They thundered against British imperial rule in Ireland, but wanted a Home Rule parliament in Dublin that would presumably be modelled on Westminster. Under its sway Ireland would be able to continue to participate in all the benefits of Empire, such as they were. Even in appearance these men, with their beards and pince-nez, began to have an outmoded air. Their politics were associated with the shame of the Parnell affair and a failed initiative. It was as if they were marking time, waiting for the dawn of some anticipated new initiative. They had been weighed in the balance by the

Church, suspicious of their anti-clericalism, and found wanting. Young people were growing up, conscious that the aspiration for independence had been frustrated, and that meanwhile Ireland was losing its distinctive identity. There was also developing a voguish and sentimental, but genuine, enthusiasm for reviving the Irish language and Gaelic culture.

This turning back to an older ethnic culture was not, of course, peculiar to Ireland at the time. Once again we are called on to witness the chemical interaction which occurs when influences from outside Ireland are allowed to play upon the quintessential Irish compound. This impulse came from central Europe where, within the confines of the Austro-Hungarian Empire, artists and intellectuals were seeking to recover submerged national identities by cultural rather than political means. In all these regions, cultural revival was to prove a potent stimulus to revolutionary movements. And so it was in Ireland.

There were other influences at work in late nineteenth-century Europe, less well defined but equally part of the *Zeitgeist*, among them the cult of physical fitness and athletic prowess – the Olympic Games were revived in 1896 by the Baron de Coubertin – and the scientific study of 'race'. The careful delineation of racial characteristics and the division of mankind into distinct groups seemed at the time to be a popular advance in scientific knowledge. Heads were measured and racial features classified to create mountains of statistics, and inevitably theories of superiority and inferiority were constructed on them. The malign development of these theories in the twentieth century, particularly in Nazi Germany, stripped the science of all respectability and created an atmosphere in which the very word race is taken to be an incitement to hideous crimes against humanity.

The subject was one of some sensitivity for Irish public opinion. The traditional English prejudice against the Irish had been reinforced by a succession of terrorist outrages, and the Irishman was regularly depicted in the pages of *Punch* and elsewhere as an ape-like creature with a long simian upper lip, dressed in ragged clothes and carrying a weapon. By contrast Irish women were generally portrayed as sad and beautiful, and this was the customary representation of Ireland itself, an indication, perhaps, of England's ambivalent reactions. A new enthusiasm for 'the Gaelic race' or 'the Irish race' was, therefore, to some extent a compensation, and these terms are still used unselfconsciously, especially by Irish Americans. In the terms of the time this implied an actual belief that the

Irish were genetically separate from the hated Saxon, a myth finally laid to rest by research into DNA.

The Gaelic Athletic Association was formed in 1884 in imitation of the Czech gymnastic clubs, with the blessing of Archbishop Thomas Croke of Cashel; under the association's code, 'such foreign and fantastic field-sports as lawn tennis, polo, croquet, cricket and the like' were banned.[3] The GAA quickly established a strong rural network, which was later put to political and paramilitary use. In 1893 the Gaelic League was founded to foster the use of the Irish language. Its leading light and first president was Douglas Hyde, the son of a Church of Ireland clergyman. The previous year Hyde had made a seminal contribution to the new consciousness in a lecture entitled 'On the Necessity for De-Anglicising the Irish People'. The Gaelic League was the vanguard for a whole plethora of literary, artistic and cultural movements, which collectively added up to the Gaelic Revival and which powerfully underpinned the new politics.

One strand in this was the kind of romantic nationalism associated with figures such as W.B. Yeats and Lady Gregory, who founded the Irish Literary Theatre – later the Abbey – in 1899. Yeats's play *Cathleen ni Houlihan* of 1902, in which Ireland appears symbolically, first as an old woman and then as a beautiful young girl, evoked an overwhelming emotional response from the public. Many years later, at the end of his life, its author was to ask

> Did that play of mine send out
> Certain men the English shot?[4]

The answer is 'Probably not', but, as happens in art, the play caught the exact mood of the time. It was also the last brief appearance of the Ascendancy in the house of nationhood.

Crisis

The period between 1891 and 1916 was, to quote Conor Cruise O'Brien, not so much a lull between storms as an interval between a verdict and a sentence.[5] In retrospect it is startling to discover that, as early as 1885, the pattern of much that has happened since was already abundantly clear. It was in fact revealed in the elections of that year, the first to be held on the household franchise created in 1884. These indicated large nationalist majorities in every county except in eastern Ulster. Neither the divisions within the Irish Parliamentary Party, nor the eventual disappearance of that party in 1918, altered that basic and menacing religious pattern. The nationalism which underlay the Home Rule majority was after all more durable than the party, which was merely its transient and expendable vehicle. If Home Rule had been won in 1886, it would not have for long, or even at all, fulfilled Irish hopes.

Nor would it have been accepted by the Ulster Protestants. Many of them had been loyal Gladstonian Liberals, keeping alive (some have argued) the traditions of the Presbyterian radicals of the 1790s; but when Gladstone announced his conversion to Home Rule, they became unionists overnight. This had important economic implications for Ireland, because the crisis occurred at the apogee of Belfast's meteoric rise to industrial prosperity. The Liberals had performed strongly there in the elections of the 1860s. Now, when Belfast was the world's linen capital and boasted the world's largest shipyards, ropeworks and engineering manufacture, the Liberal industrialists became unionists, moving in the opposite direction to their counterparts in Belfast today.

The basic facts of the Irish situation were these, from whatever side you looked at them. The independence of Ireland was inevitable, but it could not come about without a civil war in some form or other. Once again, as in 1689 and 1798, it seemed that the issue of Ireland's independence would be tested by armed conflict. Indeed the *fin de siècle* coincidence was a menacing pattern in Irish history by itself.

The absolute determination of the Ulster Protestants to resist, if necessary by force, being brought under the authority of an independent Irish government, despite all the assurances that might be given to them from either the English or the Irish side, was already the real Irish question. This is, of course, a matter of controversy. There are those, not least among them Irish Protestants, who argue that if only Gladstone's Home Rule Bill of 1886 had been allowed to pass, the Irish question would have been solved, or would, at the very least, never have assumed the acute form which it took on in the twentieth century. If this is true, then the Bill's rejection by the House of Commons has proved to be one of the most expensive mistakes in its history.

However, there is much evidence to suggest that it is not true. Another of the unlighted areas of Irish history is the determination in Ulster in 1886 and 1893 to raise and arm a militia, and, if necessary, to set up a provisional government for the north. Again, it is argued that if Lord Randolph Churchill and other Conservative politicians had not encouraged the Ulster resistance for their own political ends, Irishmen would have solved their difficulties peacefully in the long run. But the plain fact is that the Orangemen, and those who thought like them, needed no Churchill to tell them how to act. They would have acted in the same way, come hell or high water, as they were to do in 1912. They might, of course, have been swiftly overwhelmed by the British army, but if that had been allowed to happen, it would not have solved the Ulster problem but exacerbated it, and Ulstermen would have turned against a nationalist government in Dublin all those devices of sabotage and civil disobedience at which the Irish are so fatally adept.

The culmination of the long and bitter Home Rule struggle was the Ulster crisis of 1912–14, when the northern Protestants were obliged (as they saw it) to put into operation their plan of armed defiance by raising a citizen army of almost 100,000 men, the Ulster Volunteer Force, and by appointing their own provisional government. They were led by Sir Edward Carson, a Dublin Protestant lawyer and one of the leading advocates of the time, who had risen to high political office as Solicitor-General for England in 1900. Carson, after careful thought, risked his career by putting himself at the head of the unionist opposition to the Home Rule Bill introduced in the Commons in 1912 by the Liberal Prime Minister, H.H. Asquith. A leader of the utmost determination, Carson soon showed that, with the support of powerful elements in British politics and society, he was prepared to go outside the constitution to defeat the Bill. In unionist eyes the proposed legislation was extra-constitutional, to be resisted by every means inside and outside parliament, while their opponents accused them of blatant treason. Though the crisis seemed at times almost to threaten civil war (not just in Ireland, but also in Britain), the government dared not arrest Carson and the Ulster leader Sir James Craig, so broad was their support throughout the United Kingdom.

At this point it is worth remembering that 'unionist' is not a word of fixed content between 1886 and the present. Unionism was, to begin with, a political creed held by half the British nation. In the course of the successive Home Rule crises it came to mean in a more limited sense the platform of unionists in every part of the island of Ireland, and finally, after the 1921 settlement, it was restricted to meaning the unionists of Ulster. Undoubtedly the Ulster resistance was the trump card in Carson's hand, and when he lost the game in 1921, the Ulster unionists did not completely understand his feelings. He had declared that the Union was the lodestar of his existence, and when it set, for Ireland as a whole, he experienced the full bitterness of an irrevocable defeat. At this point, however, the Ulster unionists floated clear of the wreckage and accepted their own form of Home Rule.

The Ulster crisis was undoubtedly an influence, though not the only one, on the events leading to insurrection in Dublin in 1916. When, in later years, Eoin MacNeill was asked what the decisive factor was in bringing about the Easter Rising, he replied with one word: 'Carson'. Yet to suggest, as is so frequently done, that the Ulster unionists by their determination to stay British, in some way unleashed the violence that was to ravage Ireland between 1916 and 1923 is to misread the varied and complex factors which brought that conflict about, and to suggest that the history of Ireland since 1800 was other than it was.

The blood sacrifice of 1916, rejected at the time by the vast majority of the Irish population, is now seen as one of the birth-pangs of modern Ireland. It brought forward the last revolution of the period, the astonishingly swift transfer of sympathy from John Redmond and the Irish Parliamentary Party to Sinn Féin, which took place between the military executions of 1916 and the general election of 1918.

It has another significance, however, because it was, like the revolt of the American colonies, not a revolution in the fullest sense. It did not overturn or destroy the structure of society. The republicanism it proclaimed had been the most conservative force in nineteenth-century Ireland. It had not changed in substance since Tone's day, and, as we have seen, Tone had totally missed the signs of the coming industrial revolution, when he recorded the increase in the use of machinery around Belfast in 1792. The Rising was a sudden flash of lightning that revealed to what extent the main features of the surrounding landscape had altered.

Blood Work

S ome perplexing questions remain. Why was it necessary for the Union
to end in an Anglo-Irish war? At Easter 1916 the administration of
Ireland was, as far as local government was concerned, already largely in
Irish hands. Augustine Birrell was confident that he would be the last
Chief Secretary. Home Rule had been on the statute-book for two years,
its implementation merely suspended for the duration of the world war.
But Dublin Castle was still there, and the Lord Lieutenant was, as his
predecessors had been throughout the Union, still the symbol of ultimate
English authority over the other island. Why did Britain so tenaciously
refuse to let go? Why had a military struggle to take place, and why was it
so murderously bitter, with all the characteristics of a civil war, poisoning
Anglo-Irish relations, and North–South relations in Ireland itself, right
down to the present? And why did it provoke a real civil war among the
victors?

One obvious element was to be found in the tangled history of the
north, which disastrously complicated the whole question of withdrawal.
In the end it led the English to focus all their odium and frustration not on
their Irish enemies but on their Irish friends, as on a difficult but loyal
elderly relative who had not the good taste to die. Between 1912 and 1922
the attitude of the English press to unionists changed from one of en-
thusiastic support to one of coldness and criticism.

But another part of the answer is to be found in an element which is
often ignored because it is silent and unobtrusive: the existence of English
nationalism – English in a precise sense, for, as Gladstone pointed out in
1886, Scotland and Wales would have granted Ireland its independence in
an instant, an earnest, perhaps, of their own future aspirations. The history of the 120 years of the Union shows that England was prepared to
concede, if reluctantly, every important point except one: its national
security and strategic military defence.

On the Irish side the guerrilla campaigns of 1919–21 provided the War
of Independence which created the national legend of the new Ireland.
That Irish freedom could be achieved only by the gun and the bomb
accorded with earlier Irish history, and came to be accepted by the Irish
people. The price of such acceptance has been incalculable, and the
Anglo–Irish Treaty of 1921 left Ireland with tensions more terrible than

those created by the Union. It changed the form but not the substance of Irish problems. Far from bringing peace, it was immediately followed by the Irish Civil War, not the terrible civil war between Catholic and Protestant which is always impending in Irish history, and so far always averted, but a war between brothers, between Catholic and Catholic, Free Stater and Republican.

Yet the Catholic Irish state which emerged so bloodily from the turmoil of 1916–23 was the Ireland of O'Connell, not that of the terrorists and extremists. The war was fought in the south and west over the future of the six north-eastern counties, which the Treaty had allowed to opt out of the newly independent state and to remain in the United Kingdom. The 'Ulster' problem has been at the core of Anglo–Irish difficulties ever since. It is a double problem, combining the historic antagonism between the Protestant and Catholic populations within Northern Ireland with the nationalist determination to 'free' the six counties from British rule. They are by no means the same thing, although they are so regarded in England and abroad. The first is mistakenly identified as the cause of the second, but in fact the opposite is true.

The classical rhetoric of separatism always represents Britain as the invader and conqueror, who for eight centuries has occupied Ireland by force. But, for over a century now, Britain's problem has not been how to get into Ireland, but how to get out of it.

Sinn Féin's landslide victory in the election of 1918, and the virtual elimination of the old Irish Parliamentary Party which had fought the Home Rule campaign for so long, astonished observers at the time. They sensed that some new and dangerous force was at work in Irish society. Afterwards it was seen as the first direct consequence of the 1916 Rising, and particularly the insensitivity of the British in executing sixteen of the rebel leaders. Any Irish person could have told them the consequences, but it was George Bernard Shaw who put it in memorable words. They were canonising their prisoners.

> It is impossible to slaughter a man in this position without making him a martyr and a hero, even though the day before the Rising he may have been only a minor poet. The shot Irishmen will now take their places beside Emmet and the Manchester martys in Ireland, and beside the heros of Poland and Serbia and Belgium in Europe; and nothing in heaven or on the earth can prevent it.[6]

Moreover, Shaw accurately predicted that a time would come, after 'Romance has covered their graves with flowers', when 'the last of the Irish rebellions will be a stock subject of British heroic verse'.

In the background, however, two factors were at work in 1918 which have received much less attention. David Lloyd George sprang his 'coupon' election on the United Kingdom within a month of the armistice. It is impossible to read the newspapers of that time without being oppressed by a sense of desolation and tragedy. Half the columns are taken up with the names and photographs of soldiers who died in the last hours of the conflict, and the other half with the names of those dying in the influenza outbreak. Again one is reminded of Huizinga's words about the fourteenth century: 'An everlasting call of memento mori sounds through life.' For the next five years, the period of revolution and extreme violence in Ireland, the shadow of the Great War still hangs over society. Human life had become very cheap. The young men in the trenches had seen things that few at home in civilian life could begin to imagine. The survivors, including the mutilated, the gassed and the shell-shocked, were promised they would return to 'a land fit for heroes'. Instead they faced illness and unemployment, and, in Ireland, a changed political landscape and civil unrest. The shadow of the unemployed ex-serviceman would materialise in Ireland a year or two later as a Black and Tan or Auxiliary, and even sometimes as an IRA gunman. Both Joseph O'Sullivan and Reginald Dunne, the IRA men who assassinated Field-Marshal Sir Henry Wilson on the steps of his home in London in June 1922, had fought on the Western Front, O'Sullivan in the Munster Fusiliers and Dunne in the Irish Guards.[7] In Ulster the war had another effect. The decimation of the 36th (Ulster) Division on the Somme in 1916 made the Ulster Protestant's stance on Home Rule secure, because it had claimed the flower of the pre-war Ulster Volunteer Force.

There was a second factor in the demoralisation of Irish society in 1918, which most history books do not even mention – Spanish 'flu. The influenza pandemic which swept the world in 1918 and 1919 is ranked with the Black Death as one of the worst in recorded history. It killed more people than the world war, something like 20 million in all. But because many more recovered, it caused less panic than bubonic plague. It took its name from the fact that it appeared first in Spain in 1917, before spreading to the battle fronts. It reached the Turkish, Austro-Hungarian and German lines a few weeks before affecting the Allies, perhaps therefore having an impact on the conduct of the war in its last stages. The Germans called it *Blitz Katarrh*, the British 'Flanders grippe'.[8]

It was on the home front, however, that it caused most devastation. From the French seaports it reached Britain and Ireland, and then crossed the Atlantic and caused fearful havoc in the United States. Spanish 'flu was of the most virulent kind, often causing death among young people after only a few hours of fever. The US medical authorities could not contain it. In the cities of New York, Boston and Philadelphia all public meetings were cancelled; churches, theatres and bars closed; mortuaries were full, coffins became scarce and there were mass burials. In all, half a million Americans died. Who, reading the conventional history of the United States in the twentieth century, would guess at such scenes?[9]

Ireland, too, had its fair share of Spanish 'flu, and this was the gloomy background of the 1918 general election. If the history books have little to say about its effect on Irish politics and society, at least one very distinguished historian has given us his vivid childhood memory of the experience. In a personal afterword to his book *Crisis and Decline* R.B. McDowell has recorded:

> Shortly before the war ended I was involved in a major world catastrophe, the 1918 'flu epidemic. I clearly remember one autumn morning lying back in a large chair in the morning room, feeling very ill (a new, unpleasant sensation) with my parents and the doctor looking down at me with deep concern. I next remember waking up in bed, wondering why my pyjamas had been slashed. I had been unconscious for days with double pneumonia, and on one occasion the doctor had been compelled to break the news to my parents that I would not survive the night.[10]

The Irish Free State which emerged from the wreckage of revolution and civil war was not the independent country of which nationalists had dreamed. It consisted of only twenty-six of the thirty-two counties of Ireland; it was not an Irish Republic but a dominion within the British Commonwealth; it was not the 'New Ireland' of turn-of-the-century aspirations but essentially O'Connell's polity of the Catholic middle class. Moreover, it faced the most alarming perils. The republicans had surrendered to superior force, but they had no intention of giving up their campaign, and they enjoyed considerable and increasing sympathy as the new government of W.T. Cosgrave established itself. On the other hand any administration had to avoid a complete and obvious subservience to the Catholic Church, or the encouragement of those elements in Irish society who wanted to follow the example of Mussolini's Italy. Then there was the stark reality of the economy. Stripped of any further reliance on the British Treasury, the Free State had to face some unpalatable choices, like cutting pensions and benefits or keeping them to pre-1922 levels. The political separation was more drastic than the economic, however, for 98 per cent of all Irish exports still went to Britain.

The Free State survived by being ruthlessly pragmatic, and it enjoyed two considerable advantages. The first was that it could deal with subversion against the state in ways which the British could not employ. Britain had changed the course of Irish history, and affronted world opinion, by the military execution of sixteen Irishmen for the crime of treason in wartime; the Free State executed seventy-seven republicans during the Civil War, including the English-born writer Erskine Childers, without the world paying much attention. As the IRA continued attacks on police stations and assassinations, culminating in 1927 in the murder of the Minister for Justice, Kevin O'Higgins, its adherents were rounded up and given long prison sentences. Yet at no time during these years did the Free State cease to be a democracy.

The second advantage was that the Free State was overnight freed from the problem of governing the northern Protestant population which made up a quarter of the island's total, a problem which was the fatal inheritance of centuries of sectarian hatred and mistrust. It was able to intensify the campaign of protest and propaganda against partition without the risk of having to deal with any of the practicalities. The unionist government of the North was vilified on every possible occasion, and both moderate nationalists and republicans gave their fullest support to, and expressed solidarity with, the northern Catholic community in its grievances. By contrast the government of Northern Ireland never interfered after 1922 in the affairs of independent Ireland.

The downside of this advantage was that the Free State was able to develop into an all-but-homogeneous Catholic state, in which the Church exercised enormous influence over political decisions, especially in areas like health and education. The Protestant population was relatively small, and has since dwindled to something like 5 per cent; and, in the absence of any unionist or other representative political organisation, it was docile. Even Orangeism became just a cultural event, though one, it must be said, generously tolerated at official level. The partition of Ireland was never intended to be a permanent solution, but the steady development of the southern state as a predominantly Catholic state instead of a pluralist one meant that the gap between the two parts of Ireland widened.[11]

The alienation progressed further when, in 1932, the republican Fianna Fáil party won the general election, and Eamon de Valera led his followers (some armed with handguns) back into the Dáil, the Irish parliament. Cosgrave handed over the seals of authority to de Valera in what must be a very rare political occurrence: 'the victors in a civil war peacefully re-linquishing office to the representative figures among the losers in that war'.[12] Once in power de Valera began a policy of unilaterally repudiating the provisions of the Anglo–Irish Treaty. He also ceased the payment of arrears to Britain on the land annuity debt, provoking an economic war with Britain which imposed great hardship on the Irish people. In 1937 the Free State adopted a new constitution which claimed sovereignty over Northern Ireland and recognised the special position of the Roman Catholic Church. A year later de Valera negotiated a settlement with the British Prime Minister, Neville Chamberlain, which ended the economic war and cancelled the defence clauses of the Treaty. Britain handed back the so-called 'Treaty ports' – the retained naval bases – at the very moment when they were about to be needed. When war with Nazi Germany came in September 1939, de Valera chose to remain neutral, and the South's 'refusal to allow the Allies use of her western and southern coastlines, even though she herself depended largely upon the supplies the convoys brought her, contributed immensely to the Allied losses in the Atlantic'.[13] This caused great bitterness and completed the alienation of Northern Ireland, a situation hardly affected by the South's leaving the Commonwealth in 1949 and declaring itself the Republic of Ireland.

For Northern Ireland the situation was very different. There the minority Catholic population amounted to a third of the total, and despite differing party loyalties it never formed a political opposition in the conventional sense. This was because its representatives not only opposed almost every action of the government but did not want it to exist at all. From 1920 until the suspension of the Northern Ireland government and the imposition of direct rule from London in 1972 most of their political energy was devoted to the government's destruction, rather than co-operative attempts to re-form it, or make the system more democratic. The attempts of the IRA to destabilise the fledgling administration froze it into a mode of depending on Special Powers legislation against republican activists, interning suspects and banning flags and emblems.

When the Treaty was signed in 1921 Northern Ireland was allowed to exclude itself from the settlement only on condition that unionists accepted a Boundary Commission to redraw the border – in 1920 a line had simply been drawn round county boundaries. The Irish Civil War had delayed its meeting until 1924, by which time Northern Ireland as constituted was a secure and stable political entity. The Boundary Commission recommended the transfer of some small areas of Tyrone, Fermanagh and south Armagh to the Free State, and one in Donegal to Northern Ireland,[14] but on the eve of the findings being announced in November 1925, they were leaked to the *Morning Post* in London. A constitutional crisis ensued, both governments refusing to give up territory. The Northern Ireland Prime Minister, Sir James Craig, had won an election the previous April on the slogan 'Not an inch'. The British Prime Minister, Stanley Baldwin, invited the two Irish premiers to Downing Street, and an agreement was reached to leave the border as it was. It was a pragmatic decision, well oiled with further financial aid, but it horrified nationalists whom it permanently trapped within Northern Ireland, and added considerably to the security problems of the northern government.

There is, besides, another factor which is all but overlooked in all the debate over the existence of Northern Ireland. By the Government of Ireland Act of 1920 the British government expressly made itself the guarantor of the rights of the minority by withholding from the northern government the power to make any law 'so as either directly or indirectly to establish or endow any religion, or prohibit or restrict the free exercise thereof, or give a preference, privilege or advantage, or impose any advantage or disadvantage, on account of religious belief or religious or ecclesiastical status'.[15]

The history of Northern Ireland since 1920 falls into two parts. From 1920 until 1969, despite its internal problems, it operated as a recognisable part of the United Kingdom, and as such it went to war with Germany in 1939, playing, as it turned out, a vital role in keeping open the one remaining route for supplies of food and armaments from America at the height of the Battle of the Atlantic; it was also the area chosen for the assembly and training of the massive American military force built up for the invasion of Europe in June 1944. The Luftwaffe, having a more precise sense of the frontiers of the United Kingdom than most English people, thoroughly bombed Belfast in 1941.

In 1969, however, the pent up social and political grievances of the Catholic population erupted in serious disorders, which led to the deployment of troops in the North, and ultimately the suspension of the government of Northern Ireland. What began as social protest developed into an insurrection, which inevitably fuelled a sectarian war. The IRA intervened, now with the considerable Catholic support, and began a planned campaign of bombing and assassination in Northern Ireland, in Britain and at British military installations in Europe. The result was the beginning of a complex process of hurt and political restructuring which has led to the situation of Northern Ireland today. None of the detail of the wearisome politics and social disintegration can disguise the simple historical fact that the Irish question has been reopened and the clock set back to 1921. It all has to do with the geography of religion.

The Cain–Abel Business

> Abnegation — self-sacrifice, means something. Fraternity means nothing unless the Cain–Abel business. That's your true fraternity.
>
> JOSEPH CONRAD[1]

The Mosaic

A major component in the difficulties of Anglo–Irish relations has always been the geographical distribution of the two main religious groups. The Irish census of 1911, on which the Boundary Commission based its findings, revealed that of the total population (4,390,219) roughly a quarter were Protestant. Though Protestants lived in every part of Ireland, most of them were concentrated in the six north-eastern counties. Yet, taking the nine-county province of Ulster as a whole, the population was almost equally divided between Catholic and Protestant, thus creating a fiendish equation. In three of the Ulster counties (Cavan, Monaghan and Donegal) Protestants were in a minority. In the counties of Fermanagh and Tyrone the population was evenly balanced, but in four Ulster counties (Antrim, Down, Armagh and Londonderry) Protestants were in an overwhelming majority.

One thing which this pattern shows is that the concentration of Protestant population is not just, as is commonly supposed, the result of James I's carefully planned and formally implemented plantation. Much of it derives from the free-enterprise Scots colonisation of Antrim and Down, for these counties were specifically excluded from the Plantation of Ulster. This in turn was built upon centuries of Scottish migration into Antrim. The earlier migration from Scotland was Catholic, and established a Catholic population in the Glens of Antrim, adding yet another complicating strand to the religious map. The mosaic has changed very little over the last three centuries.

In the eighteenth century Belfast was a small, predominantly Presbyterian town, not unlike one of the neat burghs of the Scottish Lowlands in its appearance and culture, with an Episcopalian minority and very few Catholic inhabitants. Under the laws then prevailing, however, the Episcopalian Protestants controlled the town's affairs and determined its representation in parliament. Its phenomenally rapid rise to the status of a modern industrial city radically altered the religious balance, because Belfast's industrial revolution drew in, from parts of Ireland far beyond its hinterland, large numbers of Catholic workers, who naturally tended to settle in areas close to their churches, and already lived in by their co-religionists.[2]

There was thus endless scope for controversy when the partition of

Ireland became a reality, and later for gerrymandering to maintain or extend these boundaries. Although the unionist campaign of 1912–14 against Home Rule had been conducted on a province-wide basis (units of the Ulster Volunteer Force were raised in Cavan, Monaghan and Donegal) the Ulster Unionists – in contrast to unionists in general – eventually accepted that the six north-eastern counties constituted the maximum they could govern.

Even this definition meant the inclusion of Fermanagh and Tyrone, where a slight change in population might put Protestants in a minority. Though Antrim and Down were the counties most densely settled with Protestants, they contained, in north Antrim and in south Down, large, if isolated, enclaves of Catholics. And, although Belfast lay between these two predominantly Protestant counties, it contained substantial numbers of Catholics, particularly in west Belfast, making the Catholic proportion of the city's population much higher than in the surrounding countryside. All this religious geography is perfectly well known and understood by the inhabitants themselves, but not by outside observers, whose knowledge of Northern Ireland may be on a par with our knowlege of Kosovo or the West Bank.

These peculiarities and anomalies bedevilled relations between the two communities long before partition; violent clashes over territory have been occurring since the eighteenth century at least.[3] Territory is what this form of the conflict is about, and explains phenomena like the serious annual disorders at Drumcree, which so baffle outside observers but would be well understood in Yugoslavia or Cyprus.

The Labyrinth

'If a war has lasted twenty years,' wrote Lichtenberg, 'it can well go on to last a hundred. For war has now become a *status*. Polemocraty. People who have enjoyed peace die out.'[4] Since 1972 Northern Ireland has been a 'polemocraty', for polemics have replaced the normal process of government. The will of the people can no longer be determined, because the institutions through which it was expressed have all but collapsed. In such circumstances, the terrorist war, whether hot or cold, has generated emotions which have completed the polarisation of the entire community. Instead of extremists, who can be managed in a democracy, government (wherever it resides) has to deal with two hostile populations who cannot agree on definitions. Words like 'democracy', 'liberty', 'rights', 'esteem' become porous, and the parrot-cries of party no longer offer any guide to truth. And no one involved in the situation can really be impartial, for, to quote Lichtenberg again, 'even impartiality is partial. He was of the party of the impartial.'[5] How many public figures in the North have found this to their cost? This is the labyrinth out of which the politicians must find a way.

During the last thirty years of the twentieth century, all the irreconcilables of Irish history came to dwell in the North. The historian who, in time to come, attempts to steer an objective course through the complex story of insurrection and civil protest, terrorism and reprisal, lost lives and ruined hopes, will not be hindered by the paucity of evidence, as the researcher into early history is. The paper mountains which wearied Carlyle have become Himalayan ranges, and they are augmented by enormous amounts of visual, auditory and electronic information. The voices are myriad, and the opportunities for special pleading limitless. Already the digestive process of history is at work.

The revolution in methods of communication is altering not only the content and quantity of historical evidence, but the way in which it is interpreted. We cannot know that coming generations will judge events by the same criteria which we have so far employed. Knowledge, writes Lévi-Strauss,

> no longer filters down slowly from one generation to the next within a family or a professional milieu but is propagated at disconcerting speed in a horizontal direction and at levels with ruptures between them. Henceforth, each generation will communicate more easily with its members than with the generation that precedes or follows it. Loyal still to the old system, the school is being invaded from all sides and, with the family losing one of its essential functions, can no longer take over that function or expand it. The school is no longer ready to serve as a relay station between past and present in a vertical direction, or between family and society in a horizontal direction.[6]

One can already trace some of this influence in the widespread and incessant debate on the Northern Ireland crisis. Most of those who contribute to it are obsessed with symptoms rather than causes, unable to see the wood for the trees because the superficialities are of an all-embracing complexity. But underneath the manoeuvres and concessions of governments, the rage of party, the rise and fall of paramilitary organisations, and the memory of outrage, the fundamentals of Irish history remain largely unchanged. And the general direction is retrogressive. A new set of bitter memories of wrong has been added to that of the 1920s, which is still raw, so that the population is more polarised than at any time in the last century. One can but hope that the fragile ceasefires and peace processes, which are not yet agreements, will hold long enough for the direction to be reversed.

The nature of the troubles in Northern Ireland is frequently misunderstood by outsiders, and to a large extent even by people who live there. One major source of error is the confusion between terrorist violence and sectarian violence. They are not the same, though they appear so. Since the Belfast peace agreement of April 1998 the bewilderment of television newsreaders in Britain is very marked when they have to report incidents of mob action on the streets. Surely that was all over? Does it mean that the agreement has broken down? Not at all.

Terrorist violence consists of a deliberately planned campaign of outrages intended to achieve a political purpose, and is directly aimed at coercing governments. Sectarian violence, on the other hand, is the continuing consequence of environmental and historical circumstance. It would occur just the same if Ireland were one united republic; the reaction to it might be a different matter. Confusion of the two kinds of violence is natural, because they interact at many levels. Rage at terrorist murders of members of one community or the other can provoke sectarian disorder in Belfast, Derry and smaller towns such as Lisburn and Portadown. Equally, sectarian disorders provide a convenient cloak for planned terrorist activity. The IRA, which was quiescent for many years after the ending of the 1956–62 border campaign, suddenly reappeared when serious civil disorders began in 1969. In turn the thirty years of war with the IRA caused to spring up retaliatory Protestant terrorist organisations, which did not exist during the period of unionist government between 1922 and 1972.

While it is important to draw a distinction, in historical terms, between the two manifestations of violence, it can hardly be denied that, as far as Northern Ireland is concerned, the conflict has become over the years every bit as sectarian as that which rages in Jerusalem. The republican movement in the North is entirely Catholic, though not all Catholics are republicans. There are no Protestants in the IRA, and whatever political or social principles are bandied about for the benefit of the outside world, the Northern Ireland conflict remains in essence a war between two religious cultures.

But not quite a holy war. The analogy is rather that of a family which is quarreling over a will. Both sides profess to be Christian, and for much of the business of everyday life the total community operates as an integrated unit of modern western society. One does not call on the bus driver or the person at the supermarket checkout to declare their religion or political convictions. They can do that endlessly on the television screens after work. The community is united for some purposes and divided for others. In any event, most of the population are not going to resort to violence under any circumstances short of a final confrontation. That is why all efforts to promote 'reconciliation' are singularly futile. The people who are being preached at are already reconciled, and those who are not are impervious to such exhortation. Nor is it enough for clergy and others to 'condemn' violence; what would you think of a Christian who did not? It is a kind of religious tautology, as if a doctor were to condemn disease.

It is scarcely to be wondered at that English people have long since wearied of Ulster's genetically-modified feuds. They are colour-blind to that particular form of religious division, since it does not determine the government under which they live. Nonetheless, they desire earnestly to have it explained to them. Every native of Northern Ireland is familiar with the interrogation. Because there is in fact a very long history of all this, whether most people know it or not: commissions of inquiry, arming and then disarming the police, deploying troops, outbreaks of inter-communal violence. The troubles of 1969 occurred because two generations had grown up which had no personal memory of the horrors of the 1920s.

All those who appeal, sometimes in despair, to reason and common sense in Ireland should ponder these words of the historian Albert Sorel, written in the nineteenth century:

> Pure reason is the concern neither of politicians, who are ruled by *raison d'état*, nor of peoples, who are ruled by their passions. But both states and

peoples have traditions, as old as their history, which spring from the same source as their history and follow a course parallel with it. Their action on men's minds is entirely instinctive, and the less men are conscious of their influence, the more imperious they are. In crises which take them unawares, men find no other resource: whether they wish it or not, whether they are aware of it or ignore it, lend themselves to it, or try to escape it, they undergo the influence of received ideas and of the passions which have found a lodgement in their minds and their environment.[7]

Rivers of Coffee

In the spring of 1899 Joseph Conrad was invited by his friend R.B. Cunninghame Graham to take part in a peace rally in London on the theme of international fraternity. Graham had many attributes which Conrad admired, above all his courage and intellect, but on the question of human nature the two men were poles apart. Conrad's reply was good-humoured but frank.

What would you think of an attempt to promote fraternity amongst people living in the same street? Two ends of the same street. I don't even mention two neighbouring streets. There is already as much fraternity as there can be – and that's very little and that very little is no good. What does fraternity mean? Abnegation – self-sacrifice, means something. Fraternity means nothing unless the Cain–Abel business. That's your true fraternity.[8]

Conrad knew what he was talking about. His real name was Korzeniowski, and he was the son of the Polish poet and patriot Apollo Korzeniowski. As a child he had gone with his mother to share his father's exile in Russia, and seen him die there, a martyr, in Polish eyes, to Russian imperialism. Apollo was an idealist who combined a passionate love of his country with a belief in the perfectibility of man. His son's novels were a lifelong commentary on the moral questions posed by cowardice and trust, courage and humanity, civilisation and the heart of darkness. He had in his bloodstream the age-old hatred that existed between Poles and Russians, both Christian peoples, and he knew that no one born in Britain could even begin to understand it. His challenge as an artist was somehow to rise above it, to explore how it was that human beings were able to reach into some source of decency within themselves.

But one had to start from a different premise, which he put to Graham in French: 'L'homme est un animal méchant. Sa mechanceté doit être organisée.' (Man is a wicked animal. His wickedness must be organised.) Where Graham went wrong, Conrad thought, was by his naïve faith that human nature could be reformed, when even institutions cannot be reformed. The experience of all history is that human nature will do what it wants. 'Your faith will never move that mountain. Not that I think mankind intrinsically bad. It is only silly and cowardly.'[9] Depressing as it sounds, this is merely a reiteration of Kant's dictum: 'Out of the crooked timber of humanity, no straight thing can ever be made.'[10]

Such words are never popular, and the truer they are, the less welcome, but Conrad's pessimism is justified on all sides. Somewhere here is the explanation of the failure of every people-based initiative to bring peace in conflict areas like Northern Ireland. When it comes, it arrives by other means. Why do mass demonstrations, peace movements, the exhortations of the clergy, the visits of world leaders, spiritual and unspiritual, poems by schoolchildren, all fail to make the slightest difference to terrorists? Why, when trades unions plaster the city with posters warning 'Sectarianism kills workers', do the workers go on rioting? Of course each of the campaigning groups attributes the violence to some other group of people, and has its own solution to promote.

The Israeli novelist and academic Amos Oz, who has given much thought to peace processes in his own country, defined the problem accurately. People assume, for sentimental reasons, that if the parties in conflict get to know each other better, the conflict will go away. 'It is the other way round. First you must find a solution for the real-estate dispute. Once this is resolved, the ground will be ready for emotional reconciliation.'[11] In Northern Ireland, uncertainty about the real estate is the principal factor which kept the troubles going for thirty years. Is Northern Ireland still part of the United Kingdom or is it now attached to the Irish Republic, or is it jointly governed by both, divided up according to population? Politicians may know the answer to this, but the people do not. They do not know if a settlement has been reached, or if it *can* be reached.

The mind-set of our times is to assume that a settlement can always be reached. 'There is,' declares Oz,

> a popular European inclination to assume that every conflict is essentially a misunderstanding, and with family counselling and group therapy everyone will live happily ever after. But there is no misunderstanding between Israeli Jew and Palestinian Arab. The Palestinians want the land they call Palestine – and all of it – because they regard it as theirs. The Israeli Jews want the same country for the same reasons, which creates a terrible tragedy. Rivers of coffee cannot resolve the issue of land. We need compromise.[12]

Similarly, there is no misunderstanding between Catholic and Protestant in Northern Ireland, none whatsoever. Nor do they need to get to know each other better. They know each other only too well, having lived alongside each other for four centuries, part of the same society yet divided by politics and history. This is not just a clash of cultures; it is a culture in itself, a point overlooked by most observers. An enormous amount of the unceasing debate on Northern Ireland is beside the point. If any of the remedies put forward could solve the problem, they would have been adopted long ago, and there would be no problem.

The past is dead, and nothing that we choose to believe about it can either harm or benefit those who were alive in it. On the other hand, it has the power to harm us. There are many people of good intentions who would persuade us that if only we could discover the truth about our history, some of that harm might be neutralised. This is an illusion, for the myth is often more potent than the reality, and perhaps a different kind of truth. History is not a branch of social welfare, and the only respectable motive for studying it is to explore the past for its own sake. Academic historians must resign themselves to the fact that they have little real influence on a nation's view of its past. What a nation thinks of its history is shaped rather by colourful narrative and the need for a political myth. The reality which is disinterred by patient scholarship is not so much disputed as simply ignored. 'There are two kinds of truth,' wrote Raymond Chandler, 'the truth that lights the way and the truth that warms the heart.'[13]

The thought that, though there may be patterns in history, events can never repeat themselves in exactly the same form is a comforting one for those who seek to free us from the burden of history. They are, for the most part, sincere, and the intention is good, but the quest is hopeless. We may try to forget history, but it will not forget us. To say we can do without it is like saying we can breathe without oxygen. It has made us what we are, and is in our bloodstream, in the language we speak, the culture we proclaim, the houses, streets and cities we live in. The call of the past to us is insistent; we cannot ignore it. It presses irredentist claims upon us, impatient for us to pass under its sway. We must remember its bias against our actuality; in so far as we exist, we deny its power.

Already we are someone else's past. One day libraries will be full of books about us, about our wars and politics and the funny clothes we wore. Students will spend hours trying to analyse us, and lecturers will give little talks about us to earnest people in draughty halls on winter evenings, people who 'want to know a little more history'. They will come to the conclusion that our lives were fairly dreadful, but will draw comfort from our high standards of morality and the steadiness of our principles, such a contrast to the depravity of their own times. We would be very amused at the things they say about us, if only we could hear them. Every historian should have two small notices on his desk, one reading 'I do not know' and the other 'Everything is older than you think it is'.

'Human events display two faces,' wrote Saint-Exupéry, 'one of drama, the other of indifference. Everything changes according to whether the event concerns the individual or the species.'[14] Carlyle was profoundly aware of this aspect of history. At the high point of his description of the fall of the Bastille on 14 July 1789 he pauses to consider. 'How the great Bastille clock ticks (inaudible) in its Inner Court there, at its ease, hour after hour; as if nothing special for it, or the world, were passing.'[15] Life goes on. Not everyone in France needs to be on stage. The cows are to milk, the flocks to be brought down from the pasture. 'O evening sun of July, how at this hour, thy beams fall slant on reapers and peaceful woody fields; on old women spinning in cottages; on ships far out on the silent main ...'[16] That day Louis XVI wrote a single word in his diary: 'Nothing'.

Somewhere out on that great silent main there has been a shipwreck. Time has brought its flotsam to our shores, to our schools and universities, our galleries and antique shops. It gives us some idea of what happened, but we shall never quite know how it was for the poor souls on board.

Notes

THE WALLED GARDEN

1 This is part of the epigraph chosen by
Dorothy L. Sayers for her detective
novel *Gaudy Night*.

2 Pen-name of the novelist Flann O'Brien
(itself a pen-name for Brian O'Nolan),
who for many years wrote a satirical
column, 'Cruiskeen Lawn', for the *Irish
Times*.

3 *Sunday Times*, 20 October 1822.

4 C. Litton Falkiner, *Essays Relating to
Ireland*, p. 82.

5 John Vincent (ed.), *The Diaries of Edward
Henry Stanley, 15th earl of Derby*, p. 55.

6 Fernand Braudel, *Identity of France*,
vol. 1, p. 1.

7 Falkiner, *Essays*, p. 83.

8 Thomas Carlyle, *The French Revolution*,
vol. 2, p. 347.

9 Ibid., pp. 257–8.

10 Thomas Carlyle, *Oliver Cromwell's
Letters and Speeches*, vol. 1, pp. 5–6.

11 Thomas Carlyle, *Critical and
Miscellaneous Essays*, vol. 2, p. 181.

12 Ibid., p. 182.

13 Claude Lévi-Strauss, *The Savage Mind
(La Pensée Sauvage)*, p. 257.

14 Sir Isaiah Berlin, 'The Concept of
Scientific History', in *The Proper Study
of Mankind*, ed. by H. Hardy and
R. Hausheer, p. 31.

THE NIGHT OF TIME

1 Sir Thomas Browne, *Hydriotaphia, or
Urn Burial* (1658), ch. 5.

2 *Dictionary of National Biography*; Glyn
Daniel, *A Short History of Archaeology*,
pp. 34–5.

3 Evan Hadingham, *Secrets of the Ice Age*,
p. 41.

4 Daniel, *Archaeology*, p. 138.

5 E. Estyn Evans, 'The Irishness of the
Irish', a paper read to the Irish
Association, reprinted in *Ireland and the
Atlantic Heritage*, pp. 36–7.

6 Ibid., p. 37.

7 Ibid.

8 E. Estyn Evans, *The Personality of
Ireland*, p. 41.

9 Ibid., p. 5.

10 Virginia Crossman and Dympna
McLaughlin, 'A Peculiar Eclipse:
E. Estyn Evans and Irish Studies',
Irish Review, no. 15 (Spring 1994),
pp. 79–86. The quotation is from
p. 83.

11 Evans, *Ireland and the Atlantic Heritage*,
p. 32.

12 A.G. Richey, *A Short History of the Irish
People*, p. 4.

13 Ibid.

14 Richard Twiss, *A Tour of Ireland in 1775*,
p. 33; J.P. Harrington, *The English
Traveller in Ireland*, p. 29. See also the
comments by the Chevalier de La
Tocnaye (Jacques Louis de Bougrenet)
in *A Frenchman's Walk through Ireland,
1796–7*, pp. 51–3.

15 Evans, *Irish Heritage*, p. 24.

16 George Bernard Shaw, Preface to
John Bull's Other Island, in *The Complete
Prefaces*, ed. by Dan H. Laurence and
David J. Leary, vol. 1, p. 197.

17 Antoine de Saint-Exupéry, *Wind, Sand
and Stars (Terre des Hommes)*, p. 53.

18 R.L.S. Bruce-Metford, *Recent
Archaeological Excavations in Britain*,
p. 275.

19   Peter Harbison, *Pre-Christian Ireland*, p. 10.
20   Michael Baillie, *A Slice through Time*, *passim*.
21   *Sunday Times*, 22 March 1998.
22   Harbison, *Pre-Christian Ireland*, p. 19.
23   Peter Woodman, *Excavations at Mount Sandal 1973–77*.
24   Simon James, *The Atlantic Celts*, p. 17.
25   Harbison, *Pre-Christian Ireland*, p. 51.
26   Liam de Paor, *The Peoples of Ireland*, pp. 24–6.
27   Harbison, *Pre-Christian Ireland*, pp. 66–86.
28   Ibid., p. 114.
29   Ibid., p. 133.
30   Ibid., p. 146.
31   Ibid,. pp. 110–11.
32   Barry Rafferty, *Pagan Celtic Ireland* (ch. 5 'The Road to God knows where'), pp. 98–111.
33   Harbison, *Pre-Christian Ireland*, p. 171; James, *Atlantic Celts*, pp. 37–40.
34   David Crystal, *The Cambridge Encyclopedia of Language*, pp. 302–3.
35   Evans, *Personality of Ireland*, p. 43.
36   M. Chapman, *The Celts: The Construction of a Myth*, p. xiii.
37   James, *Atlantic Celts*, p. 16.
38   P.C.N. Stewart, 'Inventing Britain: The Roman Creation and Adaptation of an Image', *Britannia*, vol. 26 (1995), pp. 1–10.
39   Julius Ceasar, *Gallic War*, Bk V, 13, in S. Ireland, *Roman Britain*, p. 15
40   Andrew R. Burn, *Agricola and Roman Britain*, p. 125: 'In these words Ireland enters the field of formal European history.'
41   Sheppard Frere, *Britannia*, p. 127.
42   Ian A. Richmond, *Roman Britain*, p. 37.
43   Gildas, *De Excidio Britanniae, Liber Querelus*, quoted in Norman Davies, *The Isles*, p. 160.
44   Peter Salway, *The Oxford Illustrated History of Roman Britain*, p. 296.
45   Harbison, *Pre-Christian Ireland*, p. 182; Raftery, *Pagan Celtic Ireland*, p. 207.
46   Raftery, *Pagan Celtic Ireland*, p. 210.
47   Ibid., p. 218.
48   Ibid., p. 219.
49   Michael Baillie, *Exodus to Arthur*, pp. 132–4.
50   Helen Waddell, *The Wandering Scholars*, p. 61.
51   In the 1960s the distinguished Celtic scholar Daniel A. Binchy dismissed 'the imaginative and conflicting

speculations of archaeologists and the devotees of that curious science which calls itself prehistory'. Harbison, *Pre-Christian Ireland*, p. 9; Evans, *Personality of Ireland*, p. 34.
52   F.J. Byrne, 'Ireland Before the Norman Invasion', *Irish Historical Studies*, vol. 16, no. 61 (1968), p. 1.
53   Ibid.
54   Ibid., p. 2
55   Ibid., p. 8.

HIBERNIA ANTIQUA

1   Sir Thomas Browne, *Hydriotaphia*, or *Urn Burial* (1658), Epistle Dedicatory.
2   George Bernard Shaw, Preface to *John Bull's Other Island*, in *The Complete Prefaces*, ed. by Don H. Laurence and David J. Leary, p. 32.
3   Peter Harbison, *Pre-Christian Ireland*, p. 10.
4   Marie Thérèse Flanagan, *Irish Society*, pp. 137–64.
5   Sir George Carew to Sir Robert Cecil, 28 June 1602, Carew MSS, iv, 258. 'I wish that Ireland were a fishpool, for this age shall never see it settled in peace.'
6   Giraldus Cambrensis, *Expugnatio Hibernica*, ed. by A.B. Scott and F.X. Martin, Bk I, ch. xxxiv; Bk II, ch. vi.
7   Robin Frame, 'The Defence of the English Lordship', in Thomas Bartlett and Keith Jeffery (eds.), *A Military History of Ireland*, p. 76.
8   Ibid., p. 85.
9   J.C. Beckett, *A Short History of Ireland*, p. 27.
10   George C. Kohn, *Encyclopedia of Plague and Pestilence*, p. 255; A.J. Otway-Ruthven, *A History of Medieval Ireland*, pp. 267–70; James L. Bolton, 'The Black Death', *The Historian*, no. 39 (1993), p. 3.
11   Otway-Ruthven, *Medieval Ireland*, p. 268.
12   Bolton, 'Black Death', p. 8.
13   Ibid.
14   Jonathan Bardon, *A History of Ulster*, p. 55.
15   Bolton, 'Black Death', p. 3.
16   Kohn, *Encyclopedia of Plague and Pestilence*, p. 152.
17   An Act that the King of England, his Heirs and Successors, be Kings of Ireland, *Irish Statutes*, vol. 1, pp. 176–7.
18   Beckett, *Short History*, p. 48.
19   Cormac Mac Baron O'Neill to King Philip of Spain, 20 May 1596, in Hiram

Morgan, *Tyrone's Rebellion*, Appendix, p. 224.

20 Graham Danby, 'The Spanish Armada of . . . 1597?', *The Historian*, no. 55 (1977), p. 15.

21 Ibid., p. 16.

22 Ian Colvin, *Life of Lord Carson*, vol. 2, p. 193.

23 E. Estyn Evans, *Ireland and the Atlantic Heritage*, pp. 216–17.

24 J.W. Blake, *Northern Ireland in the Second World War*, pp 229–30.

HOLY DISORDERS

1   Sir Thomas Browne, *Hydriotaphia, or Urn Burial* (1658), ch. 4.

2   Thomas Carlyle, *Oliver Cromwell's Letters and Speeches*, vol. 1, pp. 2–4.

3   For discussion of the earls' motives see N.P. Canny, 'The Flight of the Earls, 1607', *Irish Historical Studies*, vol. 18 (1972–3), pp. 380–99, and J.C. Beckett *The Making of Modern Ireland 1603–1923*, pp. 43–4.

4   Aidan Clarke, *The Old English in Ireland*, pp. 15–27.

5   Beckett, *Making of Modern Ireland*, p. 82. For the panic in England and Wales see Keith Lindley, 'The Impact of the 1641 Rebellion upon England and Wales, 1641–5', *Irish Historical Studies*, vol. 18 (1972–3), pp. 143–76.

6   J.C. Beckett, 'The Confederation of Kilkenny Reviewed', in J.C. Beckett, *Confrontations*, p. 48.

7   Beckett, *Making of Modern Ireland*, p. 98.

8   Ibid., p. 102.

9   C.H. Firth, *Cromwell*, p. 260.

10 Toby Barnard, *Cromwellian Ireland*, p. 1.

11 Beckett, *Making of Modern Ireland*, p.120.

12 Revd. Aubrey Gwynn, 'Some Notes on the History of the Book of Kells', *Irish Historical Studies*, vol. 9, no. 34 (1954), pp. 158–9.

13 Ibid., p. 150.

14 Ibid., pp. 160–1.

15 J.G. Simms, 'The Civil Survey', *Irish Historical Studies*, vol. 9, no. 35 (1955), p. 253.

16 Beckett, *Making of Modern Ireland*, p.126.

17 Essex papers, *Camden Society*, new series, no. 47, 2 vols., 1890.

18 Beckett, *Making of Modern Ireland*, p.140.

19 Ibid., p. 142.

20 Ibid., p. 145.

21 E. Curtis and R.B. McDowell (eds.), *Irish Historical Documents 1172–1922*, p. 172.

22 W.J. McCormack, *The Dublin Paper War of 1786–1788*, p. 16.

HIBERNIA CURIOSA

1   Sir Thomas Browne, *Hydriotaphia, or Urn Burial* (1658), additional passage.

2   C. Litton Falkiner, *Essays Relating to Ireland*, p. 82.

3   Marianne Elliott, *The Catholics of Ulster*, p. 177.

4   E. Curtis and R.B. McDowell (eds.), *Irish Historical Documents 1172–1922*, p. 186.

5   Jonathan Swift, *The Drapier's Letters*, ed. by H. Davis, pp. 40, 67–87.

6   Bonamy Dobrée, *English Literature in the Early Eighteenth Century*, p. 438.

7   David Dickson, *Arctic Ireland*, p. 51.

8   *The Groans of Ireland in a Letter from a Member of Parliament*, Dublin, 1741.

9   Michael Drake, 'The Demographic Crisis of 1740–41', in *Historical Studies 6*, ed. by T.W. Moody, p. 104.

10 Ibid., p. 115.

11 John Wild, *George Berkeley: A Study of his Life and Philosophy*, pp. 405–6.

12 T.W. Moody and W.E. Vaughan (eds.), *A New History of Ireland*, vol. 4, p. 33.

13 *The Tanner Letters*, p. 371.

14 Gráinne Henry, 'Ulster Exiles in Europe', in Brian Mac Cuarta, *Ulster 1641*, pp. 39–40.

15 Edmund Spencer, *A View of the Present State of Ireland*, ed. by Andrew Hadfield and Willy Maley, pp. 101–2.

16 Graham Gargett and Geraldine Sheridan (eds.), *Ireland and the French Enlightenment*, p. xiii.

17 Voltaire, *Complete Works*, vol. 3, p. 67.

18 Ibid., vol 3B, p. 161.

19 Ibid, vol. 1, p. 160.

20 Gargett and Sheridan, *Ireland and the French Enlightenment*, p. 72.

21 *Belfast News Letter*, 27 July 1753.

22 Gargett and Sheridan, *Ireland and the French Enlightenment*, pp. 73–4.

23 Ibid., p. 159.

24 For a discussion of Mercier's predictions see I.F. Clarke, *The Pattern of Expectation*, p. 26. *L'An 2440* ran through eleven editions between 1771 and 1793, four English, two American,

and Dutch and German translations.

25   Sir Jonah Barrington, *The Ireland of Sir Jonah Barrington*, ed. by H. Staples, p. 249.
26   Lord Charlemont to Dr Alexander Haliday, 29 May 1786, Charlemont MSS, vol. 2, 37.
27   Dr Alexander Haliday to Lord Charlemont, 1 June 1786, Charlemont MSS, vol. 2, 37–8.
28   Barrington, *Ireland of Sir Jonah Barrington*, p. 183.
29   R.B. McDowell, *Ireland in the Age of Imperialism and Revolution 1760–1801*, p. 618.
30   J.T. Gilbert, *A History of the City of Dublin*, vol. 3, pp. 279–82.
31   Ibid., p. 281.
32   H.J. Butler and H.E. Butler, *The Black Book of Edgeworthstown*, p. 191.
33   Ibid., pp. 136–40.
34   Ibid,. p. 193.

LIBERTY AND THE HOUR

1   Pierre Vergniaud, as he awaited the guillotine. Alphonse Lamartine, *Histoire des Girondins*, vol. 4, p. 20.
2   Journal of the Duke of Rutland's Tour of the North of Ireland (*Hist.* MSS *Com.*), 14th Report, vol. 3, pp. 419–23.
3   *Beresford corres.* vol. 2, pp. 169–70.
4   William Hazlitt, *Table Talk*, p. 191n.
5   Ibid., p. 191n.
6   S. Jones, *Hazlitt: A Life*, pp. 3–4.
7   Pauline Gregg, *Oliver Cromwell*, p. 138; C.H. Firth, *Cromwell*, p. 179.
8   John Milton, *Prose Works*, vol. 3, pp. 297–8.
9   William Drennan to Samuel McTier, 21 May 1791, Public Record Office of Northern Ireland, Belfast, D. 591/300.
10 Albert Sorel, *Europe and the French Revolution*, pp. 81–2.
11 William Drennan, *The Letters of Orellana*, p. 6.
12 Theobald Wolfe Tone, *Autobiography*, ed. by R. Barry O'Brien, 2 vols., vol. 2, p. 336.
13 W.E.H. Lecky, *History of Ireland in the Eighteenth Century*, vol. 4, pp. 412, 414.
14 Tone, *Autobiography*, vol. 1, pp. 104, 113.
15 Marianne Elliott, *Wolfe Tone*, p. 181.
16 Sorel, *Europe and the French Revolution*, p. 142.
17 Tone, *Autobiography*, vol. 1, p. 85.
18 Thomas Pakenham, *The Year of Liberty*, p. 148.
19 L.M. Cullen, 'The 1798 Rebellion in Wexford: United Irish Organisation, Membership, Leadership', in *Wexford: History and Society*, pp. 248–95.
20 Graham Gargett and Geraldine Sheridan (eds.), *Ireland and the French Enlightenment, passim*.
21 Thomas Babington Macaulay, *History of England from the Accession of James* II, vol. 1, ch. i.
22 R.B. McDowell, *Public Opinion and Government Policy in Ireland 1801–1846*, pp. 232–3.
23 *Belfast Monthly Magazine*, January, May 1809.
24 Alphonse Lamartine, *Histoire des Girondins*, vol. 4, p. 20.
25 Shevawn Lynam, *Humanity Dick*, p. 50; *Irish Sword*, no. 7 (1955), pp. 228–9.
26 Tom Dunne, *Theobald Wolfe Tone: Colonial Outsider*.
27 Tone, *Autobiography*, vol. 2, pp. 309–10, 317.
28 Ibid. See, for example, vol. 1, pp. 103, 124, 129, 134, 135, 138, and vol. 2, pp. 18, 20, 45.
29 Georg Christoph Lichtenberg, *Aphorisms*, Notebook K (1793–1796), no. 70, p. 176.
30 Tone was intensely interested in the career of General Wolfe, whose great-grandfather was Irish (*Dictionary of National Biography*). His own second name derived from his connections with the Wolfes of Blackhall. See Frank MacDermot, *Theobald Wolfe Tone*, pp. 3, 96.
31 *Journal of the Society of Army Historical Research*, vol. 6, no. 249 (October 1927); *Notes and Queries*, 4th series, vi, 321.

THE RESTLESS NATION

1   Gustave de Beaumont, *L'Irlande Sociale, Politique et Religieuse*, vol. 1, p. ii.
2   James Boswell, *Life of Johnson* (Tuesday, 12 October 1779), p. 1038.
3   Oliver MacDonagh, *Ireland*, p. 4.
4   Ibid.
5   E. Curtis and R.B. McDowell (eds.), *Irish Historical Documents 1172–1922*, p. 232.
6   A.V. Dicey, 'England's Case against Home Rule' (1887), quoted in J.C. Beckett, *Confrontations*, p. 143.
7   Frank McDermot, *Theobald Wolfe Tone*, p. 53.
8   L.M. Cullen (ed.), *The Formation of the*

Irish Economy, p. 113.

9   H.A.L. Fisher, *History of Europe*, vol. 1, p. 7 (Preface).

10 J.C. Beckett, *The Making of Modern Ireland 1603–1923*, p. 304.

11 For the terms of the Act of Union see Curtis and McDowell, *Historical Documents*, pp. 208–13.

12 *Hansard*, second series, vol. 15, col. 259.

13 Louis Hyman, *The Jews of Ireland*, p. 120.

14 John Killen (ed.), *The Famine Decade*, p. 249.

15 A.B. Cooke and J.R. Vincent, *The Governing Passion*, passim.

16 Patrick Buckland, *Irish Unionism*, p. 273.

17 Curtis and McDowell, *Historical Documents*, p. 290.

REVOLUTION

1   Pierre Vergniaud, in Alphonse Lamartine, *Histoire des Girondins*, vol. 3, p. 212.

2   Conor Cruise O'Brien, *The Shape of Modern Ireland*, p. 13.

3   The quotation is from Archbishop Croke, in J.C. Beckett, *The Making of Modern Ireland 1603–1923*, p. 417.

4   W.B. Yeats, from 'The Man and the Echo', in N. Jeffares, *W.B. Yeats*, p. 311–12.

5   O'Brien, *Shaping of Modern Ireland*, p. 1.

6   George Bernard Shaw, Letter to the *Daily News*, 10 May 1916, in George Bernard Shaw, *The Matter with Ireland*, ed. by David H. Greene and Dan H. Laurence, p. 112.

7   Keith Jeffery, *Ireland and the Great War*, p. 65. See also pp. 28, 117.

8   *Macmillan Dictionary of the First World War*, p. 240.

9   George C. Kohn, *Encyclopedia of Plague and Pestilence*, pp. 205–6.

10 R.B. McDowell, *Crisis and Decline*, pp. 197–8.

11 Dennis Kennedy, *The Widening Gulf*, pp. 133–49.

12 Máire O'Brien and Conor Cruise O'Brien, *Ireland: A Concise History*, p. 155.

13 Liddell Hart, *A History of the Second World War*, p. 411.

14 Geoffrey Hand (ed.), *Report of the Irish Boundary Commission*.

15 Government of Ireland Act 1920, c. 1.4.

THE CAIN-ABEL BUSINESS

1   Frederick R. Karl and Laurence Davies (eds.), *The Collected Letters of Joseph Conrad*, vol. 2 (1898–1902), p. 159.

2   J.C. Beckett and Robin Glasscock, *Belfast: The Origin and Growth of an Industrial City*, pp. 78–119.

3   For example, on the road from Benburb to Armagh in 1788 (David M. Miller, *Peep O'Day Boys and Defenders*, pp. 59–61); at Lisnagade, Co. Armagh, in 1789 (Miller, pp. 80–1); at the Diamond near Loughgall, Co. Armagh, in 1795 (Miller, pp. 117–22); and at Dolly's Brae near Castlewellan, Co. Down, in 1847 (Jonathan Bardon, *A History of Ulster*, pp. 302–4). Between then and the Drumcree confrontations there have been hundreds of lesser encounters.

4   Georg Christoph Lichtenberg, *Aphorisms*, Notebook J (1789–1793), no. 229, p. 156.

5   Ibid., Notebook F (1776–1779), no. 78, p. 92.

6   Claude Lévi-Strauss, *The View from Afar* (*Le Regard Éloigné*), p. 270.

7   Albert Sorel, *Europe and the French Revolution*, p. 32.

8   Joseph Conrad to R.B. Cunninghame Graham, 8 February 1899, in Karl and Davies (eds.), *Collected Letters*, vol. 2, p. 159.

9   Joseph Conrad to R.B. Cunninghame Graham, 23 January 1898, in ibid., vol. 2, p. 25.

10 Immanuel Kant, *Gesammelte Schriften*, vol. 8, 23: 'Aus so krummen Holze, als woraus der Mensch gemacht ist, kann nichts ganz Gerades gezimmert werden.'

11 Amos Oz, 'Islands of Sanity', interview in *Times Higher Educational Supplement*, 8 July 1998.

12 Ibid.

13 Raymond Chandler, *Notebooks*, p. 7.

14 Antoine de Saint-Exupéry (as a war correspondent in Spain, 1936), *Wind, Sand and Stars* (*Terre des Hommes*), p. 147.

15 Thomas Carlyle, *The French Revolution*, vol. 1, p. 151.

16 Ibid., p. 154.

Select Bibliography

AKENSON, DONALD HARMAN, *The Irish Diaspora: A Primer*, P. D. Meany, Toronto; Institute of Irish Studies, Belfast, 1996

BAILLIE, M.G.L., *A Slice through Time: Dendrochronology and Precision Dating*, Batsford, London, 1995
Exodus to Arthur: Catastrophic Encounters with Comets, Batsford, London, 2000

BARDON, JONATHAN, *A History of Ulster*, Blackstaff Press, Belfast, 1992

BARNARD, TOBY, *Cromwellian Ireland: English Government and Reform in Ireland, 1649–1660*, Oxford University Press, Oxford, 1975

BARRINGTON, SIR JONAH, *The Ireland of Sir Jonah Barrington*, ed. by H. Staples, Peter Owen, London, 1967

BARTLETT, THOMAS, *The Fall and Rise of the Irish Nation: The Catholic Question, 1690–1830*, Gill and Macmillan, Dublin, 1992

BARTLETT, THOMAS, and JEFFERY, KEITH (eds.), *A Military History of Ireland*, Cambridge University Press, Cambridge, 1996

BECKETT, J.C., *A Short History of Ireland*, Hutchinson, London, 1952
The Making of Modern Ireland 1603–1923, Faber and Faber, London, 1966
Confrontations, Faber and Faber, London, 1972
The Cavalier Duke, Pretani, Belfast, 1990

BECKETT, J.C., and GLASSCOCK, ROBIN, *Belfast: The Origin and Growth of an Industrial City*, BBC, Belfast, 1967

BENNETT, MARTYN, *Historical Dictionary of the British and Irish Civil Wars, 1637–1660*, Scarecrow, London, 2000

BERESFORD, J., *Correspondence*, 2 vols., Woodfall and Kinder, London, 1854

BERLIN, SIR ISAIAH, *The Proper Study of Mankind*, ed. by H. Hardy and R. Hausheer, Chatto and Windus, London, 1997

BEW, PAUL, *Conflict and Conciliation in Ireland, 1890–1910*, Clarendon Press, Oxford, 1987

Ideology and the Irish Question: Ulster Unionism and Irish Nationalism, 1912–1916, Oxford University Press, Oxford, 1994

BLAKE, J.W., *Northern Ireland in the Second World War*, Blackstaff Press, Belfast, 2000

BOSWELL, JAMES, *Life of Johnson*, Oxford University Press, Oxford, 1953

BOYCE, D. GEORGE, *Nationalism in Ireland*, Gill and Macmillan, Dublin, 1983

BRAUDEL, FERNAND, *The Identity of France*, vol. 1, Collins, London, 1988

BROWNE, SIR THOMAS, *Hydriotaphia, or Urn Burial*, in *Selected Writings*, ed. by Sir Geoffrey Keynes, Faber and Faber, London, 1968

BRUCE-METFORD, R.L.S., *Recent Archaeological Excavations in Britain*, Routledge and Keegan Paul, London, 1956

BUCKLAND, PATRICK, *Irish Unionism 1885–1923: A Documentary History*, HMSO, Belfast, 1973

BURN, ANDREW R., *Agricola and Roman Britain*, English University Press, 1953

BUTLER, H.J., and BUTLER, H.E., *The Black Book of Edgeworthstown and Other Edgeworth Memories, 1585–1827*, Faber and Gwyer, 1927

CARLYLE, THOMAS, *Oliver Cromwell's Letters and Speeches*, 3 vols., Dent, London, 1926
The French Revolution, 3 vols., Chapman and Hall, London, 1894
Critical and Miscellaneous Essays, vol. 3, Chapman and Hall, London, nd

CHANDLER, RAYMOND, *The Notebooks of Raymond Chandler*, ed. by Frank McShane, Weidenfeld and Nicolson, London, 1977

CHAPMAN, M., *The Celts: The Construction of a Myth*, St Martin's Press, New York, 1992

CLARKE, AIDAN, *The Old English in Ireland*, MacGibbon and Kee, London, 1966

CLARKE, I.F., *The Pattern of Expectation*, Cape, London, 1979

COLLINS, PETER (ed.), *Nationalism and Unionism: Conflict in Ireland 1885–1921*, Institute of Irish Studies, Belfast, 1994

COLVIN, IAN, *Life of Lord Carson*, vol. 3, Victor Gollancz, London, 1934

COOKE, A.B., and VINCENT, J.R., *The Governing Passion*, Harvester, London, 1974

CRYSTAL, DAVID, *The Cambridge Encyclopedia of Language*, Cambridge University Press, Cambridge, 1987

CULLEN, L.M., *An Economic History of Ireland since 1660*, Batsford, London, 1972
The Emergence of Modern Ireland, Batsford, London, 1981

CULLEN, L.M. (ed.), *The Formation of the Irish Economy*, Mercier Press, Cork, 1968

CURTIS, E., and MCDOWELL, R.B. (eds.), *Irish Historical Documents, 1172–1922*, Methuen, London, 1943

CURTIS, L.P., *Coercion and Conciliation in Ireland, 1880–92*, Princeton University Press, Princeton, N.J., 1963

DANIEL, GLYN, *A Short History of Archaeology*, Thames and Hudson, London, 1981

DAVIES, NORMAN, *The Isles: A History*, Macmillan Press, London, 1999

DE BEAUMONT, GUSTAVE, *L'Irlande Sociale, Politique et Religieuse*, C. Gosselin, Paris, 1839

DE LA TOCNAYE, CHEVALIER (Jacques Louis de Bougrenet), *A Frenchman's Walk through Ireland, 1796–97*, Blackstaff Press, Belfast, 1984

DE PAOR, LIAM, *The Peoples of Ireland*, Hutchinson, London, 1986
Ireland and Early Europe: From Prehistory to Modern Times, Four Courts Press, Dublin, 1997

DICKSON, DAVID, *Arctic Ireland*, White Row Press, Belfast, 1997

DICKSON, DAVID, KEOGH, DAIRE, and WHELAN, KEVIN (eds.), *The United Irishmen: Republicanism, Radicalism and Rebellion*, Lilliput Press, Dublin, 1993

DOBRÉE, BONAMY, *English Literature in the Early Eighteenth Century*, Clarendon Press, Oxford, 1959

DOHERTY, RICHARD, *The Williamite War in Ireland*, Four Courts Press, Dublin, 1998

DRENNAN, WILLIAM, *The Letters of Orellana*, Dublin, 1785

DUNNE, TOM, *Theobald Wolfe Tone: Colonial Outsider*, Tower Press, Cork, 1982

EDWARDS, R.W. DUDLEY, and O'DOWD, MARY, *Sources for Early Modern Irish History, 1534–1641*, Cambridge University Press, Cambridge, 1985

EDWARDS, RUTH DUDLEY, *Patrick Pearse: The Triumph of Failure*, Faber and
Faber, London 1979

ELLIOTT, MARIANNE, *Partners in Revolution: The United Irishmen and France*,
Yale University Press, New Haven and London, 1982
Wolfe Tone: Prophet of Irish Independence, Yale University Press, New
Haven and London, 1989
The Catholics of Ulster, Allen Lane, Penguin, London, 2000

EVANS, E. ESTYN, *The Personality of Ireland: Habitat, Heritage and History*,
Cambridge University Press, Cambridge, 1973
Ireland and the Atlantic Heritage: Selected Writings, Lilliput Press, Dublin,
1996
Irish Heritage: The Landscape, the People and their Work, Dundalgan Press,
Dundalk, 1942

EVANS, RICHARD J., *In Defence of History*, Granta, London, 1997

FALKINER, C. LITTON, *Essays Relating to Ireland: Biographical, Historical and
Topographical*, Longmans, Green and Co., London, 1909

FIRTH, C.H., *Oliver Cromwell and the Rule of Puritans in England*, Putnam,
1900

FISHER, H.A.L., *History of Europe*, Eyre and Spottiswoode, London,
1935

FLANAGAN, MARIE THÉRESE, *Irish Society, Anglo-Norman Settlers, Angevin
Kingship: Interactions in Ireland in the Late Twelfth Century*, Clarendon
Press, Oxford, 1989

FOSTER, ROY, *Modern Ireland 1600–1972*, Allen Lane, London, 1988

FRERE, SHEPPARD, *Britannia: A History of Roman Britain*, Routledge and
Kegan Paul, London, 1978

GARGETT, GRAHAM, and SHERIDAN, GERALDINE (eds.), *Ireland and the French
Enlightenment*, Macmillan Press, London, 1999

GILBERT, J.T., *A History of the City of Dublin*, 3 vols., James Duffy, Dublin,
1861

GIRALDUS CAMBRENSIS, *Expugnatio Hibernica*, ed. by A.B. Scott and F.X.
Martin, Royal Irish Academy, Dublin, 1978

GREGG, PAULINE, *Oliver Cromwell*, Dent, London, 1988

GUIFFAN, JEAN, VERRIERE, JACQUES, and RAFROIDI, PATRICK, *L'Irlande: Milieu et
Histoire*, Librarie Armand Colin, 1970

HADINGHAM, EVAN, *Secrets of the Ice Age: The World of the Cave Artists*, Heinemann, London, 1980

HAND, GEOFFREY (ed.), *Report of the Irish Boundary Commission*, Irish University Press, Shannon, 1969

HARBISON, PETER, *Pre-Christian Ireland: From the First Settlers to the Early Celts*, Thames and Hudson, London, 1988

HARRINGTON, J.P., *The English Traveller in Ireland*, Wolfhound Press, Dublin, 1991

HART, LIDDELL, *A History of the Second World War*, Cassell, London, 1970

HAZLITT, WILLIAM, *Table Talk*, Dent, London, 1959

HYMAN, LOUIS, *The Jews of Ireland: From Earliest Times to the Year 1910*, Irish University Press, Shannon, 1972

IRELAND, S., *Roman Britain: A Source Book*, Croom Helm, London, 1986

JAMES, SIMON, *The Atlantic Celts: Ancient People or Modern Invention?*, British Museum Press, London, 1999

JEFFARES, A.N., *A Commentary on the Collected Poems of W.B. Yeats*, Macmillan Press, London, 1968

JEFFERY, KEITH, *Ireland and the Great War*, Cambridge University Press, Cambridge, 2000

JOHNSTON, EDITH M., *Great Britain and Ireland, 1760–1800: A Study in Political Administration*, Oliver and Boyd, Edinburgh, 1963

JONES, S., *Hazlitt: A Life*, Oxford University Press, Oxford, 1989

KANT, IMMANUEL, *Gesammelte Schriften*, vol. 8, George Reiner, 1912

KARL, FREDERICK R., and DAVIES, LAURENCE (eds.), *The Collected Letters of Joseph Conrad*, vol. 2 (1898–1902), Cambridge University Press, Cambridge, 1986

KENNEDY, DENNIS, *The Widening Gulf: Northern Attitudes to the Independent Irish State, 1919–49*, Blackstaff Press, Belfast, 1988

KILLEN, JOHN (ed.), *The Famine Decade: Contemporary Accounts, 1841–1851*, Blackstaff Press, Belfast, 1995

KOHN, GEORGE C., *Encyclopedia of Plague and Pestilence*, Wordsworth, Ware, Herts, 1998

LAMARTINE, ALPHONSE, *Histoire des Girondins*, 4 vols., Libraire Fume, Paris, 1847

LECKY, W.E.H., *History of Ireland in the Eighteenth Century*, 5 vols., Longmans, Green and Co., London, 1906

LÉVI-STRAUSS, CLAUDE, *The Savage Mind (La Pensée Sauvage)*, Weidenfeld and Nicolson, London, 1966
The View from Afar (Le Regard Éloigné), Blackwell, London, 1985

LICHTENBERG, GEORG CHRISTOPH, *Aphorisms*, Penguin, London, 1990

LITTON, HELEN, *The Irish Famine: An Illustrated History*, Wolfhound Press, Dublin, 1994

LYNAM, SHEVAWN, *Humanity Dick*, Hamish Hamilton, London, 1976

LYONS, F.S.L., *Ireland since the Famine*, Weidenfeld and Nicolson, London, 1971

MACAULAY, THOMAS BABINGTON, *History of England from the Accession of James* II, Macmillan Press, London, 1914

McCORMACK, W.J., *The Dublin Paper War of 1786–1788: A Bibliographical and Cultural Inquiry*, Irish Academic Press, Dublin, 1993

MAC CUARTA, BRIAN, SJ (ed.), *Ulster 1641: Aspects of the Rising*, Institute of Irish Studies, Belfast, 1993

MACDERMOT, FRANK, *Theobald Wolfe Tone*, Macmillan Press, London, 1939

MACDONAGH, OLIVER, *Ireland*, Prentice Hall, Englewood Cliffs, New Jersey, 1968
States of Mind: A Study of Anglo-Irish Conflict, 1780–1980, George Allen and Unwin, London, 1983
The Hereditary Bondsman: Daniel O'Connell, 1775–1829, Weidenfeld and Nicolson, London, 1988

McDOWELL, R.B., *Public Opinion and Government Policy in Ireland 1801–1846*, Faber and Faber, London, 1952
Ireland in the Age of Imperialism and Revolution, 1760–1801, Clarendon Press, Oxford, 1979
Crisis and Decline, Lilliput Press, Dublin, 1997

MACINTYRE, ANGUS, *The Liberator: Daniel O'Connell and the Irish Party, 1830–1847*, Hamish Hamilton, London, 1965

Macmillan Dictionary of the First World War, Macmillan Press, London, 1995

MAGUIRE, W.A., *Up in Arms: The 1798 Rebellion – A Bicentenary Exhibition*, Ulster Museum, Belfast, 1998

MANSERGH, NICHOLAS, *The Irish Question, 1840–1921*, George Allen and Unwin, London, 1965

MARWICK, ARTHUR, *The Nature of History*, Macmillan Press, London, 1970

MAXWELL, CONSTANTIA, *Irish History from Contemporary Sources, 1509–1610*, George Allen and Unwin, London, 1923
The Stranger in Ireland, Jonathan Cape, London, 1954

MILLER, DAVID M., *Peep O'Day Boys and Defenders: Select Documents on the County Armagh Disturbances, 1784–96*, Public Record Office of Northern Ireland, Belfast, 1990

MILTON, JOHN, *Complete Prose Works*, vol. 3, ed. by M.Y. Hughes, Yale University Press, New Haven and London, 1962

MITCHELL, FRANK, and RYAN, MICHAEL, *Reading the Irish Landscape*, Town House, Dublin, 1997

MOODY, T.W., and MARTIN, F.X. (eds.), *The Course of Irish History*, Mercier Press, Cork, 1967

MOODY, T.W. (ed.), *Historical Studies 6*, Blackstaff Press, Belfast, 1974

MOODY, T.W., and VAUGHAN, W.E. (eds.), *A New History of Ireland*, vol. 4, Clarendon Press, Oxford, 1986

MORGAN, HIRAM, *Tyrone's Rebellion*, Gill and Macmillan, Dublin, 1993

O'BRIEN, CONOR CRUISE O'BRIEN, *The Shaping of Modern Ireland*, Routledge and Kegan Paul, London, 1960

O'BRIEN, MÁIRE and CONOR CRUISE, *Ireland: A Concise History*, Thames and Hudson, London, 1972

Ó SIOCHRÚ, MICHEÁL, *Confederate Ireland, 1642–1649: A Constitutional and Political Analysis*, Four Courts Press, Dublin, 1999

OTWAY-RUTHVEN, A.J., *A History of Medieval Ireland*, Ernest Benn, London, 1968

PAKENHAM, THOMAS, *The Year of Liberty: The Great Irish Rebellion of 1798*, Hodder and Stoughton, London, 1969

PALMER, R.R., *The Age of Democratic Revolution*, 2 vols., Princeton University Press, Princeton, N.J., 1959, 1964

RAFTERY, BARRY, *Pagan Celtic Ireland: The Enigma of the Irish Iron Age*, Thames and Hudson, London, 1994

RICHEY, A.G., *A Short History of the Irish People*, Longmans, London, 1887

RICHMOND, IAN A., *Roman Britain*, Jonathan Cape, London, 1966

RICHTER, MICHAEL, *Ireland and her Neighbours in the Seventh Century*, Four Courts Press, Dublin, 1999

SAINT-EXUPÉRY, ANTOINE DE, *Wind, Sand and Stars (Terre des Hommes)*, Pan Books, London, 1975

SALWAY, PETER, *The Oxford Illustrated History of Roman Britain*, Oxford University Press, Oxford, 1993

SAYERS, DOROTHY L., *Gaudy Night*, Victor Gollancz, London, 1935

SHAW, GEORGE BERNARD, *The Complete Prefaces*, ed. by Dan H. Laurence and David J. Leary, Allen Lane, Penguin, London, 1993
The Matter with Ireland, ed. by David H. Greene and Dan H. Laurence, Rupert Hart Davis, London, 1962

SOREL, ALBERT, *Europe and the French Revolution: The Political Traditions of the Old Regime*, trans. and ed. by Alfred Cobban and J.W. Hunt, Collins, London, 1969

SPENCER, EDMUND, *A View of the Present State of Ireland*, ed. by Andrew Hadfield and Willy Maley, Blackwell, Oxford, 1997

STEWART, A.T.Q., *A Deeper Silence: The Hidden Roots of the United Irish Movement*, Blackstaff Press, Belfast, 1998

SWIFT, JONATHAN, *The Drapier's Letters*, ed. by H. Davis, Clarendon Press, Oxford, 1935

Tanners Letters, Irish Manuscripts Commission, Dublin, 1943

TONE, THEOBALD WOLFE, *Autobiography*, ed. by R. Barry O'Brien, 2 vols., Maunsel, 1893

TWISS, RICHARD, *A Tour of Ireland in 1775*, London, 1776

VINCENT, JOHN (ed.), *The Diaries of Edward Henry Stanley, 15th Earl of Derby*, Camden Fifth Series, vol. 4, Royal Historical Society, London, 1994

VOLTAIRE [FRANÇOIS MARIE AROUET], *Complete Works*, Les Delices, Geneva, 1970

WADDELL, HELEN, *The Wandering Scholars*, Constable, London, 1927

WALKER, BRIAN, *Ulster Politics: The Formative Years, 1868–86*, Ulster Historical Foundation, Belfast, 1989
Dancing to History's Tune: History, Myth and Politics in Ireland, Institute of Irish Studies, Belfast, 1996

WHELAN, KEVIN and WILLIAM NOLAN (eds), *Wexford: History and Society*, Geography Publications, Wexford, 1987

WICHERT, SABINE, *Northern Ireland since 1945*, Longman, London, 1991

WILD, JOHN, *George Berkeley: A Study of his Life and Philosophy*, Harvard University Press, Cambridge, Mass., 1936

WOODMAN, PETER, *Excavations at Mount Sandal 1973–77*, HMSO, Belfast, 1985

Index

Plantation of Ulster, 75, 77–80, 81, 178
plantations, 178
Plunkett, St Oliver, 6, 76, 95, 96
Poland, 130, 183–4
polemocraty, 179–80
Pope, Alexander, 111
Popish Plot, 76, 96
population
  distribution in NI, 178
  growth, 145, 154
Portadown, Co. Armagh, 181
Poynings' Law, 62–3, 98
prehistory, 16–21
  academic apartheid, 21–6
  and literary evidence, 50–3
  metalworking, 39–40
  Mount Sandal, 33–4
  scientific developments, 30–2
Prendergast, Maurice, 59
Presbyterians, 84, 86, 103, 165
  politics of, 121–3, 124
  radicalism, 125–6
  settlers, 77–8, 79, 95
  1798 rebellion, 129, 130
  Volunteers, 105
Preston, Sir Thomas, 84
Procopius, 49
Protestants
  Ascendancy, 100, 102–5, 110, 150, 161, 164
  distribution in NI, 178–9
  radicalism, 131–2
Proto-Celtic, 43
Ptolemy's map, 27
Public Record Office of Ireland, 94
Puckle, Mr, 112
Punch, 163
Puritanism, 74, 83

Quakers, 103, 111, 153
Queen's University, Belfast, 31, 46
Quit Rent office, 94

racism, 163–4
radicalism, 102–3, 105, 120–2, 165
  O'Connell, 150
  and patriotism, 131–2
  United Irishmen, 127–33
radiocarbon dating, 31, 39
Raftery, Barry, 47
railways, 145, 161
Rainsborough, Co. Thomas, 120–1
Ranke, Leopold von, 12–13
Raspe, Rudolf Erich, 39
Rathfriland, Co. Down, 126
rationalism, 131
rebellion (1641), 80–3, 87, 90–1, 112
rebellion (1798), 110, 127–30, 140, 141
rebellions, 143

Redmond, John, 146, 167
Reformation, 68–70, 78, 123
Regency dispute, 141
relapsing fever, 154
religious wars, European, 81
repeal movement, 145, 152–3
Republic of Ireland, 143, 152, 173, 184
republicanism, 102–3, 120–4, 155, 167
  O'Connell, 152
  outside influences, 4–6
  reasons for struggle, 143–4
  and United Irishmen, 127–33
Restoration, 89–91, 94–6, 121
Richelieu, Cardinal, 81
Richey, A.G., 26
Richmond, I.A., 46
Rinuccini, Giovanni Battista, Bishop of
    Fermo, 85
Robespierre, Maximilien, 10
Roche, Sir Boyle, 113
Roman Empire, 41–2
  and Ireland, 44–9
Romanticism, 124, 152, 164
Rothschild, Lionel de, 153
Rousseau, Jean Jacques, 113, 130
Rowan, Archibald Hamilton, 124
Rowlands, Henry, 35
Royal Irish Academy (RIA), 47
royalism, 132–3
Rump Parliament, 89, 90
Russell, Thomas, 137
Russia, 6, 183–4
Rutland, Duke of, 120

St Brigit's Day, 25
Saint Joseph, J.K.S., 30
St Leger, Sir Anthony, 68
St Ruth, Marquis de, 99
Saint-Exupéry, Antoine de, 30, 185
saints' days, 24–5
Sarsfield, Patrick, 99
Sassoon, Siegfried, 6
Scarampi, Pietro, 85
Schomberg, Frederick Herman, Duke of, 98
Schull, Co. Cork, 39
Scotland, 28, 29, 50, 71, 108, 154, 168
  Act of Union, 140, 142
  Bruce, 63
  Celtic, 35
  Civil War, 81, 90, 95
  and Confederates, 84–5
  folklore, 24
  plague, 63
  refugees to, 97–8
  Romans in, 46
  settlers from, 77–8, 80, 83, 145–6, 178
  western isles, 76
Scots Gaelic, 35, 43